What Readers Are Saying

"The most selfless and amazing book I have ever read. Thank you Annie Grace for your wisdom, intelligence, sense of humor, and love. I do believe you have saved my life. Today my youngest child got her final exam results and the next phase of her life begins. She will not be alone. Thank you, Annie Grace, for this gift."

Bernie M., Dublin, Ireland

"Without sounding too extreme, this book has significantly – and I think permanently – changed me and my attitude toward drinking. I have used Annie's wisdom and done some things alcohol-free that I would never have thought I could do. I can't say enough good about it and advise those who are ambivalent about drinking and not drinking to read it. Thanks again, Annie Grace, you've given me my life back, seriously."

Katy F., Albuquerque, New Mexico

"As a huge fan of Jason Vale, I was really interested to read *This Naked Mind*. It was so interesting to read more about the science behind addiction and the unconscious mind. It added a new level to my understanding of why I want to live a sober and happy life! I highly recommend this book to anyone, whether they are interested in cutting down or staying alcohol-free, there are so many practical tips and suggestions. I loved it!"

Sarah L., London, United Kingdom

"*This Naked Mind* brought clarity and focus on my drinking and ten-year struggle with sobriety that I had never paused to examine. Annie methodically brings the reader along a logical path of discovery. I highly recommend this excellent book to anyone seeking a refreshing approach to seeing alcohol in the full light of the day with eyes wide open."   Sam G., Sydney, Australia

"*This Naked Mind* delves into the psychology and physiology behind addiction and addresses these exceedingly well with thoughtfully structured chapters and memorable analogies. You will realize how alcohol truly has no place in your life and the myths we use to justify its consumption. Really, really cannot recommend this neat little book enough."   Cheryl W., Melbourne, Australia

"What an amazing book! *This Naked Mind* has been an eye-opener for me. I thought I could consciously decide to give up alcohol, and now I understand the necessity of informing the subconscious mind of the evils of drinking and then the cravings just disappear! I have also read and applied the work of Dr. John Sarno and knew the power of the subconscious mind but cannot believe how effective the book and method was for me. Thank you!"
Theresa G., Chapel Hill, North Carolina

"Reading *This Naked Mind* has been nothing short of a miracle. It has helped me to see alcohol for what it is and ended a twenty-five-year cycle of binge drinking and 'trying' to stop or moderate alcohol. I have not had a single craving since reading it, which is unheard of for me. I'm totally comfortable in situations where other people are drinking, and I don't feel the need to avoid temptation, because there isn't any! I feel happier, I'm regaining confidence, and my health is getting better every day. A must-read for anyone who wants to take control of their drinking but doesn't want a lifetime of struggle."
Kay W., The Lake District, United Kingdom

"*This Naked Mind* has allowed me to view my drinking habits from a new perspective. Now I know the science behind my addictive tendencies, sobriety has become less of a struggle and more of a celebration because I am finally free to live life on my own terms rather than under the control of alcohol. The message in *This Naked Mind* is truly liberating."   Marcus J., London, United Kingdom

"As a wife, parent, and counselor, I was increasingly distressed by my pattern of daily drinking and increasing dependence on alcohol. However, *This Naked Mind* gave me the critical insights into my own mind that I needed in order to overcome my problems. Now I have my energy, vitality, and health back. I highly recommend *This Naked Mind* for anyone concerned about their drinking."
Rhiana N., Sydney, Australia

"Annie Grace's book is the key to regaining control. It's an honest, eloquent look at the dangerous realities of our drinking culture, which gives you all of the tools you need to take back control of your life and unlock the door to a new, happier life."
Victory W., Perth, Australia

"Prior to reading *This Naked Mind*, I was a moderate drinker with what I considered a very healthy relationship with alcohol. I figured that this probably wasn't targeted at me, but I decided to give it a try anyway. How wrong I was! By the time I was done reading the book, I had come to believe that there is no such thing as a healthy relationship with alcohol. The author's examples, analogies, and personal stories are incredibly compelling. My perspective changed entirely. I questioned why I drank at all, realizing that I received little if any value from drinking. Immediately upon reading this book, I lost the desire for my evening drinks, and I found the strength to have dinner with friends without drinking a couple of beers. Don't get me wrong – I haven't completely stopped drinking. I still have a drink or two occasionally. But it is far less frequent, and it is on my terms rather than out of habit or social pressure.

If this book can have such a strong impact on somebody who didn't want to change, I can only imagine how powerful it can be for people who are truly looking for a change in their life."

John D., New Jersey

"I never realized how powerless I was against alcohol until I got my power back. A moderate to heavy drinker in my twenties, I desired to drink less as I got older. To my surprise, the desire was not enough, and I struggled to stay in control of my cravings. After reading *This Naked Mind* I feel, for the first time in my life, an extraordinary sense of freedom and happiness about my relationship with alcohol. I am eternally grateful to Annie Grace for this amazing gift!"

Mary P., Brooklyn, New York

"This is an honest book. It is genuine. It is told in a simple manner that is cogent and memorable. It helped me, and I will likely read it again sometime. Thank you, Annie Grace."

Steve G., Toronto, Ontario

"There is nothing but truth in your words. *This Naked Mind* is an awesome book that has filled my life with hope for the future."

Jacob K., Springvale, Minnesota

"Your voice in the book is clear as a bell and brings amazing clarity to the situation of drinking and drinkers and addiction, and the circularity of the substance itself causing the discomfort that we think the imbibing fixes. Skeptic that I am, your little book holds a big universe of hope."

Heidi M., Plymouth, Massachusetts

THIS NAKED MIND

Control Alcohol, Find Freedom,
Discover Happiness & Change Your Life

Annie Grace

ONE PLACE. MANY STORIES

HQ
An imprint of HarperCollins*Publishers* Ltd
1 London Bridge Street
London SE1 9GF

This paperback edition 2018

5
First published in Great Britain by
HQ, an imprint of HarperCollins*Publishers* Ltd 2018

A catalogue record for this book is
available from the British Library.

ISBN: 978-0-00-829343-7

Printed and bound in Great Britain by
CPI Group (UK) Ltd, Croydon, CR0 4YY

MIX
Paper from
responsible sources
FSC™ C007454

This book is produced from independently certified FSC™ paper
to ensure responsible forest management.

For more information visit: www.harpercollins.co.uk/green

To He Who Is:

Because you loved me before I knew your name and taught me there is always room at the bottom.

Husband:

Thank you for your incredible strength and amazing grace.

Get in touch:

thisnakedmind.com
thisnakedmindcommunity.com
hello@thisnakedmind.com
Twitter: @thisnakedmind
Facebook: This Naked Mind

TABLE OF CONTENTS

PREFACE

3:33 a.m. I wake up at the same time every night. I briefly wonder if that is supposed to mean something. Probably not, probably just a coincidence. I know what's coming, and I brace myself. The usual thoughts begin to surface. I try to piece the previous evening together, attempting to count my drinks. I count five glasses of wine, and then the memories grow fuzzy. I know I had a few more, but I've now lost count. I wonder how anyone can drink so much. I know I can't go on like this. I start to worry about my health, beginning the well-trodden road of fear and recrimination: What were you thinking? Don't you care about anything? Anyone? How will it feel if you end up with cancer? It will serve you right. What about the kids? Can't you stop for the kids? Or Brian? They love you. There's no good reason why, but they do. Why are you so weak? So stupid? If I can just make myself see the horror of how far I've fallen, maybe I can regain control. Next come the vows, my promises to myself to do things differently tomorrow. To fix this. Promises I never keep.

I'm awake for about an hour. Sometimes I cry. Other times I'm so disgusted that all I feel is anger. Lately I've been sneaking into the kitchen and drinking more. Just enough to shut down my brain, fall back asleep, and stop hurting.

These early mornings are the only time I'm honest with myself, admitting I drink too much and need to change. It's the worst part of my day, and it's always the same, night after night. The next day it's as if I have amnesia. I turn back into a generally happy person. I can't reconcile my misery, so I simply ignore it. If you ask me about drinking I'll tell you I love it; it relaxes me and makes life fun. In fact, I'll be shocked if you don't drink with me. I will wonder, "Why on earth not?" During the day I feel in control. I am successful and busy. The outward signs of how much I drink are practically nonexistent. I am so busy that I don't leave room for honesty, questioning, and broken promises. The evening comes, the drinking starts, and the cycle continues. I am no longer in control, and the only time I am brave enough to admit it (even to myself) is alone, in the dark, at three in the morning.

The implications of what it could mean are terrifying. What if I have a problem? What if I am an alcoholic? What if I am not normal? Most terrifying, what if I have to give up drinking? I worry that my pride will kill me because I have no intention of labeling myself. I am afraid of the shame and stigma. If my choice is to live a life of misery in diseased abstinence or drink myself to an early grave, I choose the latter. Horrifying but true.

What I know about getting help, I know from my brother who spent time in prison. Prison in the U.S. often involves Alcoholics Anonymous (A.A.) meetings. He says you start every meeting admitting that you are an alcoholic, powerless against alcohol. He says they believe alcoholism is a fatal illness without a cure. And I personally know self-proclaimed alcoholics who, rather than finding peace, fight a daily battle for sobriety. It seems miserable in our culture to be sober. To live a life avoiding temptation. Recovering appears synonymous with accepting life as just OK and adjusting to a new reality of missing out.

The idea of recovering seems to give alcohol more power even, and, maybe especially, when I am abstaining from it. I want freedom. It's now clear that alcohol is taking more from me than it's giving. I want to make it small and irrelevant in my life rather than allowing it more power over me. I want change. I have to find another way. And I have.

I now have freedom. I am back in control and have regained my self-respect. I am not locked in a battle for sobriety. I drink as much as I want, whenever I want. The truth is I no longer want to drink. I see now that alcohol is addictive, and I had become addicted. Obvious, right? Not exactly. In fact, in today's drinking society, it's not obvious at all. Admitting that alcohol is a dangerous and addictive drug like nicotine, cocaine, or heroin has serious implications. So we confuse ourselves with all sorts of convoluted theories.

I've never been happier. I am having more fun than ever. It's as if I have woken up from the *Matrix* and realized that alcohol was only dulling my senses and keeping me trapped rather than adding to my life. I know you may find this hard, if not impossible, to believe. That's OK. But I can give you the same freedom, the same joy, and the same control over alcohol in your life. I can take you on the same journey—a journey of facts, neuroscience, and logic. A journey that empowers you rather than rendering you powerless. A journey that does not involve the pain of deprivation.

I can put you back in control by removing your desire to drink, but be forewarned, getting rid of your desire for alcohol is the easy part. The hard part is going against groupthink, the herd mentality of our alcohol-saturated culture. After all, alcohol is the only drug on earth you have to justify *not* taking.

Experts imply that it takes months, even years, of hardship to stop drinking. A tough riddle can make you crazy, taking forever to solve. But if someone gives you the answer, solving the riddle becomes effortless. I hope this book will be the answer you are looking for.

I offer a perspective of education and enlightenment based on common sense and the most recent insights across psychology and neuroscience. A perspective that will empower and delight you, allowing you to forever change your relationship with alcohol. And remember, sometimes what you are searching for is in the journey rather than the destination.

All my best,
Annie Grace

THIS NAKED MIND

Control Alcohol, Find Freedom,
Discover Happiness & Change Your Life

INTRODUCTION

"We can't be afraid of change. You may feel very secure in the pond that you are in, but if you never venture out of it, you will never know that there is such a thing as an ocean, a sea." —C. JoyBell C.

What if, by reversing years of unconscious conditioning, you could return to the perspective of a non-drinker? Not a recovering (sober) alcoholic but a person with the same desire, need, and craving for alcohol as someone who has never picked up a bottle—a true non-drinker. Well, you can. By the end of this book, you will be free to weigh the pros and cons of drinking and determine alcohol's role in your life without emotional or illogical cravings. You can remain happy about your choice because it will be yours alone, decided from a place of freedom rather than out of obligation or coercion. Your desire to drink will be gone, so no matter what you choose you won't feel like you are missing out. You won't be pining for a drink or avoiding social situations because of temptation. Without desire there exists no temptation. Importantly, you won't have to label yourself as diseased or powerless.

This book will change your perception by showing you why you drink, both psychologically and neurologically. You may believe you already understand why you drink—to relieve stress, engage socially, or liven up a party. These are your rationalizations for drinking, but you actually drink for subtler and less conscious reasons. Understanding these reasons will put you back in control. It will end your confusion and eliminate your misery. But first, we must undo years—decades—of unconscious conditioning about alcohol.

And don't beat yourself up for anything you have struggled with in the past (including unsuccessful attempts to quit). It's counterproductive. There is a powerful misconception that people who can't control their drinking are weak-willed. In my experience it's often the strongest, smartest, and most successful people who drink more than they should. Drinking, or wanting to drink, does not make you weak. You may find it hard to believe, but an inability to control how much you drink is not a sign of weakness. So let's stop any self-loathing right now.

You may find it impossible to believe drinking less won't involve deprivation. The idea of drinking less fills you, as it did me, with dread. You worry that parties and social occasions will become tedious and difficult to attend. If you drink to relieve stress, the thought of losing the added support you believe alcohol provides can be terrifying. But it's true. With this approach you can effortlessly drink less and feel happy about it. What a euphoric, life-changing experience! You'll be excited to go out with friends, even to bars, knowing that not a drop of alcohol will cross your lips.

Does drinking less mean drinking nothing? Do you need to quit forever? That will be up to you. You will make your own decision based on information that empowers you, giving you back control rather than imposing rules on you. We will explore all aspects of the drinking cycle. Don't worry about making a decision about how much or how often you will drink now. What is important in this moment is that you have hope. You need to know this approach can and will work—that you will be released from the clutches of alcohol.

Maybe you think I don't grasp your situation, how dependent you've become on booze. Perhaps you've been drinking heavily for many years, and these claims seem absurd. That's OK. Skepticism won't impact the result.

No matter why you picked up this book, you'll find nothing but great news here. If you read, critically consider, and absorb the information in these pages, you will be inspired to sever or cut back on your relationship with alcohol without feeling deprived. In fact, you'll be happy, possibly euphoric, about your decision. You will feel in control and empowered to make conscious, logical, fact-based choices about the role alcohol will play in your life. I encourage you to read between one and two chapters a day, progressing with momentum, yet allowing sufficient time to absorb the content.

Don't change your day-to-day routine, even if it includes drinking. You heard correctly—feel free to continue to drink while reading the book. This may seem counterintuitive, but you will see that it is important to the process. Of course, if you have already stopped drinking there is no reason to start, and I am absolutely not encouraging you to do so. What's important is that you continue your regular routines so you don't create stress and foster a sense of deprivation while trying to absorb this information. You will need to focus and critically consider what *This Naked Mind* presents to you. However, it is important, if possible, to read sober in order to fully grasp the material. And don't skip ahead. The concepts build on themselves. This book will challenge you, so please be willing to open your mind and question long-held beliefs.

Finally, be hopeful. You are about to accomplish something incredible—regaining control. I know it hasn't happened yet, but you can be excited about it now. So, throughout the book, do your best to maintain a positive state of mind. Change often occurs when the pain of the current situation becomes so great you become willing to change without fully understanding what the future holds. You probably imagine a life without alcohol as painful, even scary.

This perception encourages you to put off change as long as possible. I will show you how altering your drinking habits will not cause pain, but instead allow you to enjoy your life more than you ever thought possible. With this approach, you are not clutching to the proverbial burning platform. You do not have to choose between the lesser of two evils (continuing to drink or living a life of deprivation). Rather, you will make the simple choice between your current state and a bright and exciting future. It's OK, even encouraged, to allow yourself to feel hopeful. This book contains a revolutionary approach. It will change your life for the better.

1.
THIS NAKED MIND:
HOW AND WHY IT WORKS

unconscious: un·con·scious | /ənˈkänSHəs/ *noun.*
The part of the mind that a person is not aware of but that is a powerful force in controlling behavior.

conscious: con·scious | /ˈkänSHəs/ *adjective.*
Aware of something (such as a fact or feeling), knowing that something exists or is happening.

consciousness: con·scious·ness | /ˈkänSHəs-nəss/ *noun.*
The condition of being conscious
: the quality or state of being aware especially of something within oneself
: the upper level of mental life which the person is aware of as contrasted with unconscious processes.

Definitions sourced from Merriam-Webster's.

Conscious or Unconscious Thought?

Did you know your unconscious mind is responsible for your desires? Most of us don't think about the distinction between our conscious and unconscious thoughts, but that distinction forms a vital piece of the alcohol puzzle. Studies confirm we have two separate cognitive (thinking) systems—the conscious and the unconscious.[1] The give-and-take between unconscious choices and our rational, conscious goals can help explain the mystifying realities of alcohol.[2]

We are all fairly familiar with the conscious (or explicit) mind. Conscious learning requires the aware, intellectual grasp of specific knowledge or procedures, which you can memorize and articulate.[3] When we want to change something in our lives, we usually start with a conscious decision. However, drinking is no longer a fully conscious choice in your life. Therefore, when you make a conscious decision to drink less, it's almost impossible to adhere to that decision because your larger, more powerful unconscious mind missed the memo.

Unconscious learning happens automatically and unintentionally through experiences, observations, conditioning, and practice.[4] We've been conditioned to believe we enjoy drinking. We think it enhances our social life and relieves boredom and stress. We believe these things below our conscious awareness. This is why, even after we consciously acknowledge that alcohol takes more than it gives, we retain the desire to drink.

The neurological changes that occur in your brain as a result of alcohol compound this unconscious desire. Thad A. Polk, neuroscientist, professor, and author of *The Addictive Brain* (a 2015 course on the newest science of addiction), says viewing addiction through the eyes of neuroscience allows us to "look beyond the seemingly bizarre behavior of addicts and see what is going on inside their brain."[5] In my early days on this journey, the undermining of my desire to drink less by a strange desire to drink more seemed nothing if not bizarre.

The mind, specifically the unconscious mind, is a powerful force in controlling our behavior. Information suggesting the benefits of alcohol surrounds us, yet we rarely become conscious of it. According to the Neuro-Linguistic Programming (NLP) communication model, we are assaulted with over two million bits of data every second, but we are only consciously aware of seven bits of that information.[6] Television, movies, advertising, and social gatherings all influence our beliefs. From childhood we've observed, with few exceptions, our parents, friends, and acquaintances appearing to enjoy moderate, "responsible" drinking. These images teach our unconscious minds that alcohol is pleasurable, relaxing, and sophisticated.

Your opinions about alcohol and your desire to drink spring from the lifelong mental conditioning of your unconscious mind. This desire has likely been compounded by specific neurological changes in the brain. The goal of *This Naked Mind* is to reverse the conditioning in your unconscious mind by educating your conscious mind. By changing your unconscious mind, we eliminate your desire to drink. Without desire, there is no temptation. Without temptation, there is no addiction.

Like most things that have been ingrained in us since childhood, we believe in alcohol without question, like we believe the sky is blue. Through this book, you will think critically about your deeply-held beliefs about alcohol and strip away those that are false. This will convince the all-powerful unconscious mind and allow harmony and agreement between your conscious and unconscious minds.

When the Brain Causes Pain

I cannot overstate the importance of your unconscious mind. I learned this lesson from Dr. John Sarno, a renowned physician who investigates the connection between physical pain and emotions. A *Forbes* article calls Dr. Sarno "America's Best Doctor,"[7] and his methodology has successfully healed all sorts of people, including controversial radio personality Howard Stern. Sarno coined the term The Mindbody Syndrome, the theory that your mind, below your conscious awareness, rather than any physical injury or ailment, may be responsible for your pain. After the birth of my second son, I experienced crippling back pain. Incapacitated for weeks at a time, I spent thousands of dollars on treatment. I tried chiropractic care, acupuncture, traditional doctors, muscle relaxants, and painkillers. I attended weekly physical therapy, including traction and massage. For three years I was unable to pick up my kids, and no type of treatment helped.

Through Sarno's work I learned the true source of my affliction, and through reading his book I was cured. I know this is hard to believe. Yet here I sit—I've remained pain-free for years. Many thousands of people have been forever cured of chronic pain through Dr. Sarno's work. There is even a website set up by individuals Dr. Sarno has cured. The purpose? To provide a place for people to write thank-you letters to Dr. Sarno to express their gratitude for giving them their lives back. It's truly amazing and can be found at thankyou drsarno.org. Dr. Sarno's approach of targeting and speaking to your unconscious mind is the same approach I employ for regaining control over alcohol.

Dr. Sarno methodically proved to me that the back pain I felt—pain that no medical professional could diagnose—was related to suppressed stress and anger.[8] How do we accumulate all this suppressed stress and anger? Imagine a young father. His wife (who no longer has time for him) hands him their screaming baby. She is exhausted and needs a break. He takes the child and tries everything to comfort him. Forty minutes later the baby is still screaming. The father is frustrated and angry. How can he not be? His needs are not being met, the baby's actions are illogical, and he feels useless. In his mind, it is unacceptable to feel angry at a helpless baby, so these emotions remain buried in his subconscious, or as psychiatrist Carl Jung calls it, "the shadow."[9]

We hide emotions that we feel to be abhorrent in "the shadow." We are unwilling to accept this part of us. So, we assert, "I am a good person; there is no way I want to harm this helpless baby," and we unconsciously repress our negative emotions. In order to deeply bury reprehensible emotions, your brain can cause physical pain to distract you. The pain is real. Laboratory tests demonstrate that the pain is caused when your brain cuts off oxygen to the afflicted area. Epidemiologists call this transfer of symptoms *amplification*.[10] Amplification prevents unacceptable ideas from surfacing.

Your Unconscious Mind at Work

"Anything unconscious dissolves when you shine
the light of consciousness on it."
—*Eckhart Tolle*

Why am I telling you all this? Drinking and back pain seem like two very different problems. So what do "the shadow" and amplification have to do with drinking? It's hard to believe that reading a book cured my back pain, but perhaps you can see how physical pain could originate in your emotions. Your conscious mind may now be willing to entertain this theory. But if I only needed to consciously accept the fact that the pain stemmed from my emotions rather than a physical injury, the cure would have been instant. Simply hearing the theory and accepting it consciously would have been enough to heal my back. But while my consciousness could grasp the concepts relatively easily, the pain remained. This is because it was my unconscious, rather than conscious, mind that needed to understand, to grasp the reality of the situation. And that process, the process of Dr. Sarno speaking to my unconscious mind, took me reading a 300-page book.

The unconscious mind is not logical; it's all about feelings. It is the source of love, desire, fear, jealousy, sadness, joy, anger, and more. The unconscious mind drives your emotions and desires. When you make a conscious decision to quit or cut back on alcohol, your unconscious desires remain unchanged. You have unknowingly created an internal conflict. You want to cut back or quit, but you still desire a drink and feel deprived when you do not allow yourself one.

Also, the unconscious mind often works without the knowledge or control of the conscious mind.[11] Studies from as far back as 1970 prove our brains actually prepare for action 1/3 of a second before we consciously decide to act. This means that even when we think we are making conscious decisions, our unconscious mind actually makes the decision for us.[12]

You can easily test this and reveal the extent to which your unconscious mind controls your conscious decisions. Remember a day when you were in a bad mood for no reason. You couldn't pinpoint what was wrong; you just felt grumpy. If your conscious mind controlled your emotions, you could simply think, "I am going to be happy," and your mood would change from grumpy to sunny. Have you tried that? Did it work?

When I am in a bad mood, a conscious thought to try to be happier—or, worse, someone telling me to just be happy—does nothing to improve my mood. It does the opposite. Why? Because your conscious mind doesn't control your emotions. Granted, you can train your conscious mind in more positive or negative thought patterns, which ultimately alters how you feel. These repeated conscious thoughts eventually influence your unconscious and therefore your feelings.

So how does your unconscious mind feel about alcohol? Today's society has conditioned your unconscious mind to believe alcohol provides pleasure, enjoyment, and support—that it is vital to social situations and stressful situations alike. This book reverses that conditioning by stripping away your false beliefs about alcohol. We will do this with the help of Liminal Thinking, a method developed by author Dave Gray. Liminal Thinking defines how, through the conscious exploration and acceptance of new ideas and truths, you can influence your unconscious mind. This gives you back your ability to make rational and logical decisions about alcohol, no longer influenced by illogical, emotional, or irrational desires. It will give you control and freedom by changing your understanding of and therefore your relationship with alcohol. While tradition, advertising, and societal norms condition our unconscious to believe that alcohol is beneficial, Liminal Thinking and the material in this book will expose that unconscious conditioning and recondition your unconscious, exposing alcohol and giving you freedom.

Experience and the Unconscious Mind[13]

In order to influence the unconscious mind, we need to first talk about the way in which personal experience ties to the unconscious. Perhaps you've heard the ancient story about the blind men and the elephant. Three blind men are brought into a room with an elephant, and each man touches a different part. One touches the tail, one the trunk, and one the side. When asked what they are touching they begin to argue. The one touching the trunk believes he is touching a snake; the one touching the body, a wall; and the one touching the tail, a rope.

Each blind man is saying what he believes to be true. And their experience proves it. Since we tend to trust our experiences implicitly, we understand how the argument started. Of course, the truth is that none of them are correct. They are all experiencing a piece of reality and forming their own, very different, opinions.

Gray explains that we only see and experience part of reality, and no matter how many experiences we have had, our brains are not

powerful enough to experience and observe everything. Gray makes the point that we are limited by what we pay attention to: "In any given moment, the more you focus on one aspect of your experience, the less you notice everything else."[14] We usually notice only the things specific to our immediate reality: the society we grew up in, the media, the influencers in our lives, and our actual life experiences.

Gray states that upon those relevant experiences and observations we make assumptions, from those assumptions we draw conclusions, and from those conclusions we form beliefs.[15] Gray defines belief as everything we "know" to be true.[16]

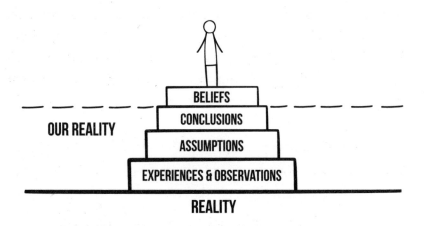

This illustration demonstrates that the things we "know" to be true are not actually formed by reality, but by reality as we have interpreted it from our experiences, observations, assumptions, and conclusions. Consider how this applies to alcohol. Collectively held beliefs are not built directly on the foundation of reality.

These beliefs can include statements like:

· Alcohol provides enjoyment.
· Alcohol provides relief.

- Alcohol is the key to social situations.
- A party can't really be a party without booze.
- Alcohol makes us funnier or more creative.
- Alcohol can relieve our stress or boredom.
- For some it can be hard, if not impossible, to stop drinking.
- The very definition of alcoholic and alcoholism.

These beliefs can be particularly difficult to change for several reasons. One reason is that we unconsciously self-seal them by seeking out things that are congruent with them. This is called confirmation bias, the tendency to search for or interpret information in a way that confirms one's preconceptions. We can find confirmation for our preconceptions about alcohol in many forms, including the media, the people we drink with, and our internal rationalizations. Adages about drinking found hanging in so many households illustrate a confirmation bias. Some of my favorites are:

- It's not drinking alone if the kids are home.
- We have too much wine, said no one ever.
- It's not a hangover; it's wine flu.
- I cook with wine; sometimes I even put it in the food.
- Wine! Because no great story started with someone eating a salad.

The kicker is that these beliefs have become so ingrained in our minds and our society, and so repeatedly self-sealed, that they are programmed into our unconscious. And our unconscious controls our emotions and our desires.[17] By definition the unconscious is not readily accessible or easily changed.[18] We need a specific process to dive into the foundation of our beliefs, examine them, and change our perceived reality.

So what happens when your experiences with alcohol start to contradict your bubble of self-sealing belief? Perhaps your experiences are no longer wholly positive, and you start to question your drinking. Or maybe you hear new information about the dangers of drinking.

Gray says that one of the ways we make sense of these new ideas that don't fit with our current beliefs is to look for external validity. Can we take the new information and test it out to prove its merit? However, especially with alcohol, we often don't make it that far. This is because the new information doesn't have internal coherence— it doesn't fit with what you "know" to be true. And because it is lacking in internal coherence, you will *unconsciously reject it before you have a chance to consciously consider it.* This happens all the time. We both consciously and unconsciously disregard information we don't want to hear. And when we do this, we never have a chance to see if this new information is indeed true; we never move to test it against reality.[19]

Why does this happen? Because we like certainty; it feels safe. Gray explains this unconscious behavior helps us deal with the realities of life, many of which are uncomfortable. It allows us to outsource some of the fear that attacks us when we confront certain truths. Reality is uncertain, and uncertainty causes fear. We try to protect ourselves from this fear by staying inside our bubble of belief until something happens that we cannot ignore. At that point we are forced to confront reality.

For me, it was one hangover too many, leaving me unable to function during the day as a result of my heavy drinking at night. I reached a point where I could no longer ignore the fact that alcohol was affecting my career and my relationships. This forced me to confront new information that said wine was not the joy juice I believed it to be.

But at this stage, attempting to drink less felt practically impossible. Why? I lived with a huge bubble of self-sealing belief around my drinking. I believed alcohol enhanced my creativity, made me funnier and more outgoing, allowed me to enjoy social situations, relieved my stress at the end of a long day, and comforted me when something went wrong. Giving up drinking felt like an incredible sacrifice, like the loss of a close friend. These were beliefs I had never previously questioned that had been built up over a lifetime of experiences, observations, assumptions, and conclusions.

I *knew* these beliefs to be true. I felt I would never be able to relax without a glass of wine. I honestly believed social situations would be boring and even depressing without alcohol. Even when I realized these beliefs were illogical, they still *felt* true because they were embedded in my unconscious and were much stronger than my logical, conscious reasoning. As Gray says, "construction of belief is not something we do consciously, it's something we do unconsciously."[20] In the illustration below you can see how everything shaded in below the line of our beliefs represents the things we are not consciously aware of.

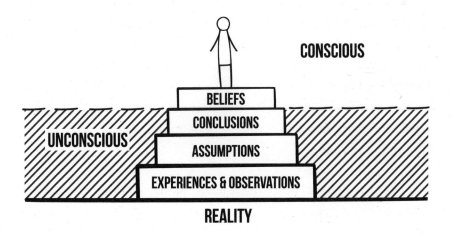

So what can we do? How can we explore reality and change our unconscious belief that alcohol is the "elixir of life" to fit with our conscious desire to drink less? It's relatively simple. We need to bring unconscious experiences, observations, assumptions, and conclusions into conscious thought. This allows your unconscious to change. The concept is scientifically proven—scientists now realize that the brain is able to change and adapt in response to new experiences, in a process called neuroplasticity.[21]

The process of illuminating your unconscious foundation of belief will influence your unconscious mind. To do this, I will logically and critically provide you with information about alcohol and addiction. I will expose your beliefs, assumptions, and conclusions by presenting you with methodical, factual, and rational arguments for you to question and evaluate. You'll be completely in control: I will strip away misinformation and present new concepts you have not yet critically considered. I will give you the tools to discover your own truth, your own reality, to understand that the rope you think you are holding might really be the tail of an elephant. Let's get started.

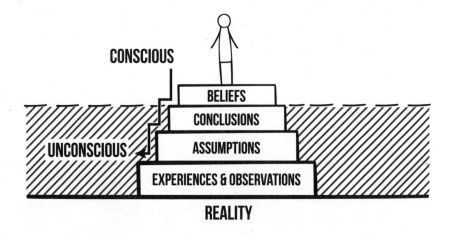

Alcohol: The "Elixir of Life"?

Alcohol is addictive. This fact has been proven over and over again. It is the nature of the substance, and it doesn't matter who you are or how in control you believe yourself to be. Your physical response when you drink alcohol is to want more. Alcohol hooks you through its addictive and dehydrating nature. Again, this is a physiological fact. Before you drank alcohol, you didn't miss it; you didn't think about it. You were happy and free.

If you're having problems with alcohol, you've already realized alcohol is not a miracle elixir. You know it's costing you money, health, friendships, and maybe even your marriage. Your conscious mind knows all of this. The problem is that your unconscious is continuously assaulted with messages about the "joy" it brings and the stress it relieves. These messages come from external sources, friends, family, and of course, advertising. These messages are confirmed by internal sources—your past experiences with alcohol. This book will address both.

Over the next day, notice how many messages you are exposed to about the "pleasures" and "benefits" of alcohol. Look around—from your friends to what you watch on television, almost everything in our society tells you, both *consciously* and *unconsciously*, that alcohol is the "elixir of life," and without it your life would be missing a key ingredient.

The Twelfth Juror

"Truth rests with the minority . . . because the minority is generally formed by those who really have an opinion." —Søren Kierkegaard

Alcoholism appears complex because it is misunderstood, not only by drinkers and their families but also by experts. We must see through these illusions. In short, we need to become detectives and lay bare the information, evaluate it, and discover the truth.

You may wonder, if common knowledge about alcohol and addiction is false, why do we believe it? How do we, as a society, accept untrue propositions as fact? Great questions. To answer them, let's look at a jury deliberating in a trial. It's a large jury with twelve jurors. Eleven of them are convinced of the defendant's guilt and one believes in his innocence. Do we believe the eleven jurors or the one? For the single juror to detain an exhausted jury (the decision must be unanimous), he must be absolutely sure of his position. In fact, you could argue that he is more certain than the eleven. Going against the grain is not easy. He must see something the rest do not. Suppose the eleven are experts? How much firmer in his stance must that single juror be? It appears the one juror is considering a perspective the eleven are not.

One of my favorite authors, Terry Pratchett, famously said, "We must be able, at any time, to accept the fact that we could all be absolutely and utterly wrong." It can be difficult to accept that the majority might be wrong, but it is a possibility we must entertain. It's amazing how drinkers can be incredibly open-minded about many things, yet close-minded when it comes to alcohol. This is because of the compartmentalization that happens within the mind of any substance-addicted person. So keep your mind open.

Visualize Success!

You are now ready to suspend judgment. To explore your unconscious desire to drink, to understand the reasons why you drink. This is great, and if you are willing to be honest with yourself and look deep into your belief system, you will find success.

This Naked Mind will help you explore your unconscious—and therefore influence it—as you work through the book. This type of book encourages your mind to consider the information when you are not actually reading and even when you sleep. That being said, you can take certain steps to ensure success. You may notice repetition throughout the book. You're a busy person and want me to cut to the chase. Rest assured, it is repetitive for a reason. For most of your life you have been repeatedly exposed to media, peer pressure, and many other influences. Repetition is vital to undoing a lifetime of ingrained beliefs. Despite the repetition, I've tried to make the content as interesting as possible.

Emotions and images—not necessarily images you see but images in your mind—comprise the language of your unconscious mind.

When you experience emotions related to the content, you will speak more directly to your unconscious. Importantly, you should feel hopeful when reading this book. The theory is sound, and I've included the most up-to-date scientific, medical, and psychological information. It works. It will work for you. Concentrate on that, and be hopeful.

Visualizing success always helps. A growing body of research suggests our unconscious minds cannot actually tell the difference between a real experience and a vividly imagined fake experience.[22] So visualize success—like being incredibly happy, laughing, and having a great time out with friends while drinking lemonade. You can even spend a few minutes each morning and night imagining the life you want while feeling positive emotions. This inspires success.

Get excited about what the future holds. Cultivate feelings of success even before you are successful. You hold all the tools you need to regain control of your drinking. Begin to think about the power of your mind and the strength of your body. This is exciting! In fact regaining control of my life through *This Naked Mind* is one of the most exciting and life-affirming things that has happened to me. It can be the same for you.

Don't dwell on past experiences. Your past is in the past. You have been caught, and through this book you will see that your alcohol problem is not your fault. Forgive yourself. You are the hero of this story. There is no reason to dwell on the negativity of the past and every reason to forgive yourself. Look forward to an incredible future.

Finally, relax! Let go of expectations, remain positive, and just let it happen. In Shawn Achor's book *The Happiness Advantage,* he states, "positive emotions broaden our scope of cognition and behavior . . . they dial up the learning centers of our brains to higher levels. They help us organize new information, keep that information in the brain longer, and retrieve it faster later on. And they enable us to make and sustain more neural connections, which allows us to think more quickly . . . and see new ways of doing things."

Do what you can to put yourself in a positive frame of mind while reading. There is so much to look forward to! Trust the approach, and more importantly, trust your unconscious to do the right thing for you. You can't control or micromanage your unconscious. Worry and stress are conscious activities—don't bother with them.

2.
THE DRINKER OR THE DRINK?
PART 1: THE DRINKER

"The world we have created is a process of our thinking.
It cannot be changed without changing our thinking."
—Albert Einstein

To find a cure we must understand the problem. What causes the alcohol epidemic in society, the drinker or the drink? We will look carefully at each.

The Blame Game 1.0: Me

Who is to blame? It seems society would have you believe that it is you, the drinker. You probably believe that your inability to control drinking—unlike "regular" drinkers who can "take it or leave it"—is due to a flaw you possess and they don't. What if that's not true?

I bet when you drink more than you should or when you wake up with a hangover, you beat yourself up. I know I did. I would drink a bottle or more of wine each evening and fall asleep quickly. But I awoke at 3 a.m. when the carbohydrates and energy from the alcohol flooded my system. Every night, I lay there and chastised myself for overindulgence, vowing to be better tomorrow.

The next day seemed invariably long and tiring, and by late afternoon I craved my wine. When evening came, I pushed the vows I'd made to the back of my mind. Sound familiar? For you it may be a different drink, a different cycle. Perhaps your drinking is not quite as bad, or maybe it's worse. The bottom line is that when we discover we are unable to control our alcohol, we blame ourselves. It's easy to do. Society blames us; our families blame us; our friends look at us with pity, wondering why we can't get our lives under control. We live in a state of constant self-loathing. What if it's not your fault?

It is difficult to be drinking more than you would like. You start to hate yourself, feeling weak and out of control. If you hadn't hid your problem so well more people would judge you, wondering why you can't simply "get it together," "be responsible," and "take control." After all, they drink but don't seem to have a problem.

If you are like most problem drinkers, you interpret your inability to control your drinking as weak willpower or a personality flaw. If only you had more willpower, you could drink less or abstain. If only you could quit for some unknown length of time, your desire for alcohol would diminish. You would finally be like all the people you know who seem to be in control of their alcohol, who seem to be able to take it or leave it. But wait. Are you weak-willed in other areas of your life or is alcohol a strange exception? I am distinctly not weak-willed, as people who know me can attest. Isn't it strange that I seem to lack willpower in this area?

Does it make any sense that alcoholics—those who need to control their drinking most—are the same people unable to do so? Why can't they simply exercise their free will and stop? Is there something, apparently undiagnosable, that makes certain people less able to control their alcohol consumption than others?

Am I an Alcoholic?

So what is an alcoholic? And how do I know if I am one? The majority of adults drink. According to the National Institute on Alcohol Abuse and Alcoholism, a whopping 87% of adult Americans drink.[23] What differentiates the casual drinker, the moderate drinker, the heavy drinker, the problem drinker, and the full-blown alcoholic?

According to *Paying the Tab* by Philip J. Cook, if you drink a single glass of wine each night you're in the top 30% of all drinkers. If it's two glasses, you're in the top 20%.[24] That means that 80% of adults drink *less* than you. But many people who imbibe a glass or two of wine with dinner do not fit the stereotypical description of an alcoholic. Alcoholism isn't strictly defined by how much or how often you drink. There is an invisible and ill-defined line that categorizes the "true alcoholic." Since the line is arbitrary, and alcoholism does not have a standard definition, how are you supposed to know if you actually have a problem?

A quick Google search reveals dozens of test questions intended to answer the question, "Am I an alcoholic?" They all carry a disclaimer saying they cannot provide a diagnosis for alcoholism. They say that is a decision I have to make.

How is it that the majority of Americans drink, yet for a self-diagnosed select few, a fun, social pastime turns into a dark, destructive secret? And why then do we deny the problem and put off asking for help as long as possible, until the problem becomes truly unmanageable?

It's quite easy for us to self-diagnose as "non-alcoholics" when we start to think we have a problem. Most people believe that alcoholics are somehow different from other people, different from "us." Many assume that alcoholism results from some type of defect. We're not sure if the defect is physical, mental, or emotional, but we're sure that "they" (alcoholics) are not like "us" (regular drinkers).

Jason Vale explains that most doctors belong to the "state the obvious" brigade. They pronounce something like: "You are drinking a lot, and it is starting to affect your health. My recommendation is that you moderate or stop drinking."[25] Then the doctor goes on to say that only you can decide if you are an alcoholic. Really? I might have a fatal illness, but no one can diagnose me? As a drinker, the suspicion that I have a serious problem will likely cause me to drink more. And why not? We believe alcohol relieves stress, and the journey to overcome denial, put away my pride, and determine if I am an alcoholic is terribly stressful.

If there is a specific physical or mental attribute responsible for alcoholism, why can't we test for it and segment the population into alcoholics and regular drinkers? That would enable us to prevent the afflicted individuals from falling victim to drink. If there is something inherently different about alcoholics, surely we could find some indication of it before they harm themselves, their family, and society as a whole.

With good reason, we applaud the strides scientists have made in medicine. Amputees with prosthetic limbs can now control the prosthetics' movements with their thoughts, which are translated to the limb by electrical signals from the brain.[26] Dr. Sergio Canavero, an Italy-based neuroscientist, is preparing to transplant a human head.[27] Recent advances in medicine blow our minds. If there is a specific physical or mental defect responsible for alcoholism, I find it hard to believe that we can't, in this day and age, diagnose and prevent it.

Am I saying every person responds the same way to alcohol, no matter their genetic or physical disposition? Not at all. Like the way one glass of wine affects two people differently, long-term exposure to alcohol has different effects on each of us. I am not debating this. Nor am I saying there is no evidence for a gene that increases a proclivity for alcohol addiction. We have discovered many loose relationships between genes and alcohol use but none definitive enough to declare responsible.

The genetics lab at the University of Utah, a department that studies the role of genes in addiction, says that someone's genetic makeup will never doom them to becoming an addict.[28] Polk confirms that, despite any genetic connections, someone cannot become an alcoholic without repeatedly drinking alcohol.[29]

It seems strange to use the term "alcoholic." We don't have cigarette-o-holics but rather people who have smoked and therefore become addicted to cigarettes. Similarly, you don't hear about people who are cocaine addicts suffering from cocaineism.[30] If you consider yourself a regular drinker, you probably take issue with this sentiment. Why? Because if we agree that no specific, diagnosable physical defect separates alcoholics from the population of "responsible" drinkers, everyone who drinks is susceptible and perhaps on the path to alcohol dependence. I assert that over time, with the right level of exposure, anyone can develop a physical dependence on alcohol. And since we are all built differently, no one can determine at what point an individual will develop dependence. This message isn't popular; it flies in the face of our thriving alcohol industry, our societal dependence on the drug, and the attitudes of "regular" and "responsible" drinkers who pride themselves on maintaining control.

The Blame Game 2.0: A.A. and the Alcohol Allergy Theory

I used to accept the notion that alcoholics were different than regular drinkers. Why not? The alcoholics I knew said they had a disorder or defect, so who was I to argue? Since that time I have done a tremendous amount of research. It took me some time to find out where the belief started and why it was accepted. I discovered at once how genetics play into the diagnosis. Neuroscientist Thad Polk says, "There is no single addiction gene; dozens of genes have been identified that affect addiction susceptibility, and most of them only have a small effect by themselves."[31] We have not yet found a way to diagnose or prevent addiction based on genetics.[32] Understanding why alcoholics themselves believe they are different from the normal population proves more difficult.

We accept this theory for a handful of simple reasons. Regular drinkers like it because it allows them to believe they are in control—safe to continue drinking without any worry that they will cross the arbitrary line into alcoholism. Alcoholics like the theory because once you "come out" as an alcoholic, your friends make an effort to help you abstain, rather than pressuring you to drink. They mix you mocktails and support your journey to fight the disease. It is easier to abstain when no one offers you alcohol. Also, physical difference means you receive less blame. We don't blame people who get cancer; disease allows for forgiveness. Finally, it is easier to maintain sobriety if you believe one slip will bring a fatal disease out of remission.

A.A. is the world's most prolific approach to treating alcoholism, with more than two million members in 175 countries.[33] Let's examine A.A.'s approach to alcoholism to understand what assumptions we, as a society, have made and how these assumptions translate into beliefs about alcoholism. A.A.'s primary documentation is informally called "The Big Book." Its official title is *Alcoholics Anonymous, the Story of How Many Thousands of Men and Women Have Recovered from Alcoholism*. This book describes Dr. William D. Silkworth, who treated but did not cure Bill Wilson, founder of A.A. Dr. Silkworth specialized in treatment of alcoholism, and in 1934 he unsuccessfully treated a patient who he concluded was hopeless. When A.A. later cured this patient, Dr. Silkworth wrote this letter to Bill Wilson:

> *We doctors have realized for a long time that some form of moral psychology was of urgent importance to alcoholics, but its application presented difficulties beyond our conception. What with our ultra-modern standards, our scientific approach to everything, we are perhaps not well equipped to apply the powers of good that lie outside of our synthetic knowledge.[34]*

Here, Dr. Silkworth recognizes that the solutions A.A. forwarded are successful beyond what the medical profession was able to offer. And the "ultra-modern" medicine of 1939 is still in use today.

The letter goes on to speak about how, where medical procedures fell short, the "unselfishness and community spirit of recovered A.A. members, who want to help those afflicted, has been an astounding success."[35]

I will quote the most important part of the letter directly:

> *We believe . . . that the action of alcohol on these chronic alcoholics is a manifestation of an allergy; that the phenomenon of craving is limited to this class [of people] and never occurs in the average temperate drinkers. These allergic types can never safely use alcohol in any form at all; and once having formed the habit [they have] found they cannot break it, once having lost their self.[36]*

The letter discusses the inadequacy the doctor feels in helping these alcoholics and that he is astounded to see how a psychological change—like inclusion in A.A.—allows alcoholics to heal. You may notice this letter contains a contradiction. How can alcohol be an allergen that is only activated once the habit is formed? It seems to indicate they believe alcohol to be a manifestation of an allergy but that they also must "form the habit" for that allergy to manifest. It makes more sense to believe that alcohol is an addictive substance to which any human can become addicted once enough is consumed.

The idea that alcoholics differ physically from the rest of us was hypothesized without any corroboratory lab findings by a doctor who suspected some people suffered from an allergy to alcohol. Allergens are relatively easy to diagnose, and 76 years later we have not found an allergy to be responsible for the disease of alcoholism. But Dr. Silkworth needed an explanation for A.A.'s success in helping alcoholics for whom medical prowess failed.

How did this belief, that a physical flaw differentiates regular drinkers from alcoholics, become so widely held? A.A.'s response to Dr. Silkworth's theory is telling:

> *In this statement he [Dr. Silkworth] confirms what we who have suffered alcoholic torture must believe—that the body of the alcoholic is quite as abnormal as his mind. It did not satisfy us to be told that we could not control our drinking just because we were maladjusted to life, that we were in full flight from reality, or were outright mental defectives. These things were true to some extent, in fact to a considerable extent with some of us. But we are sure that our bodies were sickened as well. In our belief, any picture of the alcoholic which leaves out this physical factor is incomplete.[37]*

What a relief the pioneers of A.A. must have felt. It is wretched to feel that your mind is not strong enough to resist alcohol. How much better to believe something is wrong with your body, something out of your control. A physical flaw, in a sense, lets us off the hook for our inability to maintain control when drinking. The A.A. literature of today continues to perpetuate the theory that alcohol is an allergen. A booklet that is distributed at today's meetings states,

> *As far as we are concerned, alcoholism is an illness, a progressive illness which can never be 'cured,' but which, like some other illnesses, can be arrested . . . We are perfectly willing to admit that we are allergic to alcohol and that it is simply common sense to stay away from the source of our allergy.[38]*

"Us" and "Them"

While A.A. saves many from alcoholism, I must point out the danger of the physical-flaw theory. Given the widespread drinking in our society, this theory can be dangerous. We continue drinking unchecked, often overlooking the danger of addiction, because we have come to believe alcoholism can only happen to other people. By the time we realize we have a problem, we are faced with self-diagnosing a fatal and incurable illness or admitting to being weak-willed and lacking self-control. We tend to avoid this horrific diagnosis until things have gotten so out of control we can no longer avoid the problem. In some ways this approach has defined alcoholism as a disease of denial. It is standard practice for drinkers to hit rock bottom before they seek help. When I told a friend I had stopped drinking, her immediate response was, "I can't imagine what you must have been through in order to make that decision." The assumption was clear: I must have had a rock-bottom experience.

We see this physical-flaw theory play out in every A.A. meeting. The meeting starts with a round-robin of, "Hello, my name is _____, and I am an alcoholic." By forcing me to name the problem—I am an alcoholic, a person with a physical flaw that gives alcohol unreasonable control over me—they make the affliction easier to deal with. Members of A.A. enjoy the fellowship of like-minded people fighting a similar battle, and through that community and support they find sobriety. But how does this physical-flaw theory affect drinkers who don't (or won't) consider the possibility that they have an incurable illness? Those who don't (or won't) consider themselves alcoholics?

Instead of treating alcohol with caution because we know it to be dangerous and addictive, we reassure ourselves that we are different from those flawed people we know as alcoholics. I speak from experience. And no one treats this as an insult. The alcoholics themselves confirm they are "different" from the normal population. So, millions of "regular" drinkers go through their drinking lives with no fear that they might become alcoholics.

We also believe that addiction to alcohol varies from other addictions because the rate of addiction happens differently for each person. We see many people who seem to "control" their drinking and can "take it or leave it." So it's difficult to understand why some people's first sips launch them into full-blown dependence while others never reach that point. But it is not just alcoholics who systematically increase the amount they drink. Regular drinkers start off with just a few drinks and are soon consuming a nightly glass of wine. In fact, alcoholics start off as "regular" drinkers. In many cases it takes years for them to cross the indistinct line into alcoholism.

The Blame Game 3.0: Alcoholic Genes

The Big Book claims that alcoholism "is limited to this class [of people] and never occurs in the average temperate drinkers."[39] The idea is that alcohol is not a problem for normal people and that many people can drink and suffer no physical, mental, or social ill effects, implying that alcohol is not a problem for normal people. Since 87% of the population drinks,[40] with those drinkers ranging from the person who only drinks during toasts at weddings to the degenerate sleeping in the gutter, it is not hard to see why society struggles to understand this disease.

A.A. members describe themselves as a group of men and women who have discovered they cannot control their drinking.[41] While I don't agree that alcoholics have lost control due to a physical, mental, or emotional defect, I concur that an alcoholic should be defined as someone who no longer has the ability to restrain their drinking.

I realize under this definition many alcoholics don't recognize that they have lost control. Many more drinkers dwell in limbo. Usually, years separate the point where you start to wonder if you have a problem and the moment you accept it. Ten years after a tiny voice in my head began to question my nightly drinking I determined I had to stop denying it and change how much I drank. It saddens me to think of the damage I did to my body, the havoc I wreaked in my relationships, and the pain I caused my husband. I want *This Naked Mind* to be a life raft, a wake-up call well before we reach "rock bottom" and our drinking becomes unmanageable.

If about 87% of people drink, it seems fair to assume that the majority believe themselves to be in control.[42] To be clear, I am not saying that everyone who drinks has developed a physical and neurological dependence on alcohol. It is not that everyone who sips alcohol is addicted but that everyone who drinks alcohol has a chance of becoming addicted. Furthermore, the point of addiction or dependence is unknown to the drinker and is generally not known until the drinker attempts to cut back. The obvious problem is that you can't know when you are in control. Nothing seems different, and in fact as humans we tend to feel in control until something significant shows us that we are not. Even then we will vehemently deny we have lost control.

The End of the Blame Game

Why is it hard for us to admit that alcohol itself is the primary issue? That alcohol, like any other drug, is addictive and dangerous? That life circumstances, personality, and conditioning lead some victims down into the abyss of alcoholism faster than others, but that we are all drinking the same harmful, addictive substance? That alcohol is dangerous no matter who you are? Have you heard the saying, "When you hear hoof-beats, think horses, not unicorns?" Perhaps we need to take another look and realize the simpler answer makes more sense.

If you are not convinced, that's OK. We will talk more about this. What is important now is that you entertain the idea that you might not be fully in control of your drinking. After all, you cannot solve a problem you don't realize you have.

So that begs the question, when exactly did we lose control?

3.
THE DRINKER OR THE DRINK?
PART 2: THE DRINK

"First you take a drink, then the drink takes a drink,
then the drink takes you."
—F. Scott Fitzgerald

A Dangerous Delight: The Nectar of Death

Allen Carr, an author and addiction expert best known for helping smokers overcome nicotine addiction, uses a perfect analogy for how addiction works: the pitcher plant.[43] This analogy is powerful, both in making sense of addiction in your conscious mind and in reconditioning your unconscious mind.

Have you heard of a pitcher plant? It's a deadly, meat-eating plant native to India, Madagascar, and Australia. Imagine you are walking by a Krispy Kreme doughnut shop, and you smell the doughnuts frying. It's hard to resist the smell of doughnuts. A pitcher plant is like Krispy Kreme for insects. You are an unsuspecting bumblebee flying through the woods. Suddenly, you fly through blissfully perfumed air. It makes your little bee tummy start to rumble, and you want to get a taste.

You fly closer to the plant; it looks like a delicious treat of fresh nectar. It smells great. To get a taste you must fly inside the rim. You land in the nectar and start to drink. But you don't notice the gradual slope under your feet. You are caught up in the moment, enjoying the treat. You begin to slide down into the plant without realizing it. You only notice the intoxicating nectar. Then you begin to sense the slight slide; gravity conspiring against you, but you have wings. You are confident you can fly out of the plant at any time. You need just a few more sips. The nectar is good, so why not enjoy it?

You think, as most drinkers do, that you are in control; you can leave the plant at any time. Eventually the slope becomes very steep, and the daylight seems farther away as darkness closes in around you. You stop drinking just enough to see dead, floating bodies of other bees and insects around you. You realize you are not enjoying a drink; you are drinking the juices of other dead and dissolving bees. You are the drink.

But can't we have the best of both worlds? Enjoy the nectar and then fly away? Maybe you can put limits on yourself and monitor your intake. Tons of people can do this and do it well—for a while, until something changes in their lives, some additional stressor or a tragedy. Or perhaps nothing changes and, like me, you gradually find you are drinking more than you ever set out to.

All doctors and alcohol experts agree that alcohol is addictive. How many people do you know who drink consistently less over time? For the moment, let's focus on "responsible," adult drinking patterns. Sure, students are well known for binging while attending university, leaving the party-heavy environment of frat houses for steady jobs and family life can reset the amount they regularly drink. But once they've set their long-term patterns, isn't it true that people tend to drink more, not less, over time?

We used to tease one of my friends because she was tipsy after half a glass of wine. Her low tolerance was the butt of jokes for years; however, when I saw her last week, she drank two large glasses at dinner and felt sober enough to drive home. Alcohol is addictive, and your tolerance increases over time. It's a dangerous road no matter how little you drink or how in control you think you are. In fact, recent neurological studies demonstrate that the brain changes in response to alcohol. These changes increase tolerance, diminish the pleasure derived from drinking, and affect the brain's ability to exercise self-control.[44] We will talk in detail about the effects of alcohol on the brain in a later chapter.

A Neglected Warning: The Homeless Drunk

Why aren't we forewarned by the dead bees at the bottom of the pitcher plant? We have all seen people who've lost everything to addiction, who beg on the street with a bottle of booze in a brown paper bag. Isn't this vagabond like the rotting bodies of the other trapped bees? Does this person help us to see the danger? Perhaps for a few. But most of us hide behind the arbitrary line we have drawn between "alcoholics" and "regular drinkers." We don't blame the addictive drug in our glass. Instead, we believe that there is something wrong with the addict on the street.

Thinking the alcoholic on the street is different allows us to believe ourselves to be immune. What has happened to him cannot possibly happen to us. We are not in danger of becoming one of "those" people. Of course, we don't know his backstory, that he was a smart, successful businessman with a growing family. We don't know how alcohol ensnared him, and he lost everything to the most accepted, deadly, and widely used of all drugs.[45]

Let's look at it a different way. We see the homeless man on the street like a bee views an ant that has crawled into the pitcher plant. The ant doesn't have wings; therefore, he is not like me, the bee. I have wings; I am in control. I can escape whenever I want to. But in reality both the ant and the bee are in mortal danger.

The last time I was on the Las Vegas strip everyone, everywhere was drinking. I mean, hey, it's Vegas. The drinkers came in all varieties, from giggling girls with the "yards" of fruity drinks to the bachelor-party boys with their 40 oz. beers. They were young, vibrant, and full of life. I watched them walk right by a beggar with his bed on the street. He had no food but clutched a bottle of alcohol hidden in a paper bag. It was clear to any passerby that drinking had destroyed his life. All of the "regular" drinkers looked directly at him. Many even gave him spare change.

But did they question the substance in their own cups? Did they realize they were drinking the same life-destroying poison as the homeless man? Did it prevent them from ordering their next drink? Sadly, no.

The Descent: When Did I Lose Control?

Is it so hard to accept that the youngsters, experimenting with alcohol, are like the bee landing on the edge of the plant and tasting the nectar? That the homeless man begging for food is just at a more advanced stage in the descent?

A recent study by the Prevention Research and Methodology Center at Pennsylvania State University measured the college binge drinking habits of students whose parents had allowed them to drink in high school. The findings demonstrate that teens who drink in high school have a significantly higher risk of binging in college. The study also confirms how much influence parental behavior has on teenagers and children. And it's not just boys modeling their dads or girls modeling their moms. If either parent drinks at home, both the son and daughter are influenced.

Starting to drink in high school leads to more drinking in college.[46] Why? Because when the descent begins at an early age, kids enter the college years farther down the slope than those who waited until college to sample the "nectar."

I didn't realize how my drinking increased over time. I shut my mind to the fact that I was drinking more than I ever had antici-pated. Are you drinking more or less than you did three, five, or even ten years ago? What about your friends? Are they drinking at the same level, or do they drink more as time goes on? When we realize we are drinking more than we want, we begin the battle to quit or cut back. But, like the bee in the pitcher plant, the more we struggle, the more stuck we become.

When does the bee lose control? When she begins her gradual slide downward? When she tries to fly away and is unable to? That's certainly when panic sets in. But it's clear she lost control well before she realized it, prior to the point she couldn't physically escape. As Allen Carr theorizes, perhaps from the moment she landed on the pitcher plant, the bee was never in control.

When did you lose control? Was it the first time your spouse com-mented on your drinking? Or someone noticed the smell? When you drank so much you threw up, again, perhaps on your partner? When you got a DUI? Maybe you feel like you are still in control. I'm not asking when you realized you had a problem. That was most likely a definitive moment: another hangover, blackout, or even wrecking your car. Losing control is different from *realizing* you have lost control.

So when was it? Or are we always in control? No one insists we drink; no one holds a gun to our heads. But if we are in control, aren't alcoholics also in control? No one forces them to drink. But that has to be different, right? Is it? Or are there just different levels of the same thing? From the outside no one would have guessed how much I was drinking. I was a "high-functioning alcoholic." I didn't lose my job or miss a single meeting because of alcohol. In fact, I excelled at my job and was frequently promoted. I didn't drink and drive. There were few outward signs of how much I drank. Did that mean I didn't struggle? Or that the alcohol wasn't slowly killing me? On the contrary.

Perhaps it's like the story of the boiling frog. A frog is placed in a pot of cold water, which is moved onto a hot stove. The water heats up, yet the frog does not jump out and save himself. Why not? It happens at such a gradual pace that the moment in which he should jump out passes. When he realizes he is boiling to death, it's too late. Could it be that the 87% of adults who drink are like the frog? Are we all in the same pot of slowly boiling water?

So when did you lose control of your drinking? When you experienced a life-crisis related to alcohol? When you realized it was hurting your health, and you decided to cut back? No, it must have been before that because if you were truly in control, you would not have allowed any of those things to happen. When exactly was it? Can you pinpoint it? Chances are you don't know when normal, habitual drinking became a problem. Can you entertain the possibility that you may never have been in control? That, like the bee, you are not in control of alcohol but alcohol is controlling you? And if you are certain you are still in control and can stop whenever you want to, are you certain you will still be able to next week? Next year? Are you willing to bet your life on it?

Finding Freedom: You Can Do This

You still have many questions. What about the addictive personality? What about the fact that some people have different backgrounds and reasons for drinking? What about our intellect—surely we are smarter than a bee? What about all the people who enjoy a single drink with dinner and never seem to slide farther down? What about all the people who actually seem to be able to take it or leave it?

We'll cover these questions in future chapters. But for now, consider the possibility that since we are human, and since alcohol is addictive to humans, once we begin to drink we unconsciously begin the slow slide into addiction. Does this mean everyone descends at the same rate? Or that everyone reaches the bottom? No. Many will drink throughout their lives and never reach a point where they try to stop. Maybe this means they are sliding at a very slow pace, or maybe it means that the alcohol kills them before they realize they have become dependent. Many factors contribute to the speed of a person's slide, and we will explore those factors in detail. Keep asking these questions. Critical thought is the key to understanding.

What is important now is that you can see that alcohol is an addictive substance whose nature does not change depending on who drinks it. This means that you are not weak. It is not your willpower or character that is lacking. You are as much at fault in the situation as the bumblebee that is instinctively enticed by the nectar of the pitcher plant.

Insects in the pitcher plant do not have hope. They don't have the intellectual ability to understand, and therefore escape, their tragic fate. We do! We, as humans, have the intelligence and ability to understand what is happening in our minds and bodies. I know the pitcher plant is terrifying, but be hopeful. You can find freedom and it may be one of the most joyful experiences of your life.

When I found freedom from alcohol I felt euphoric. The realization dawned, and I cried tears of joy. You probably still believe alcohol benefits you in some way. So the idea of drinking less or quitting altogether is uncomfortable. I can relate. It is terrifying to think about giving up something you feel brings you pleasure or relief. It's OK. When you understand the concepts in this book you will not feel any apprehension, only joy. Hope is stronger than fear. Try to maintain a hopeful outlook.

And remember, this is not your fault. You have been caught in a deadly trap that was designed to ensnare and slowly kill. It is subtle and insidious, and millions of people are deceived every day. The trap is designed to keep you a prisoner for life by making you believe you drink because you want to. We will expose the truth.

4.
LIMINAL POINT:
IS DRINKING A HABIT?

"The chains of habit are too weak to be felt
until they are too strong to be broken."
—Samuel Johnson

I've organized the book in a unique way in order to use Liminal Thinking to shine the light of conscious thought on ingrained beliefs about alcohol. You will find the narrative chapters of the book interspersed with mini-chapters called "Liminal Points." A Liminal Point will take you on a journey through certain, ingrained beliefs about alcohol. I want to deal with these beliefs throughout the book, instead of all at once, to allow you to test the logic in the midst of your daily life. This will allow you to examine what you believe to be true against external sources. What observations and assumptions have you made? What experiences have you had? What conclusions have you drawn?

To deconstruct why we might believe drinking is a habit, we must look at how this belief was unconsciously created.

We have already discussed how our experiences and observations affect our unconscious mind and our desire to drink. Since it is impossible to notice, experience, or observe everything, we unconsciously put our **experiences** and **observations** through a lens of relevance that is shaped by our personal needs. From these relevant experiences and observations we make **assumptions**, and from those assumptions we draw **conclusions**. From conclusions we form our **beliefs**. Once we've established a detailed framework of why you believe what you believe, I will reveal another perspective, one that may be closer to reality, in narrative form. In this manner we will submerge beneath the surface of your conscious and deconstruct your beliefs about alcohol.

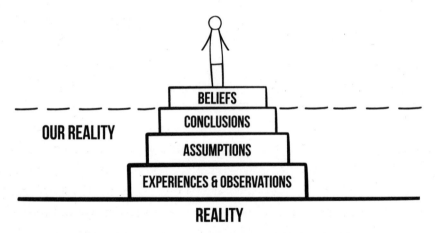

Note: With each Liminal Point we will go through the above steps, so you may want to mark this page and refer back to it from time to time.

Your **experience** is that you regularly drink. You also **observe** regular, habitual drinking around you. You **assume** because of how frequently drinking occurs, not only in your own life, but also in the lives of those around you, that drinking must be habitual. This is an easy assumption. It is more palatable than the assumption that you, and those around you, drink regularly because you have become dependent on alcohol. A habit doesn't feel threatening. You **conclude** that drinking, because it is so regular and you are afraid to look for a more sinister reason, must be a habit.

Let's explore reality:

It's Just a Habit

Many people justify their drinking by saying it is just a habit. And indeed, drinking may have started as a habitual routine. You went to a party and had a drink, or you got home from work and had a drink. The thing about habits is that they, by definition, encourage your brain to think less.[47] Once something has become habitual, like driving or brushing your teeth, you no longer consciously think about it. This is great—it frees up brainpower, allowing us to focus on new and different things.[48] So if your drinking started as a habit, there is a good chance you often drink without thinking too much about it. Over time, drinking became more than a simple habit.

If drinking was truly a habit, when I was pregnant, I would have been perfectly happy drinking non-alcoholic beers. Non-alcoholic beers tasted similar, but I couldn't bring myself to drink more than one. It was the alcohol, not the taste, I wanted. Similarly, if heroin was a habit, perhaps the addict could shoot up a syringe of saline? With some effort, aren't most habits relatively easy to break?

Would you allow your wife to leave you, your kids to hate you, your money to bleed away, and your self-respect to abandon you because of a habit? And if drinking was simply a habit, why does the alcoholic, who has been sober for fifteen years, still take it one day at a time? There is no other habit where this is the case.

When we give up a habit like biting our nails, notoriously difficult to do, we don't feel deprived because we no longer gnaw on our fingertips. We don't worry we will live our lives missing out on an authentic pleasure. We may habitually drink, but drinking is not a habit—it's an addiction. Yet the majority of drinkers believe they drink because they want to, they enjoy it, and they choose to do it.

Say I offered you two hundred thousand dollars to stop drinking. Would you? Do you have to think about it? What about a half million? You can buy a beautiful home, but you can never drink again. If drinking was a habit, there would be no hesitation. For a half million dollars you wouldn't hesitate to break a habit—no matter how much effort it took.[49]

With justifications such as these, we aim to prove we are in control. The fact that we spend so much time defending our alcohol intake proves the opposite. All drugs do this—you try to prove you are not dependent, not controlled. It is the fear that keeps us drinking, and the alcohol itself creates the fear. We fear that we will never be happy or at peace without drinking and that stopping will mean we will feel unhappy—that we are missing out. If you believe these false justifications, even after you stop, when your health has improved and your relationships have been restored, you will continue to envy drinkers. You will believe their reasons for drinking and feel jealous that they are drinking when you are not. But when you recognize that their reasons are unfounded, you're not jealous at all—you rejoice in your newfound freedom.

Is your alcohol habit truly a habit?

5.
YOU: SIMPLY NAKED

"The most fundamental harm we can do ourselves is to remain ignorant by not having the courage and the respect to look at ourselves honestly and gently."
—Pema Chödrön

You are the most awesome living organism on the planet. Your mind can do more than any computer. In fact, it creates computers. Your body is self-regulating, self-healing, and self-aware. It alerts you to the tiniest problems and is programmed to protect you, ensuring your survival. It is infinitely more complex than the most intelligent technology. It is priceless.

Since alcohol affects how your body functions, it is vital to understand how your body works when sober. When you are ensnared in the cycle of addiction, it's easy to forget how competent you really are. You are balanced and strong. You are equipped with two phenomenal guidance systems—symptoms and instincts—which help your mind to understand your body's needs.

Your Extraordinary Mind and Body: Complex

We learn more about the human brain every day. We are awed by its abilities, and, despite our technological advances, we cannot come close to replicating it. Your brain is capable of more in a single second than I could describe in hours. It can do more than I could ever explain because much of its power is still unknown. We know of nothing more powerful than the human brain. Astonishingly, the majority of your brain's activity happens without conscious thought. It's designed to keep us alive and highly functional without our direction. When we are asleep, it allows us to breathe, keeps our hearts beating, and regulates our temperature. Our immune system fights a daily battle against millions of toxins, both externally and internally. We take all of this for granted.

Your extraordinary brain is housed in a body that sustains and communicates with it. Your senses alert your brain to new information. Our abilities to smell, feel, taste, hear, and see connect us to our surroundings. They allow us to function and protect us from danger. Survival depends on our senses.

It's astounding how far we've progressed in science and medicine, yet nothing we've accomplished compares to the miracle of a single human cell. And we possess trillions of cells, each unique. Human beings are more sophisticated than anything in our known universe. It can be argued that a human being is the apex of the known universe. It is important to be aware of how awe-inspiring, complex, and powerful your body is. We've been created for the survival of our species and ourselves yet with capacity for emotion, empathy, reflection, and compassion; we are able to accomplish so much more than just survival.

Your Extraordinary Mind and Body: Balanced

One of our miraculous abilities is achieving and maintaining homeostasis. *Merriam-Webster's Medical Dictionary* defines homeostasis as:

homeostasis: ho·meo·sta·sis | /hō-mē-ō-ˈstā-səs/ *noun*
: the maintenance of relatively stable internal physiological conditions (as body temperature or the pH of blood) in higher animals under fluctuating environmental conditions
: the process of maintaining a stable psychological state in the individual under varying psychological pressures or stable social conditions in a group under varying social, environmental, or political factors

Homeostasis is a vital life force. We must remain in balance to survive. If we get too much acid (low pH) in our blood, it harms our organs. Consider how we take care of a houseplant. We need to make sure the soil is moist but not oversaturated. We need to give it sunlight but not scorch it. We do all these things to ensure the right balance of water and nutrients. We as humans instinctually do this inside our bodies. We sweat when we are hot so that water evaporates. Evaporative water is cooling, so sweating regulates our temperature. When we are trying to rid our body of unwanted intruders such as bacteria and viruses, we get a fever, but not so high of one as to kill us. By heating itself up, our body kills the intruders without harming itself. When we need oxygen to feed our cells, we naturally breathe at a faster rate. All of these, plus an uncountable number of other functions, work as your body's optimal survival thermostat, helping to maintain homeostasis.

Your Extraordinary Mind and Body: Strong

We are constantly exposed to messages from the media about the fragility of our bodies. Look at how we consume hand sanitizer by the bucket. America spends more on healthcare than most other countries, yet has a higher infant mortality rate and relatively lower life expectancy for the developed world.[50]

We often feel weak and incomplete, yet nothing is further from the truth. Despite drinking poison in increasing quantities, usually daily, we still function. By believing we are weak, we foster the misconception that we need something more to thrive.

We are not weak; we are strong. We represent the very pinnacle of existence, stronger and more capable than anything we know of. We populated and explored the entire planet and even the moon before most of our modern medical discoveries.

It's a miracle I survived all my years of heavy drinking and am healthy and thriving. It's a testament to how strong we are. When I decided to stop drinking, I expected to lose weight and improve my health. I was not disappointed—I lost ten pounds in the first month. The real surprise was how my life improved in ways I didn't expect. For one thing, my confidence skyrocketed. Also, when my body healed, I found myself amazed at the difference in how I felt every day. During my years of drinking I didn't feel particularly sick, but I didn't feel physically great either. I completely forgot how it felt to have tons of energy. Now I'm often surprised by how much I can get done, while still feeling motivated and happy. It is staggering to realize what we are capable of when we are mentally and physically strong.

We know more than ever about the dangers of alcohol and drugs, yet addiction is on the rise. As a society we find this confusing. The "Just Say No" campaign, introduced by First Lady Nancy Reagan, remains one of the most famous anti-drug campaigns of all time.[51] Between 1998 and 2004, the U.S. Congress spent almost $1 billion on national anti-drug media campaigns. Why? Because we continue to see addiction on the rise, and we just don't understand why. Youth today drink more than they did in the '80s, and though we are concerned, we can't seem to understand why the rates of drug and alcohol use are increasing. I believe part of the reason is that we inadvertently condition ourselves to believe we are weak. We believe we lack some vital ingredient necessary to the enjoyment of our lives. We conclude that we are deficient; we need substances to enjoy life and deal with stress. We've been unconsciously conditioned to believe alcohol helps us compensate for this deficiency, that it will help us feel strong, uninhibited, creative, and confident. Or maybe we think it will help us deal with the pressures and hassles of daily life.

Your Warning Mechanisms: Symptoms

Now let's look for a couple minutes at the most common way our body warns us when something isn't right: symptoms. When we feel a symptom of illness, we usually hurry to the medicine cabinet or the nearest doctor to make the discomfort go away. The pharmaceutical industry has never been bigger.

Imagine you are on a ship, and you sail into a storm. The captain can no longer see the shore or the stars and is completely dependent on the ship's navigational systems. A bright red light starts flashing. This light lets him know one of his navigational instruments is low on battery. He can't accurately navigate without it. What if, instead of replacing the battery, he removed the red indicator light? Did the captain fix the issue? Nope. He compounded it.

My mother is a health nut. She ate organic food before most people knew what organic food was. She won't even take Advil because she believes our ailments can and should be healed through natural, herbal, and food-based remedies rather than with chemicals. Although I ignored her guidance for many years, especially in college when I rebelled against my healthy upbringing with a diet of Taco Bell and Nerds candy, I have come to realize how poignant and true her advice is: We must exercise caution before doing anything that alters our normal functions. It can be terrifying to realize how little we know about the inner workings of our bodies and minds. When we mess with the functions of our bodies or numb our senses with alcohol and other drugs, we act like the captain, inviting catastrophe.

Tommy Rosen, founder of Recovery 2.0 and an addiction specialist, teaches that we have an "infinite pharmacy within," meaning inside we have every instinct, hormone, and drug we need to help us live long, healthy, and happy lives. If you look at your body's ability to produce adrenaline or endorphins, you see they are supplied in the perfect quantity at the exact time needed. We possess a phenomenal system.

Your immune system is your single most powerful weapon against disease. It is significantly more important to your health than any modern medicine. Ask any doctor and she will tell you the same thing. We've discussed how alcohol severely damages your immune system's ability to function. Drinking is like removing the red indicator light on your immune system.

A rare genetic condition aptly referred to as Congenital Insensitivity to Pain prevents a person from feeling pain. At first this might seem like a good thing. A life with no pain, who'd complain about that? It is actually one of life's scariest disorders. You wouldn't realize the shower was scalding until your skin reddened and blistered. You wouldn't know your bone was broken until it protruded from your arm. People suffering from this disorder have no chance of living a normal life. It would be hard to make it past childhood unless you lived inside a bubble. Pain gets a bad rap, but it is our friend—it keeps us alive.

As kids we longed to be older, to have our own houses, cars, and money to spend. As adults we wish we were young again because we are always tired and life seems to get increasingly stressful. It shouldn't be this way. During childhood and adolescence we undergo more changes than at any other time in our lives. In every other animal, childhood is much more stressful than adulthood.[52]

Think about how tough high school was. Remember the mental strain of the changes you underwent. As a child you don't feel in control of your life and your destiny, which generates fear and stress. When you are mentally at peace and physically strong as an adult, you experience the best of both worlds. You regain the vigor of youth, and your actual age no longer seems to matter. You feel more comfortable in your own skin. You are wiser and better adjusted. These are the best years of your life. You have more energy, joy, vigor, courage, and self-respect than ever before. Alcohol steals this from us. We drink more and more and become sicker and sicker. It is gradual, and we don't realize we no longer feel our best. We become accustomed to it and actually believe it's normal to feel fatigued, stressed, and somewhat unhappy. Now, granted, exhaustion can be caused by many things besides alcohol, but if you are drinking, there is no doubt it exacerbates these stresses, making exhaustion and even regular hangovers an unpleasant way of life. There is not a clear sign that we are doing something to hurt ourselves other than the hangover. Perhaps this chronic exhaustion is the body's way of saying that something's wrong.

These days I have so much energy it's incredible. It took time to regain my energy, but over time I healed from years of drinking poison. When you are physically strong, you feel on top of the world. You are present to fully enjoy the great moments in life. I handle stress better too. Before, my stressors multiplied because, instead of dealing with my problems, I ignored them by drinking. When left unattended, they grew inexplicably large. Without drinking, I can mindfully manage stress. In fact my ability to handle the things I once drank to ignore can be empowering. I don't mean to say I never have hard days—of course I do. But when you are healthy and happy, everything becomes easier.

Your Warning Mechanisms: Instincts

We have a staggering intellect that both helps and harms us. It's helpful when we use that intellect to recognize our bodies' warning lights—symptoms—and search for the root problems. It's harmful when we rely solely on our intelligence and ignore our bodies' instinctual knowledge. Instinct is the work of our bodies' senses alerting us to what will harm us. Sadly, we often ignore this most basic warning system.

When something goes wrong with our body, we visit a doctor. Doctors will tell you that we understand relatively little about how we are made and how to heal ourselves. We continuously learn more, disproving existing medical theories. We used to think that bloodletting—draining blood from a sick person—would cure illness by draining the malady from the body. We now realize this actually harmed the patient, sapping vital strength from an ailing body. Now, of course, our knowledge and technology is growing at an unprecedented rate. We are more informed than at any other point in the history of the world, yet we would be stupid to imagine that our knowledge is complete. You only have to read the news to realize we are constantly discovering new things and disproving existing theories.

Our health is the single most important thing we have, and without it, nothing else matters. Our instincts are specifically designed to guide us. Yet in our stubbornness, we rely heavily on our own intellect, trusting our knowledge more than our senses, even though common knowledge is often later disproven. We ignore our instincts in favor of intelligence, not realizing our instincts are designed to keep us alive and healthy. Alcohol deadens our senses and mutes our instincts. It is important that we do not ignore our natural instincts; they are the most valuable source of information we have regarding our health and longevity.

We need to see that we are strong, whole, and complete. We need to understand that alcohol, instead of acting as a support to help us deal with life, actually deadens our senses and harms our immune system. Consuming chemicals, which affect the functioning of our bodies, is reckless. And in this case, the danger is increased because our chemical of choice is addictive. In truth, you don't need alcohol to enjoy life or to relieve stress. You only think you do. And in reality, it does nothing for us. As you uncover the truth, your perception will begin to change, both consciously and unconsciously, and with this knowledge you will no longer desire alcohol. You will be free.

6.
LIMINAL POINT: ARE WE REALLY DRINKING FOR THE TASTE?

"Recovery is all about using our power to change
our beliefs that are based on faulty data."
—*Kevin McCormack*

Before you ever drank a drop you **observed** everyone around you drinking, seeming to enjoy the taste of alcohol. Yet your early **experience** probably contradicted that belief. Kids generally don't like their first sip of alcohol. Since you continue to observe others around you drinking, you **assume** there must be something good and beneficial about drinking, despite the taste. You **conclude** that you should persevere in drinking; you may even be told you need to "acquire the taste." Over time, you do indeed acquire a taste for alcohol. Now your experience is in line with your observations, and you can more easily conclude that alcohol tastes good, and you do, in fact, drink because you like the taste.

Let's consider reality:

You Just Have to Acquire the Taste

This justification is the great deceit that lures new drinkers in. My colleague, Yani, is French. She told me her parents encouraged her to have sips of wine at dinner from the age of eight, much like my parents encouraged me to at least taste the spinach on my plate. She never liked it and would tell them so, but they would insist on at least one sip telling Yani to just wait and see—she would like it when she is older. Sure enough, Yani now drinks wine every night. When we take our first sips and almost gag, there's always someone there to reassure us that alcohol is an acquired taste.

But let's consider again our awesome bodies, whose purpose is to make sure we remain alive. We know that we need food and water to survive, and if we don't eat and drink, we will die. Other animals are not consciously aware of this, so how does nature make sure they eat and drink? Instinctually, they feel hunger and thirst.

We know that certain things are poison because we are told so or because the label says so. How does a doe know what is poison, which grasses to eat and which will make her sick? It's a brilliant aspect of her design, yet quite simple: Grasses that deer are meant to eat smell and taste nice, while the grasses that will make the deer sick smell and taste bad.

Our sense of smell and taste are vital to our well-being. They help us distinguish between good and rotten food. The products in our refrigerators may carry expiration dates, but our own ability to smell when meat is rotten or taste spoiled milk is more sophisticated than the dates placed on foods. These senses ensure our survival.

I was recently in Brazil and saw ethanol for sale at the gas stations. You may be surprised to know that the ethanol you put in your gas tank is the exact same ethanol in the liquor you drink. Yep, alcohol, without additives, is ethanol. Pure alcohol tastes awful, and a very small amount will kill you. We use extensive processes and additives to make it taste good enough to drink. Unfortunately, none of these processes reduce the harms associated with drinking fuel.

Alcohol destroys our health by attacking our liver and immune system and is related to more than sixty diseases.[53] Yet because we are only peripherally aware of the harms but very familiar with pro-alcohol social messages, we often justify our drinking by saying we drink for the taste. And we believe this is true. We have an uncanny ability to unknowingly deceive ourselves.

Imagine a college kid drinking one of his first beers at a football game. It's cheap and warm, and almost certainly does not taste good. You are fairly sure he would rather be drinking a soda. If you ask him why he isn't drinking a soda, he will probably tell you he likes the taste of beer. In truth, he wants to fit in, and only kids drink soda during football games. He cannot admit this, and might not even realize it, so he tells you he likes the taste. This does not sync with reality as you watch him choke the beer down.

If you ask him a few months later, at the homecoming game, he will again tell you he likes it. Since he has been drinking for a few months, the answer may hold some truth. He has started to acquire the taste. And since the alcohol is addictive, it has created an imperceptible craving for itself, which, when satisfied, gives him the perception of enjoyment.

I don't know anyone who drank so many sodas they puked. Yet, how many people do you know who have drunk enough to throw up? Even the most moderate drinkers I know occasionally take it too far. Throwing up is awful. Awful, but when you think about it, actually incredible. Throwing up saves our lives, protecting us from alcohol poisoning. The implication is clear: Alcohol is not good for us. Yet we are not deterred. We carry on, thinking of our nights "worshiping the porcelain gods" as a badge of honor. It's college after all, and we are determined to acquire a taste for booze.

Finally, you actually like the taste of alcohol, but it is still the same chemical in your gas tank. It is still destroying your liver, your immune system, and your brain. The taste doesn't actually change—that's impossible.

Think of the guy who showers in cologne. You can smell him coming from a mile away, yet he is unaware. It's the same concept. I went to school in an agricultural town surrounded by ranches and farms. Aggie towns have a very intense smell. After a few months there, I couldn't smell it at all. It's remarkable how, given enough time, senses grow immune to the most unpleasant things.

There's no doubt alcohol tastes bad. Why else would we need to go to such great lengths to make it palatable with mixers and sweeteners? You may be a manly type who now loves to drink whiskey straight. You acquired a taste for whiskey like I acquired a smell for animal crap.

Do you really drink just because of the taste?

It Enhances the Taste of Food

The enhancement of food by a particular drink makes sense when you think about milk and cookies. You actually take a cookie and dip it into milk, changing the texture and flavor of the cookie. I can understand how this could enhance the taste. But you don't put wine in your mouth with your steak, so how can it change the way food tastes? Not to mention it's been medically proven that alcohol actually deadens your taste buds rather than increasing their sensitivity.[54]

Now, I admit the flavor of wine can be great in sauces, but so can just about anything depending on what else you mix with it. A popular cooking show forces chefs to cook with all kinds of nasty ingredients to make them palatable. I find it strange that, with thousands of beverages in existence, we only use this excuse with alcohol. We don't hear people claiming they drink Coke because it enhances the flavor of their hot dog. It strikes me, as a marketer, that this is a genius marketing tactic. If we can marry the product (alcohol) with the authentic pleasures of eating, we have a much higher chance of selling a glass of wine, at its incredible markup, every time we sell a steak.

Conversations justifying why we drink happen all the time. We don't sit around justifying other things we like, like why we eat grapefruit. Yet when you turn down an alcoholic drink, it seems everyone around you launches into a diatribe explaining in painful detail all the reasons they are drinking. If you pay attention, you will start to notice how conversations about alcohol are not balanced. When eating a doughnut we will probably mention the calorie count or how much sugar it has. And for good reason—it helps us limit ourselves to just one. Yet when discussing alcohol you never hear someone say, "This booze is delicious. It enhances the taste of my food, but I do worry about liver damage."

Why is this? Why do we group together and chat up the great things about drinking? It's so we can collectively close our eyes to the dangers. Herd mentality makes it easier to believe or do something because everyone else is saying or doing the same thing. This is exactly what happens when people start to talk about the "full-bodied, oaky, lemony, exaggerated, pompous yet fruity" flavor of a Cabernet.

Further, at least when it comes to wine, there is actual proof that almost no one can actually tell the difference between good wines and cheap wines. The American Association of Wine Economists did a study of more than six thousand wine drinkers. In these blind taste tests, wine drinkers were unable to distinguish expensive wines from cheap wines. In fact, the majority claimed to prefer the cheap wines.[55] You might be amused to know that the same association conducted a study two years later and found that people are also unable to differentiate Pâté from dog food.[56]

I Drink to Quench My Thirst

"How can I be so thirsty this morning when I drank so much last night."
—Anonymous

We think a cold beer sounds good on a hot day to quench our thirst. Since beer is about 96% water and 4% alcohol, it's logical to conclude the water content in beer should quench your thirst. Yet alcohol is a diuretic, a substance that eliminates water from your system by making you pee. The beer not only sucks away the 96% of water but further depletes your body's water content. That's why you wake up in the middle of the night with incredible thirst after a bout of drinking. Your mouth is parched, and you feel like you are dying for a glass of water. Dehydration from drinking can actually shrink your brain and its ability to function.[57] This means after one drink you are actually thirstier, and that makes it easier for the next pint to go down. You probably wouldn't drink a six-pack of soda, yet we do that with beer all the time. The more our thirst increases, the better we believe the next beer will taste because of the illusion it is quenching our thirst. Not to mention the alcohol is addictive, and your taste buds are becoming numbed.[58] You want more. What genius product marketing.

I closed my mind to the dangers of drinking. I went to great lengths to justify alcohol and encouraged others to drink with me. Drinking with other people seemed more fun, but I now see it was less stressful. It's not drinking alone, when we are by ourselves, that bothers us. It's drinking by ourselves in the company of people who are not drinking that makes us question our choice. When no one else is drinking you feel quite dumb standing around drinking something that is making you lose control of your faculties. If everyone is doing it, even if it goes against your rational judgment, you don't have to come up with reasons to justify it. If everyone is doing it, there must be good reasons—it must not be that bad. It's amazing how far we will go to delude ourselves. Tell a lie long enough and convincingly enough, and even the liar will believe it.

7.
YOU: POLLUTED

"Education is the most powerful weapon which
you can use to change the world."
—*Nelson Mandela*

I didn't intend to write this chapter. In fact, I wrote it after the first round of edits. Why? I believe a positive outlook is far more productive than a negative one. I stand by my belief that listing the horrors of alcohol doesn't help us quit. It gives us the conscious desire to quit, but if you're reading this book, you probably already have that. It is your unconscious desire to drink that is causing you so much trouble. For as long as you can remember, you have been conditioned to believe alcohol provides numerous benefits. These beliefs must be reversed in order to find freedom. A list of the harms does nothing to undo your perception of the benefits. And chapters like this one can cause drinkers stress, and we tend to drink more when we are stressed. In the end, our situation is not improved.

Before you skip on past this chapter, though, as a society, we really do need an education about what alcohol is and what it does to our bodies. I had assumed it was common knowledge that alcohol is harmful to your health. I was wrong. More than seven thousand people volunteered to be beta readers—reading early drafts of the book and providing feedback during the editing process. As their comments poured in, I realized that it is not common knowledge that alcohol is harmful. In fact, we have been so indoctrinated that we believe the opposite is true. Common knowledge actually claims that moderate drinking, defined as one to three drinks per day, benefits your health. Given these misconceptions, this chapter became vital, and I will start with the presupposition that you believe some alcohol use is good for your health.

Why All the Misinformation?

I understand where these beliefs come from. Articles come out all the time claiming that wine is good for your heart or that alcohol reduces your cholesterol. A few studies have correlated alcohol consumption and life expectancy. What is bizarre about these studies is that they ignore the cause of death (i.e., did alcohol contribute to death?) and lump all deaths together. Nonetheless, innumerable articles are published highlighting the relatively few studies that claim alcohol is good for you and ignoring the thousands of studies that prove otherwise.

So why do the supposed health benefits get so much publicity that they have become commonly believed? There are a few reasons. First, journalists need to write popular articles that get attention and exposure. This enables them to claim a higher readership, sell more advertisements, and build their business. While there are many more studies about the dangers of drinking, there are far fewer published articles. You can test this with a quick Google search. If you search "alcohol harms" or "alcohol dangers," your results will include numerous studies from organizations like the National Institute on Alcohol Abuse and Alcoholism or medical sites like the Mayo Clinic or

WebMD. My search of both of these terms turned up zero popular publications (*Times, Huffington Post, Washington Post*) on the first page. Try searching "alcohol healthy." Almost no reliable sources will show up, but you'll see dozens of articles with headlines like "Drinking for Health" from popular but unscientific media outlets. These articles invariably point to one of a small handful of actual studies.

We've been duped by media that print what is popular rather than what has been comprehensively demonstrated. But we also dupe ourselves. This is another example of confirmation bias. Articles that claim health benefits from wine or beer get thousands to tens of thousands of shares. They proliferate on social media. With our culture's short attention span and focus on headlines, it is no wonder we have come to believe that some drinking is actually good for you. When you do find an article in a popular media outlet that cautions against alcohol use, you'll notice it has fewer shares, often fewer than ten. This means that only the first line of readership sees these articles, and the information rarely goes viral.

Dr. Jürgen Rehm, PhD, Senior Scientist at the Centre for Addictions and Mental Health in Toronto, cautions that studies claiming beneficial health links to alcohol represent a small fraction of the studies conducted, which generally demonstrate harm. Yet when measured in the press, the studies claiming benefits are more often highlighted. He reiterates, "We have counted how many studies are reported in the press, and there are many more reports on the beneficial link than on the detrimental link between alcohol and health." There is ten times the evidence to support the dangers of alcohol, yet it's the small fraction of the research supporting the benefits of drinking that is published and shared, often with the purported benefits taken out context.

This is again proven with insight into the science of sharing. Why do people share on social media? One of the top reasons for sharing is "social currency." People share things that they think will make them look "good" (smart, cool, hip, informed, etc.) in the eyes of their peers. An article about happy hour doing wonders for your heart carries more social currency than the study that disproves the relationship between wine and heart health.[59]

But it is confusing. There is a lot of misleading information out there. We cannot blame ourselves for being misinformed. This chapter will educate you. The information has been compiled from statistically relevant studies, and I have included data from both sides to allow you to draw your own conclusions. I encourage you to dig deeper into the sources provided and to further your knowledge with your own research. We seem to pay more attention to the side effects of ibuprofen than we do to the beverage society consumes most. It is important that we use our intellect with discernment, keeping up-to-date on the most recent articles and understanding what the study is actually saying. We owe it to ourselves to be informed about what we put into our bodies and to make decisions based on fact.

Let's focus on what alcohol does to our bodies. We will speak more about societal harms and secondhand drinking (effects on those in proximity of the drinker) later in the book.

The Overall Harm Factor

Researchers scored twenty drugs on criteria related to overall harm, considering both the harm to the user and the harm to people who are around the user but not actually using the drug. The majority of the criteria related to the specific harm to an individual. Overall, alcohol scored as the most harmful drug, with an overall harm score of 72. Heroin came in second with a harm score of 55, and crack cocaine scored third with a score of 54.[60]

The World Health Organization (WHO) says that alcohol is a causal factor in sixty types of diseases and injuries. The report goes on to say that alcohol has surpassed AIDS and is now the world's leading risk factor for death among males ages 15–59.[61]

In the United States, excessive alcohol consumption, defined as four drinks in two hours for women (five for men) or eight drinks per week for women (fifteen for men),[62] is a leading cause of premature mortality, with 88,000 alcohol-related deaths in the U.S. every year.[63] This means alcohol causes more than twice the number of deaths as all other drugs combined, both illegal and prescription. All illicit drugs cause 17,000 deaths per year, and prescription drugs are responsible for 22,000 deaths per year.[64]

Benefits of Alcohol?

There are medicinal benefits to alcohol. It is a strong antiseptic and can be used to dull pain. Not surprisingly, doctors have found other methods, such as ibuprofen and morphine, to more effectively relieve pain. But there are numerous claims about more dubious long-term benefits of alcohol. For instance, there is evidence that wine can raise your levels of good cholesterol because of its antioxidants.[65] But is it really about the wine? Many fruit juices contain more antioxidants than wine. Yet I don't know anyone who drinks juice on a nightly basis, while I know plenty of people who habitually drink wine. If you disciplined yourself to drink a glass of antioxidant-rich juice every night, I'd wager you would get the same results. And there would be no harmful side effects or chance of becoming addicted.

We have seen many articles around the supposed heart-health benefits of alcohol, specifically wine. A new study that analyzed the drinking habits and cardiovascular health of over 260,000 people shows that drinking alcohol, even light-to-moderate amounts, provides no heart-health benefit.

The other well-publicized claim is that people who drink live longer than abstainers. One of the most famous studies to this effect is the Holahan study.[66] Charles J. Holahan tracked 1,824 individuals, ranging in age from 55–65 when the study started and 75–85 at the end of the twenty-year period. The majority (65%) were men, and

92% were Caucasian. The study found a correlation (not a causation) between drinking and living longer, meaning a higher percentage of the 345 abstainers died during the twenty-year period than the 1,479 drinkers. Cause of death was not measured or considered. The study gives a caveat to the significance of the correlation by saying that "abstainers were significantly more likely to have had prior drinking problems, to be obese and to smoke cigarettes than were moderate drinkers." The people who abstained seemed to abstain for reasons such as other health issues or prior alcohol abuse, and the reasons the 239 abstainers died between the ages of 55 and 85 is unknown. And I don't want to make decisions about my overall health based on a tiny sample size of 239 individuals. There is a correlation between the stork population and the number of babies born, but surely we aren't tempted to translate this correlation into causation.[67] Why should we treat alcohol differently?

It would not be a good idea to self-medicate with morphine, codeine, or any other prescription drug. In fact, it's probably not a good idea to self-medicate with any addictive substance. Medicating for any condition from heart disease to Parkinson's should be done under supervision with a specific treatment plan and well-documented and understood side effects. While there are correlations between alcohol consumption and health, none make a compelling case that alcohol itself should be medicinally self-administered.[68]

The Dangers of Drinking: To Your Body

As we discussed in the previous chapter, your body is arguably the most complex and capable organism on the planet. Your body's ability to ensure your survival and overcome illness lies beyond our comprehension. If you take care of your precious body, it will take care of you. I would like to outline what alcohol does to your body, so you see why it wreaks such devastation on your health and life. I've compiled this information from several studies with the primary source being the U.S. Department of Health and Human Services.[69]

Your Brain

Your brain's structure is incredibly complex. The brain communicates with neurons, trillions of tiny nerve cells, which translate information into signals that the brain and body can understand. Your brain's network of chemicals (neurotransmitters) carry messages between neurons. These chemicals are powerful, and they change your feelings, moods, and physical responses. Your brain works to balance these chemicals, either speeding up the transfer of information or slowing it down. Alcohol slows the pace of communication between neurotransmitters. It interrupts your brain's communication pathways, literally reducing the speed of communication between parts of your brain by slowing down your brain's neural highways.[70] It slows communications from your senses, decreasing your responsiveness and deadening your senses.

Your cerebellum, limbic system, and cerebral cortex are most vulnerable to alcohol. Your cerebellum is responsible for motor coordination, memory, and emotional response. Your limbic system monitors your memories and emotions. And, your cerebral cortex manages activity, including planning, social interaction, problem solving, and learning. It comes as no surprise that alcohol hinders motor coordination. After all, being tipsy or unable to walk a straight line is a classic indicator of alcohol use. But have you realized that alcohol robs you of your natural ability to manage your emotions? This is why alcohol causes unhappiness and irritability, and why some drinkers describe their binges as either crying jags or fits of rage.

It won't surprise you that severe, chronic depression and heavy drinking are closely linked.[71] What is more terrifying is that over time the artificial stimulation your brain receives from drinking makes you neurologically unable to experience the pleasure you once did from everyday activities, such as seeing a friend, reading a book, or even having sex.[72] Alcohol interferes with your ability to behave, think, and interact socially. Drinking impedes your natural capacity to remember, learn, and solve problems.

Just one bout of heavy drinking, meaning five drinks in two hours for men or four drinks in two hours for women, can cause permanent alterations in your nerve cells and reduce the size of your individual brain cells.[73]

A release of serotonin, a neurotransmitter that regulates emotion, physiologically contributes to the initial tipsy feeling. Sometimes drinking can release endorphins, the neurotransmitter responsible for feelings of euphoria. You might think this is a good thing, but actually it's not. Your brain tries to compensate. It doesn't understand the surge in neurotransmitters and tries to adjust and restore balance.[74] This is one of the reasons you build up a tolerance, become dependent, and experience physical withdrawal symptoms.

Your liver acts as your first line of defense. It breaks down the alcohol so that your body can rid itself of the poison as quickly as possible. When breaking down alcohol, your liver releases toxins and damaged liver cells into the bloodstream. These toxins are more dangerous to the brain than the alcohol itself.[75] The toxins released into your brain are responsible for bad sleep, mood imbalance, personality changes (like violence or weeping), anxiety, depression, and shortened attention span, and they can result in coma and death.

Don't be feeling too discouraged right now. Abstinence can help reverse the negative effects on thinking skills, memory, and attention. And over several months to a year structural brain changes have been shown to self-correct.[76]

Your Heart

Your heart beats over 100,000 times per day, carrying 2,000 gallons of blood through your body. As you probably know, there are two chambers in your heart. The right side pumps blood to your lungs where it exchanges carbon dioxide for oxygen. Your heart then relaxes and allows the oxygenated blood to flow back into your left chamber. When your heart contracts again, it pumps the oxygen-rich blood into your body, nourishing your tissues and organs. On the journey through your body, your blood passes through your kidneys to cleanse it of waste. Blood becomes "dirty" because it is one of our more efficient cleansing systems and constantly removes toxins from your body. Electrical signals ensure your heart beats at the right pace multiple times per second for your entire life.

Alcohol weakens the heart muscle so that it sags and stretches, making it impossible to continue contracting effectively.[77] When your heart can no longer contract efficiently, you are unable to transport enough oxygen to your organs and tissues. Your body is no longer nourished appropriately.

Drinking large amounts in one sitting, even on rare occasions, can affect the electrical system that regulates your heartbeat.[78] This can cause blood clots. During a hard drinking bout, your heart may not beat hard enough, which can cause your blood to pool and clots to form. The opposite can also happen. Your heart can beat too fast, not allowing time for the chambers to fill with blood so insufficient oxygen is pumped out to your body. As a result, binge drinking raises your likelihood of having a stroke by 39%.[79]

Your blood vessels are stretchy, like elastic, so that they can transport blood without putting too much pressure on your heart. Drinking alcohol releases stress hormones that constrict your blood vessels, elevate your blood pressure, and cause hypertension, in which the blood vessels stiffen.[80] Hypertension is dangerous and causes heart disease.[81]

Your Liver

Two million Americans suffer from alcohol-related liver disease,[82] making it a leading cause of illness and death. Your liver stores nutrients and energy and produces enzymes that stave off disease and rid your body of dangerous substances, including alcohol. As we've discussed, the process of breaking down alcohol creates toxins, which are actually more dangerous than the alcohol itself.[83] Alcohol damages liver cells causing inflammation and weakening your body's natural defenses. Liver inflammation disrupts your metabolism, which impacts the function of other organs. Further, inflammation can cause liver scar tissue buildup.[84]

Your liver function suffers because alcohol alters the natural chemicals in the liver. These natural chemicals are needed to break down and remove scar tissue. Drinking also causes steatosis or "fatty liver." Fat buildup on your liver makes it harder for the liver to operate.[85] Eventually fibrosis (some scar tissue) becomes cirrhosis (much more scar tissue). Cirrhosis prevents the liver from performing critical functions, including managing infections, absorbing nutrients, and removing toxins from the blood. This can result in liver cancer and type-2 diabetes.[86] Twenty-five percent of heavy drinkers will develop cirrhosis.[87]

Your Immune System

Germs surround us, making our immune system our most important tool for fighting off disease. Our skin protects our bodies from infection and disease. If germs make it into the body, we have two systems that provide defense: the innate system (which fends off first-time germ exposure) and the adaptive system (which retains information about prior germ invasions and promptly defeats repeat attackers). Alcohol suppresses both.[88]

Our immune system uses cytokines, small proteins, to send out chemical messages about infection in a kind of early alert system. Alcohol disrupts the production of cytokines. When working correctly, cytokines alert our immune system to intruders, and our immune system responds with white blood cells that attack, surrounding and swallowing harmful bacteria. Alcohol impairs both functions, which leaves us more susceptible to pneumonia, tuberculosis, and other diseases.[89] Further studies link alcohol to an increased susceptibility to HIV, not only increasing our chances of contracting HIV, but also impacting how rapidly the disease develops once contracted.[90]

Alcohol and Cancer

> *"Responsible drinking has become a 21st-centry mantra for how most people view alcohol consumption. But when it comes to cancer, no amount of alcohol is safe."*[91]
> —*Laura A. Stokowski*

But wait, light drinking doesn't cause cancer, does it? Yes, apparently it does. In a meta-analysis of 222 studies across 92,000 light drinkers and 60,000 non-drinkers with cancer, light drinking was associated with higher cancer risks for many types of cancers, including breast cancer.[92]

A seven-year study of 1.2 million middle-aged women highlights the direct and terrifying link between drinking and cancer. According to this study, alcohol increased the chance of developing cancers of the breast, mouth, throat, rectum, liver, and esophagus.[93]

The most frightening revelation is that cancer risk increases *no matter how little or what type* of alcohol the women drank. According to cancer.gov, the risk of breast cancer was higher across all levels of alcohol intake.[94] It's not just heavy drinkers or people who drink every day who increase their chances of getting cancer. Compared to women who don't drink at all, women who consume three alcoholic drinks per week increase their breast cancer risk by 15%.[95] According to Cancer Research UK, "There's no 'safe' limit for alcohol when it comes to cancer."[96]

Both binge drinking and daily drinking have the same cancer-causing effect. "Drinking alcohol increases the risk of cancer whether you drink it all in one go or a bit at a time."[97] It also doesn't matter what type of alcohol you drink. It's the alcohol itself that leads to the damage, regardless of whether you imbibe beer, wine, or hard alcohol.[98]

Another study links 11% of all breast cancer cases to alcohol.[99] Since 295,240 new cases of breast cancer were diagnosed in 2014,[100] about 32,476 new cases of breast cancer were connected to alcohol.

Although many of us are not aware of the relationship between alcohol and cancer, it should not come as a surprise. The International Agency for Research on Cancer (IARC) declared alcohol a carcinogen in 1988.[101] Alcohol itself, ethanol, is a known carcinogen, and alcoholic beverages can contain at least fifteen other carcinogenic compounds including arsenic, formaldehyde, and lead.[102] Alcohol causes or contributes to cancer in different ways. When your liver breaks down alcohol, it produces a toxic chemical called acetaldehyde. Acetaldehyde damages your cells, rendering them incapable of repair and making them more vulnerable to cancer. Cirrhosis also leads to cancer. Alcohol increases some hormones, including estrogen, contributing to breast cancer risk. It also causes cancer by damaging DNA and stopping our cells from repairing this damage.[103]

In summary, any level of alcohol consumption increases the risk of developing an alcohol-related cancer.[104] This is a discouraging message. However, I have good news—any reduction in alcohol intake lowers your cancer risk.

Alcohol and Death

You already know that you can die from alcohol poisoning by drinking too much alcohol in one sitting. What you may not know is that alcohol overdose can also occur from a continual infusion of alcohol into the bloodstream over time, resulting in death that does not correlate with a single binge.[105] Early death from alcohol steals more than 2,400,000 hours of human life per year in the United States.

According to the Centers for Disease Control and Prevention (CDC), alcoholism reduces life expectancy by ten–twelve years.[106]

This may lead you to ask what level of alcohol use really is safe. According to the most up-to-date research (2014 and newer), there is no risk-free level of alcohol consumption.[107] Considering how many people still drink every day, this is a sobering fact indeed.

8.
LIMINAL POINT: IS ALCOHOL LIQUID COURAGE?

"The secret to happiness is freedom. The secret to freedom is courage."
—*Carrie Jones*

You have **observed** alcohol used as liquid courage in popular media your whole life. The cowboy who takes a few shots before the high-noon gunfight. James Bond with his martinis "shaken not stirred." Even soldiers sipping from their flasks before battle. You **assumed** alcohol did provide liquid courage. You tried it, and your **experience** taking a shot to rid yourself of your nerves confirmed that your butterflies subsided. You've **concluded** that yes, alcohol helps you take on life with an extra dose of bravery.

Let's consider reality:

Liquid Courage

I get nervous every time I speak in public. Lately I've needed to speak more in front of senior colleagues. I can't recall exactly when, but somewhere along the line I figured that, since alcohol relaxed me, a quick drink before a speech would help me. I would stop at the hotel bar or buy a four-pack of single-serving wine bottles, keeping a few in my purse.

I was convinced drinking gave me confidence. I now realize alcohol actually chipped away my confidence.

In this day and age, most true danger has been eliminated from our daily lives. We live longer than ever before. We are not under attack by neighboring tribes or wild animals. We go to the grocery store rather than hunting for food. As a result we regard fear as weakness when, in reality, fear allows us to exercise caution and make better decisions. We protect ourselves because of fear. Considering that fear is key to our survival, calling someone fearless doesn't seem like much of a compliment. It is good for us to feel fear; it prevents us from taking unnecessary risks. With adrenaline pumping through our bodies we are more alert and responsive and can make faster decisions. Alcohol numbs your senses and prevents you from feeling natural fear. It is not possible for alcohol to give you courage because, by definition, if you've numbed feelings of fear you cannot be courageous. Courage means doing what is right or just, despite your fear. Ignoring, or disregarding, your fear goes against your instincts, which ensure your survival.[108]

So what's wrong with numbing my fear before a presentation? My natural nerves spurred me to prepare. They ensured I wasn't complacent and drove me to rehearse and plan. When I began to rely on alcohol to dampen my fear, I stopped preparing in advance. Instead I stayed up late, drinking the night before and putting off my rehearsals. Preparation made me a good public speaker. But once I started drugging myself with alcohol, knowing I wasn't prepared, my nerves skyrocketed. I actually worsened my fear by drinking, and so I felt I needed a few swigs before I stepped on stage. As you can guess, my speeches got worse. Thankfully it never reached a point where I was visibly drunk on stage, though if I hadn't found *This Naked Mind*, I have no doubt I was heading that direction.

Think about an athlete or a soldier who uses alcohol as liquid courage. The same thing happens—by removing natural apprehension, they rob themselves of important skills. I won't disagree that fear, nervousness, and apprehension are unpleasant feelings, but they are valuable and necessary.

In our society, we have so many ways we protect ourselves that we actually look for activities, like adventure sports, to demonstrate our bravery. I think drinking is one of those things. We know drinking has dangers, yet we brag about our ability to hold our liquor. Like a warrior demonstrating strength through his scars, we demonstrate strength by beating our bodies up and rallying the next morning. After a long night out with colleagues, comparing how much was drunk, who no longer remembers the evening, and who is feeling the best or the worst becomes a favorite topic of conversation. A hangover has become a badge of courage.

We went skiing recently (another, albeit healthier, activity we engage in to inject adrenaline into our safe and protected lives). My husband and I skied the back bowls (all double black diamond runs) while our kids took lessons. My sons, wanting to prove they were brave, courageous, and grown-up, asked to go with us to ski the bowls. When I explained the danger, it only enhanced the allure. If we can't do it, but Mom and Dad can, it must be awesome. We tried to caution them, but nothing we said was as powerful as what we did. They didn't care about the cliffs or that they weren't yet proficient skiers. We are their parents, they admire us, and if we're skiing hard stuff, they want to ski hard stuff.

This also happens during our teenage years—things our parents caution us against become available to try. We learn that some of the stuff our parents warned us about can be fun. We start to wonder if everything they've advised us against will be enjoyable. Danger means excitement, we think.

Do we believe telling our kids that "it's an adult drink" does anything to caution them? Quite the opposite—it enhances the allure.

According to the Substance Abuse and Mental Health Services Administration, more than half of Americans age twelve or older report that they are current drinkers of alcohol.[109] Thirty percent of adolescents report drinking by the eighth grade.[110] Our children do what we do, not what we say. Kids want to be brave, courageous, and grown-up. They emulate their parents; it's how they are programmed. When they see us playing with fire, whether it's on the double black diamond ski runs or by drinking poison, they also want to play with fire and prove their bravery. And there is no way we can deny that drinking alcohol is playing with fire. While illegal drugs kill 327 people per week, and prescription drugs kill 442 people per week, alcohol kills 1,692 people per week.[111] We are unintentionally conditioning our children. We are programming them to believe their lives will not be complete without drinks in their hands.

We use our brains to make choices, and choices often come down to fear. We choose what we are less afraid of. Our decisions change once the fear scales tip. For example, a woman in an abusive relationship may not leave the abuser because she fears living without him. If she has a child, however, the fear scales may tip. She may now fear for her child more than she fears being without a partner. In this way, children can be the catalyst for a woman to leave an abusive relationship. The fear scales tipped against cigarettes when new research proved smoking causes lung cancer and takes thirty years off your life. Many people quit because their fear of dying from lung cancer outweighed their fear of a life without cigarettes.

The rational decisions we make change in light of more information. Imagine you are a short, scrawny man. You've managed to piss off some guy who is 6'4" and 250 pounds. He is coming after you and wants blood. You run. You arrive at a wall and find yourself trapped. Without any other option, you turn around to fight. Your odds have not improved—your attacker is still much stronger than you, but your situation has changed. Running is no longer an option. It is not cowardly to run away, nor is it brave to turn around and fight.[112]

Let's say you are the same scrawny guy, but now you've been drinking. Drinking does nothing to improve your position; it makes it worse. You feel a false sense of bravado, and you decide to fight before you are cornered. Further, when you are fighting, your reactions are delayed, and your senses are dulled. You don't feel pain to the same extent, and instead of backing down you are severely injured. Alcohol does not make you brave because there is no such thing as bravery when it comes to the instincts, which keep us alive. Alcohol just makes you less aware of your instincts. In this instance alcohol makes you stupid rather than brave.

If you are hiking alone and see a mountain lion cub, would it be brave to try and get close enough for a photo? The mother lion, despite her natural fear of humans, will kill you to protect her cubs. She is protecting her young, showing courage. Yet, if her family was not threatened would she be showing cowardice by running away from humans? Carr says both bravery and cowardice are human concepts, which don't exist in the animal kingdom.

I believe true bravery does exist. It's shown when you make a decision to override your natural fear in order to do what is morally right, but not when you remove your fear by numbing your senses. Jumping onto the subway tracks to try to save a child is irrational but brave. Your fear of dying is surely greater than your fear of watching someone else die. Yet you can overcome that fear in order to help another person. You cannot be brave without fear. If alcohol removes your fear, it makes it impossible for you to be truly brave. And cowardice? Cowardice is when you do not act according to your moral compass, failing to do what you know to be right, because of your fear. In my experience, drinking, to shut out life and avoid actual issues I knew I needed to deal with, was, without a doubt, the act of a coward.

We fear ridicule as much as bodily harm. Say you are pressured into trying a drug for the first time. The fear of looking weak, cowardly, and stupid in front of your friends outweighs your fear of the drug. You ignore your instincts to avoid scorn. This is cowardice, not bravery. It is much harder to make the right decision, the better decision, and endure the blow to your ego. It is much harder to go against the grain, skipping the drink and showing your children a different way, than it is to be swept along in our drinking culture. That is courage. Drinking because everyone else is doing it or because you are worried about being left out is not. It takes great courage to stand up for what is right, to stand up to the majority even silently by ordering an iced tea rather than a beer. It takes courage to read this book. There is no bravery in using alcohol to rid yourself of fear.

And let us not ignore the fact that alcohol actually makes us more vulnerable. My husband is training to become a pilot. When he flies he depends on instruction and information from the ground crew. They alert him when it is clear to land and where other planes are located to ensure they don't collide. If the communication between my husband and the ground crew is cut off, he will be vulnerable. He will have less information about his surroundings and feel less in control. This is not a pleasant experience, yet we do this to ourselves willingly when we drink. Alcohol deadens the flow of information from our mind and senses. This increases our fear, as we realize we can no longer clearly hear instruction from the ground crew. We realize we are less prepared to deal with whatever situation we find ourselves in; the natural feedback our senses provide us with has been obscured. Drinking during times of danger worsens your fear because you know you are removing your defenses.

But wait, if you believe alcohol provides courage, relaxation, and enjoyment, isn't that almost the same as if it actually provided those things? Are you better off believing you have a helper to get you through life, even if it's a placebo, an illusion? But deep down you know the truth. You know an alcoholic doesn't valiantly face up to the hardships and sufferings of life. I always knew drinking revealed weakness, not bravery. I knew I had allowed myself to become some-one who could not face life on its own terms.

For many, alcohol ensnares them at such a slow pace that it's im-perceptible. The changes are subtle. You come to depend on alcohol, feeling it gives you the courage to face the day, when in reality it steals confidence from you.

9.
OH S#*%! WE'RE STUCK

"Once we accept our limits, we go beyond them."
—Albert Einstein

Trapped Without a Key

In *The Sober Revolution*, Lucy Rocca describes alcohol dependence in this way: "Breaking free from a dependency on alcohol is akin to escaping from a self-built prison . . . in the cycle of addiction you had no idea that you were effectively restricted behind bars."[113] When you're drinking more than you want to be drinking, it's as if you're behind bars. This idea is not unique to Rocca or myself—many other experts are starting to look at alcohol dependence in this way.

Imagine you're in a tight pair of handcuffs, without a key, and everyone blames you for it. You may have put them on yourself, but you don't really remember doing it, and you are very sorry that you did. You feel miserable.

Your wife takes you to see a doctor about the handcuffs. They're chafing your wrists, and your skin is infected. She is upset that you are no longer doing your part around the house. You find it hard to take out the garbage in a pair of handcuffs.

The doctor takes a look at you and tells you how bad it is for you to be in these handcuffs. The infection on your wrists could kill you if you are not careful. You need to get out of them as soon as possible. He goes on to tell you all the reasons you should take them off—they are affecting your family, your health, and your life. He tells you how difficult it is to pick up your kids with handcuffs on and that they will feel unloved. He gives you strict instructions to remove the cuffs. But he doesn't have the key, so nothing he says actually helps you get free.

What a frustrating experience. The doctor thinks you are stupid, and you think the doctor is an idiot. But doctors do this when they tell a drinker, who has become dependent on alcohol, that he needs to stop drinking or he won't live to see his children graduate. You, the drinker, already know this, and you've tried to quit. The doctor also knows his advice hasn't worked with others, and he doubts it will succeed with you either. The same thing happens when a wife threatens to leave her husband unless he stops drinking. More than anything he wants to stop and save his marriage. He would never logically or emotionally choose alcohol over his family, but he can't stop. Yet we believe addicts drink because they want to.

If I drank because I wanted to, why, when drinking began messing up my life, was I unable to stop? Instead, I wanted to stop and didn't stop. If you are making a choice, it should follow that you can reverse the choice. This is not the case with addiction. But we still believe with more willpower we could quit and release ourselves from the handcuffs.

So, we're stuck. But how did it happen? We did not smell enticing nectar like the bumblebee. Actually, alcohol initially tasted bad. So why are we tempted?

Marketing 101: What Are We Really Selling?

Look around or turn on the television. We've been conditioned to drink our entire lives. We're told alcohol calms and relaxes us, gives us courage, gets us through parties and work events, and makes us happy. Younger people even believe alcohol is good for their health.

Yet no one wants to admit that they're influenced. We want to feel in control of our destinies, free to choose our paths, uninfluenced by marketers' ploys. We feel like advertising isn't affecting us because we are not consciously aware of its power. In reality, your staunch belief that advertising does not influence you is one of the reasons it is so effective. Dr. Mark Schaller, a psychologist at the University of British Columbia, says, "Sometimes nonconscious effects can be bigger in sheer magnitude than conscious ones, because we can't moderate stuff we don't have conscious access to."[114] Makes sense, right? How can we consciously counteract a belief that bypassed our conscious understanding entirely?

An article in *Scientific American* says, "The error we often make is to assume that we can control the effects an ad has on our behavior because we are fully (consciously) aware of its content."[115] Consciously rejecting an ad's message doesn't ensure your subconscious doesn't buy the scam. We may think, "What a ridiculous car ad! A handsome guy wearing a fancy suit, zooming around a race course, and picking up a hot date. Who pays for this stuff?" But the next time we look at our worn-out old Ford, our unconscious mind revs up, and we find ourselves daydreaming about updating our ride or bemoaning the lack of cool features that newer car models include. Why? Because our unconscious is responsible for our desires and emotions, and our unconscious bought the underlying message that a new car will improve our overall happiness and success.

Studies in the last eighteen months have brought to light how profoundly our unconscious mind shapes our day-to-day thoughts and decisions.[116] When we make decisions with little to no thought that often actually means little to no conscious thought. This is why advertising influences you in profound ways, especially when you are not consciously aware of it.

In my first job out of college I worked at an advertising agency. A few times a week our founder would get on the intercom and say, "This is your captain speaking. All hands on deck, we have a brainstorming emergency." I'm not kidding; he really thought he was funny. We hailed to the boardroom, where he had plenty of "creative juice." The message was overt and clear—alcohol boosts creativity. To produce great campaign ideas, we needed to get drunk.

Was our best work done in those meetings? Not that I can remember. I actually remember the "aha" creative moments coming from other places. In fact, I don't recall a single big campaign idea from our drunken meetings. Did that stop us? Not at all. I didn't drink a lot at the time, but I was passionate about marketing and advertising. And I soon learned that alcohol was the key to my career.

The agency occasionally produced campaigns for local bars. I remember thinking hard about the methodology of selling alcohol. The marketing formula I often use is "the product's product's product." I realize that sounds confusing, so let me explain. The most successful advertising speaks very little about the product being sold and volumes about what void that product will fill in your life.

Take perfume advertisements. What's the product? A yellowish liquid that looks a bit like urine. Now that doesn't equate to compelling ad copy. What is the product's product? The yellowish liquid smells nice. Yet smelling nice is still not why people buy perfume. Advertisements selling the smell are not very successful. No, it's the product's product's product that you must sell. For perfume? Yes, it's sex.

The Wound of Existence

With this framework in mind, let's talk about another important aspect of marketing. Marketers actually create need by speaking to your vulnerabilities.

How? We play heavily on the human condition. Humans are not satisfied with simply existing. We look for more. No other animal questions their purpose in life or how they fit into the universe. This is one of the remarkable features that makes us uniquely human. But this questioning often creates a void inside us. We have more questions than answers, which causes tension. We desire more. This affliction is often called "the wound of existence."

Marketers play into this. Our natural, internal yearning can be easily and unconsciously directed. We not only sell sex when selling perfume. We also promise fulfillment, completion, satisfaction, and self-actualization. We present a lifestyle that promises to satisfy your restlessness. Through marketing, we tell you that if only you were thinner, smarter, sexier, you would find contentment; your life would be complete. You don't realize that the restlessness you feel is simply part of being human, so you look for ways to eliminate it. But ask yourself, even if you were handed everything you wanted, would it make you truly happy? Dan Harris explains this as hedonic adaptation: "When good things happen, we bake them very quickly into our baseline expectations, and yet the primordial void goes unfilled."[117] Generally, the more we consume the more we desire.

Existentialist psychotherapist Irvin D. Yalom identified what he calls humans' ultimate concerns: death, isolation (loneliness), freedom, and meaning.[118] These concerns reflect our deep fundamental needs. We search to understand the meaning of life, but no question provokes more debate. We feel desperate to experience gratification, so much so that we often rob ourselves of it by overindulging. We grapple with the inevitability of isolation and feel alone even in groups or families. We are painfully aware of the inescapability of death. We pursue pleasure and fulfillment in a never-ending search for satisfaction. Harris says, "It is the lie we tell ourselves our whole lives: as soon as we get to the next meal, party, vacation, sexual encounter, as soon as we get married, get a promotion, get to the airport check-in, get through security and consume a bouquet of Auntie

Anne's Cinnamon Sugar Stix, we'll feel really good . . . and yet the itch remains."[119] Marketing plays directly to these concerns. Alcohol commercials promise friendship, acceptance, gratification, happiness, and youth.

How to Sell Poison

Why do alcohol marketers need appeals that target the most fundamental of human needs? Let's look at this a different way. What if tomorrow we discovered alcohol for the first time, and the discovery included all the known scientific data on alcohol's effects on individuals and society, including that it's now been named the world's number one killer?[120] It's unlikely we would use or promote it recreationally. We might use it as a fuel, an antiseptic, or to dull pain. But we certainly wouldn't promote drinking it.

A good marketer can sell practically anything to anyone. Tobacco is literally dried, decaying vegetable matter that you light on fire and inhale, breathing horrid-tasting, toxic fumes into your lungs.[121] At one point marketers promoted smoking as a status symbol and claimed it had health benefits. Once you give it a try, the addictive nature of the drug kicks in, and the agency's job becomes much easier. If they can get you hooked, the product will sell itself.

Since the product is actually poison, advertisers need to overcome your instinctual aversion. That's a big hill for alcohol advertisements to climb, which is why the absolute best marketing firms on the globe, firms with psychologists and human behavior specialists on staff, are hired to create the ads. These marketers know that the most effective sale is an emotional sale, one that plays on your deepest fears, your ultimate concerns. Alcohol advertisements sell an end to loneliness, claiming that drinking provides friendship and romance. They appeal to your need for freedom by saying drinking will make you unique, brave, bold, or courageous. They promise fulfillment, satisfaction, and happiness. All these messages speak to your conscious and unconscious minds. Look at alcohol advertisements over the next few days. For each ad, try to identify the product's product's product. Try to see which of your most fundamental emotional desires the advertisement is appealing to and notice how unrelated the claim is to the reality of drinking. It's easy to dismiss alcohol advertisements as ridiculous because the claim that your chances of experiencing a threesome go up if you drink a certain kind of beer are absurd (I'm not kidding—this is a real ad). But as ridiculous as these ads seem on the surface, you must remember that consciously dismissing them as absurd is part of how they work in speaking directly to your unconscious desires. You will be amazed at who alcohol ads actually say you need to be to end your isolation, find freedom, maintain your youth (avoid death), and discover meaning in life. You may start to wonder how, as a society, we allow it.

Let's not forget, alcohol gives you no nectar. The reality, when the sexy advertisements have been stripped away, is that the actual product is ethanol.[122] It is a horrible-tasting, addictive poison. So we sweeten it with sugar and flavoring or process it to make it more palatable. The product's product is inebriation, a gradual deadening of your senses until you become completely intoxicated. And the side effects that are never disclosed are many. Think about ads for new medications, like Viagra or blood pressure medication. They are legally required to disclose all the statistically relevant side effects. Alcohol has the same cancer-causing effects as asbestos,[123] and just three drinks per week can increase a woman's chance of developing breast cancer by 15%,[124] yet there are no labeling requirements whatsoever. Yet compared to other drugs (illegal, legal, and prescription), alcohol bears the highest harm rating.[125]

When promoting alcohol, marketers sell a better human experience: relief from the human condition. And in doing so, we promise the opposite of what alcohol really provides. We sell happiness where there is pain. We sell romantic relationships when alcohol destroys healthy, fulfilling relationships. We sell sex when drinking deadens your senses and, as a depressant, actually decreases sexual desire, making it difficult to achieve erections and orgasm.[126] In fact, alcohol is a main cause of sexual dysfunction in men, including premature ejaculation, low sexual desire, and erectile dysfunction. A clinical study done in 2007 revealed that the amount of alcohol consumed was the most significant predictor of developing sexual dysfunction.[127] We sell stress relief when addiction derails your life. We sell increased mental capacity and creativity, yet drinking slows our brain function,[128] resulting in less intelligent and creative thought.

Maybe you still believe you are not affected by advertising. Most people think they're immune, but the data shows otherwise. The evidence is clear—exposure to alcohol advertising impacts subsequent use, encouraging people to start drinking and promoting heavier drinking among existing drinkers.[129] This connection is especially strong in young people.[130] Research demonstrates that your brain not only receives sensory information but also registers information at an unconscious, cellular level.[131] This can occur even when you are asleep![132]

Guess what some of most expensive commercials are for? You guessed it—alcohol. Guinness spent $20 million on the single most expensive commercial of all time. In terms of dollars per second, the priciest ad award goes to a Bud Light commercial. It cost $133,000 per second. The alcohol industry in the U.S. spends more than two billion dollars per year on advertising. Why would Guinness and Bud Light invest that type of money if advertising didn't work? They wouldn't.

Even if you accept that marketing influences you, it's hard to believe that advertisements are solely responsible for your desire to drink. You're right. As powerful as advertising is, it is not powerful enough to create a society where 87% of adults voluntarily drink cancer-causing poison. While the advertising industry contributes to that number, marketers are not solely to blame. We are most influenced by what we observe others doing, especially those we know and respect. Word of mouth is a powerful tool. Advertising is only the beginning. After it's done its job, it passes the task on to a society of walking billboards.

Case Study: The Marketing of Wine

Since marketing is my trade and wine was my drink, I want to take a minute to talk about the absolute genius behind wine marketing. I drank red wine for two reasons: It was touted as the healthiest choice, and it allowed me to feel grown-up at business dinners. I understand that the wine tasting ritual you observe at restaurants began a long time ago when wine occasionally turned sour due to the vinegar content. It was necessary to sample the bottle before it was poured. However, we've taken this ritual to a whole new level. I never thought I would admit it, but the entire thing, with its pomp and ceremony, makes me giggle.

Given my experience in marketing and the lengths I know marketers will go to in order to create a culture around certain products, it seems more likely that this is all a marketing ploy. In fact, I see the pairing of wines with foods and the elaborate tastings as one of the smartest strategies of our time. People will pay hundreds, even thousands, of dollars for a bottle of wine, yet it is consumable, so the pleasure, if there is any, is fleeting.

What we don't realize is that everyone else is likely faking it. It's worth repeating that the American Association of Wine Economists has proven that people cannot actually distinguish between "good" wines and cheap wines.[133] But since there is such a seemingly distinguished culture around wine, you probably felt, like I did, too stupid to admit you cannot tell the difference between certain vintages. So even if we don't see the point, we go along with it. I learned words like "oaky" in order to blend in, yet we had no idea what an oaky flavor actually is. I've still never licked an oak tree to find out. Another clue is that I've been part of hundreds of these rituals, all around the world, and never once was the wine, post swirl and sniff, returned.

Can you imagine if we did this for any other drink? Like milk? And wouldn't it make much more sense with milk? If the milk isn't fresh, you could actually smell the fermentation and send it back. Yet there is no milk ritual.

We start to identify with the type of wine we drink—white or red. This again goes against the idea that certain wines complement certain foods. You will notice that people who have acquired a taste for red wine drink red almost 100% of the time. Since apparently red wine only complements meat and pasta, while white wine complements fish and chicken, how do you explain these red wine drinkers drinking red with their salmon? Generally, if you enjoy the taste of wine, or in fact liquor, it's because of the sugar, not the alcohol. If I mixed enough milk, sugar, and flavorings with Drano, I bet I could make it taste like Bailey's.

Craig Beck, a self-proclaimed ex–wine aficionado describes the fine wine industry in one word: bullshit.[134] Beck says that he, by using the ritual of wine to cover his problem, managed to delude himself that there was nothing wrong. He says, "I couldn't have a problem because I was clearly a cut above the alcoholic in the park who chugged back super-strength tins of beer. I was buying and drinking the stuff of kings, an indication of my social standing and refined palette, and surely not a proclamation of a drug addiction!"[135]

Living Advertisements

Today's data-driven, intelligent marketing targets messages with such precision that the marketing department at Target is said to be able to predict pregnancy before even the mother-to-be realizes she is pregnant.[136] A successful marketing department should be known as a profit center, not a cost center. So we break target markets into audiences and drill down to specific personas. We articulate exactly who we are speaking to and craft our ad campaigns to lever the unconscious desires of the people most likely to be big profit sources. When the sales start pouring in, we increase our marketing budget and target additional segments of the population. This method maximizes bang for our buck, and we then rely on popular opinion and societal conditioning to extend our reach.

How does this societal conditioning play out in real life? As kids we're allowed juice while the adults drink beer. Soon we're teenagers, and we have a powerful urge to prove we're grown-up too. So we sneak our first drinks. And why not? Adults all around us are proclaiming the benefits of alcohol. These influential adults are living advertisements. And we believe them, not only because of their words but because of their actions. Alcohol must be incredible—why else would they drink so much of it?

Our society not only encourages drinking—it takes issue with people who don't drink. Since I stopped drinking I've been shocked by the invasive questions I receive. You wouldn't ask someone who turned down a glass of milk, "Are you pregnant?" "Are you lactose intolerant?" or "Did you struggle with milk?"

Beck explains these reactions in his book, *Alcohol Lied to Me: The Intelligent Way to Stop Drinking*. He says that all humans are motivated by just two component factors: seeking pleasure and avoiding pain. That is a key reason why your friends, no matter how much they care about you, don't want you to stop drinking. When you stop drinking they are forced to confront the fact that deep down they too know alcohol is bad for them. Beck explains, "When you stop drinking you appear to raise your standards above those of the people around you. As you raise your own standards, you automatically highlight their low standards, and this causes psychological pain to everyone around you."[137]

Is it any wonder that more people drink than ever before? And alcoholism now begins earlier in life. In "Alcoholism Isn't What It Used to Be," the National Institute on Alcohol Abuse and Alcoholism (NIAAA) states that twenty-two is now the mean age for the onset of alcohol dependence. The article says, "In most persons affected, alcoholism looks less like Nicolas Cage in *Leaving Las Vegas* and more like your party-hardy college roommate or that hard-driving colleague in the next cubicle."[138]

How do we allow the advertising industry to spend more than two billion dollars to tell us (and our children) that ingesting an addictive substance that drastically shortens our lives, destroys our confidence, causes cancer, and is responsible for death, abuse, violence, suicide, and general unhappiness will make our lives better?

Would we allow cocaine to be advertised in the same way? Can you imagine a $12 million commercial playing during the Super Bowl, with millions of young minds watching, proclaiming how amazing their lives will become if they snort a few lines? Why do we see cocaine and alcohol so differently, especially when, in the United States, alcohol kills 241 people per day[139] and cocaine kills only fifteen people per day?[140] Why do we glamorize the benefits of drinking?

There are complex answers, which lay in alcohol corporations, politics, taxes, lobbyists, and the like. But, in an effort to concentrate on what we can control, let's go back to the initial question. How did this happen?

I know plenty of people who use cocaine. Would I let them pull it out in front of my kids? Never. Between friends, restaurants, and television, my kids don't go a day without seeing someone take a drink. Yet alcohol kills 17.6 times more people than cocaine every year.[141] If we look at drunk driving, the statistics are horrific. Every night and weekend one out of ten drivers on the road are intoxicated, and alcohol-related accidents are the leading cause of death among young people.[142] Half of all fatal highway accidents are alcohol-related.[143] Imagine if a Boeing 747 aircraft carrying five hundred people crashed, killing all its passengers, every eight days. That is how many people die every eight days as a result of drunk driving.[144]

No one intends to be a statistic. We don't intentionally kill another human being by driving drunk. Most drunk drivers don't even realize they are drunk. Their inhibitions have been compromised, and their senses are no longer functioning properly—they literally no longer have the sense to avoid getting behind the wheel.[145]

While we glamorize the benefits of drinking for "responsible drinkers," being a drunk carries a heavy stigma. The stigma is so strong that we've created the belief that becoming a drunk can't happen to normal people, it can only happen to "them." It forces us to lie to others and ourselves about our drinking. Let's be honest—we all drink more than we want to sometimes. You can't tell me that moderate, "in control" drinkers don't puke on occasion or wake up with a killer hangover. No one sets out to throw up or get the spins at the end of the night. Why can't we recognize that, with alcohol, we are not as in control as we think we are?

Why can't we admit it? Why has it become painful to imagine a life without booze? Because marketing, our friends, our families, and our own experiences conspire to create a strong mental desire to drink. Drinking is so ingrained in our culture and upbringing that we've practically been trained, both consciously and unconsciously, to try alcohol. You now have a way to find freedom that will not result in tragedy or deprivation. You will not feel like you are living a boring, deprived life. You will be making a decision based on clear evidence. By the time you are ready to make a decision about how much you will drink, your unconscious mind will retain no desire to drink whatsoever.

10.
LIMINAL POINT: DRINKING HELPS ME LOOSEN UP AND HAVE BETTER SEX

"Alcohol doesn't permit one to do things better but instead causes us to be less ashamed of doing things poorly."
—W. Osler

You have **observed** people who are normally quiet and reserved become loud and obnoxious after a few drinks. You have also observed that people tend to "give it up" easier after drinking. You may have then **assumed** that drinking is vital to loosening up and getting lucky. You've personally **experienced** your inhibitions fade after drinking. Without your typical inhibitions you've become more empowered to go after sex. And maybe this has resulted in you having more sex when under the influence than when sober. The clear **conclusion** is that yes, drinking does help you loosen up and have better sex.

Let's consider reality:

I Drink to Loosen Up

More than half the population considers themselves shy; I know I do. Ironically, if you ask my friends and family, they will tell you I'm outgoing. This shows how different our perceptions are from reality. Yet shyness can be crippling, especially when you are forced to be outgoing with strangers in a social situation. As my friend Heidi calls it, "schmoozing and boozing."

For me it was business trips, networking events, and running booths at conferences. The norm for all us "shy" people was to drink. The conferences reinforced this, and there was never a shortage of free alcohol. Often booths provided free alcohol all day. If you wanted a drink, you could have one. No wonder I started believing alcohol was key to loosening up and being more gregarious while networking.

The important question is, did it work? Drinking didn't make me funnier. How could it? When my brain functioned at a slower pace my wit was dulled. It didn't make me more interesting. It just removed my inhibitions. I thought this was a good thing. I now realize we have inhibitions for a reason. They protect us, not only from physical harm, but from doing or saying things we shouldn't. Without my inhibitions, I talked to strangers like I would speak with close friends. This got me in trouble more than once. Sometimes the trouble was benign, and "drunk Annie" just resulted in a few whispers behind my back. Since I was often the youngest at these functions, people wrote off my silly behavior to immaturity. Other times my loss of inhibitions, combined with my naive nature, put me in awkward and risky situations.

More than once I found myself alone with a man who clearly wanted more from me than a business card. I'm incredibly thankful I was never harmed, but research shows how rare that is. When drinking, men perceive a greater level of sexual interest than women intend to communicate. This perception of feeling "led on" by a woman when combined with alcohol, which can increase aggressive behavior, makes a man more likely to commit assault. Drunk men are more likely than sober men to find the use of force to obtain sex acceptable.[146] Finally, alcohol affects a woman's ability to assess and react to risk. We are more likely to take risks that we would normally avoid, such as being alone with an strange man.[147]

You may argue that having a couple of drinks to loosen up is no big deal. Did you know that sexual assault, especially in universities, is at an all-time high? Authors of a 2015 study from *The Journal of Adolescent Health* say, "Sexual violence on campus has reached epidemic levels."[148] How would you like your son to be loosening up and losing his inhibitions in that environment? The majority of college rapes involving alcohol are not planned. These boys don't intend to become rapists. In a major study, a boy who forced sex on a female friend wrote, "Alcohol loosened us up and the situation occurred by accident. If no alcohol was consumed, I would never have crossed that line."[149] In the same study we find that 54% of college women have experienced some form of sexual assault.[150]

Let's put that in perspective. Last October I volunteered at my son's kindergarten and helped carve pumpkins for Halloween. The statistic above means that more than half of these sweet and innocent six-year-old girls will experience some form of sexual assault when they leave their homes for university. Again, when it comes to sexual assault, and especially alcohol-fueled sexual assault, we all seem to have a story. A close friend of mine was asleep in her dorm room when a man, with alcohol on his breath, broke through her window and raped her in her bed. Can you imagine the horror and pain she still feels, decades after the incident? Even if the sex is consensual, alcohol increases other dangers. Sixty percent of STDs are transmitted when alcohol is involved, and young adults who use alcohol are seven times more likely to have unprotected sex.[151]

Shyness and inhibitions are not negative, yet we've been conditioned to think they are. These emotions protect us, helping us to navigate life with grace. It's not a lot of fun to be shy, but it's normal. Everyone feels it. In Susan Cain's book *Quiet, The Power of Introverts in a World That Can't Stop Talking*, she discusses what a gift it is to listen, a gift to the people we are listening to and to ourselves. You won't learn anything new by talking. When our talkative nature stems from drinking, it's neither thoughtful nor eloquent. Our brains function at a slower pace, and we have fewer filters between our thoughts and our mouths. What we talk about is less filtered and less interesting—not a great combination.

Despite introversion's positive qualities, as a society, we have been conditioned to believe shyness is a curse. We have a societal bias toward extroverts[152] because we are ashamed of our natural inhibitions. It's no wonder we try to escape our true nature by drinking. We hope that our personalities will change after a few drinks, and we will become the outgoing, engaging person we aspire to be. A more effective approach is to accept ourselves, realizing everyone is in the same boat, and allow conversations to unfold naturally. When we take the time to get to know someone, asking questions instead of speaking to fill the silence, the result is amazing. It's a gift to learn from other people. Asking questions, listening, and learning, these things make *you* a more interesting person. You become the type of person others want to be around.

Losing inhibitions is dangerous in sexual interactions. It's worth repeating that a loss of inhibitions is deadly when it comes to driving. When you are sober you don't imagine you would ever get behind the wheel of the car when drunk. But when you are drunk, what seemed like a terrible idea suddenly makes sense. With your heightened sense of bravado, you feel more in control than you actually are. Before you know it, it's the next day, and you think, "Wow, I probably shouldn't have driven last night." Half of all traffic accidents are linked to alcohol.[153] The majority of drunk drivers don't mean to drive drunk, but when drinking they can no longer judge how drunk they are. The roads have become more dangerous than ever. Inhibitions are protective, both to us and the people around us.

If we agree that alcohol has some control over you once you start drinking, enough that drinkers regularly drink more than they set out to, surely alcohol can make you do something you never imagined yourself capable of. I am appalled by how many awful things I did under the influence. Addiction is humbling, and I have been humbled enough to know that I am capable of anything, no matter how abhorrent, if the circumstances are right. Anyone is. Believing yourself immune to mistakes increases your chance of committing a repugnant act. All humans are painfully capable of failure. We are only human. It only takes one slip-up, one lapse in judgment. Don't be fooled—everyone makes mistakes. No one intends to kill another person while driving drunk. Yet it happens all the time. In the U.S., someone is killed by a drunk driver every 51 minutes.[154]

Have you ever gotten so drunk you threw up? Did you set out to do that? If your judgment is perfect, would you have allowed that to happen? Even if you consistently make great decisions and keep yourself and others out of harm's way, do you want to be the person at the party who cannot shut up? The person whose breath reeks of wine but can't tell because their senses have been numbed to the smell? We all know the person who goes on and on, and unfortunately, unlike on Facebook, we can't skip to the next interesting story. I know from experience, no one wants to spend time with "drunk Annie," who can't stop talking or laughing loudly at her own jokes.

You may feel that a little alcohol is good for your conversation skills or your golf game. The problem with alcohol is that once you start drinking you can't judge the point where a little is good and a lot becomes a disaster. When you are making a fool of yourself, or when your conversation skills wane, you remain unaware. Even if you could gauge the exact amount to drink, booze doesn't make you cleverer, funnier, more creative, or more interesting. There is nothing inherent in alcohol that can do this. More often when a shy person gets drunk, they end up emotional, weepy, and repetitive. We don't realize how bad we look when drinking because we are drunk and so is everyone else. It's the old question: If everyone jumped off a cliff, would you? With alcohol, as a culture, our answer is disturbing—yes.

I Drink to Have Better Sex

We have already discussed the fact that alcohol is a main cause of sexual dysfunction in men, that it makes it harder to become and remain sexually aroused.[155] What about women? I spoke with women who no longer drink, and the overwhelming sentiment is that sex is much better sober. One said, "My libido has taken a full-on, diva-style return to center stage." Another called it a "sober mojo revolution." I agree, sex is much better when you aren't deadening your ability to feel. Not only is it easier to have orgasms, but they seem to last significantly longer.

I experienced another positive in the sexual arena when I stopped drinking. Becoming alcohol-free made me happier than I'd been in years, allowing me to get off an anti-depressant that I had been taking for a long time. The result? Libido! Sex has been more fun and more frequent these days.

The one downside everyone mentioned was that it's not all that fun to have sex sober with someone who is drunk. One woman said, "I agree that sex is so much better without booze, but I have to try and get my naughties in the mornings now because I hate wine breath on my husband." Another said, "I've discovered sex when you're both drunk is OK, and sex when you're both sober is amazing, but sex when one is sober and the other is drunk is the worst. Timing is everything, if you know what I mean, and when he is drunk things end much too soon." No matter how you look at it, alcohol does not lead to better sex. And the good news is that you don't have to take my word for it. This is something I hope you will enjoy finding out for yourself!

11.
A QUEST FOR SOBRIETY

*"Be patient with yourself. Self-growth is tender; it's holy ground.
There's no greater investment."*
—Stephen Covey

Let's imagine you've decided to try and stop drinking.

The first thing you do is research the evils of alcohol online. What you learn reinforces the reasons you want to quit, so your motivation is higher than ever. But you haven't addressed the actual reasons you drink. As Charles Duhigg demonstrates in his book *The Power of Habit*, willpower is a muscle that fatigues and eventually runs out.[156] Eventually, after a hard day, you get frustrated, your willpower muscle weakens, and you decide to have just one. One turns into many. Since you weren't successful stopping, you start to believe you are truly addicted. Quitting suddenly seems as difficult as you've heard.

When quitting is hard, it reinforces our belief that alcohol holds a great deal of power over us. It must be incredibly addictive, and we must be incredibly addicted. The more you dwell on reasons not to drink, the more upset you feel when you abstain and the worse you feel when you give in to temptation.

Yet this seems illogical. We've determined that alcohol causes us problems, and our efforts to cut back have taken the joy out of drinking. We no longer enjoy it, and drinking bouts are filled with self-loathing and regret. We are miserable when we give in but cannot understand why we can't quit. What do we need to know to find freedom? We must begin by understanding how our descent began.

My Descent

Your circumstances will differ from mine, but the principles remain. Here is where it started for me.

When I was a kid, I was full of enthusiasm and energy, without a drop of alcohol. I didn't need it to enjoy slumber parties, playgrounds, school dances, or anything else.

It all began in high school. At first I didn't like the taste. The only person I know who actually liked the taste of their first drink is my friend Jenny. She was on the beach in France drinking Malibu and Coke. Of course it tasted good—it was 95% sugar. Her surroundings were exotic, and she will tell you she liked her first drink. Let's be honest and realize she did not like the alcohol; she enjoyed the sugar and the environment. If her first drink was hard liquor in a dark basement, she would have spit it out. Even rats won't touch the stuff. In *Introduction to Learning and Behavior*, Powell and Symbaluk write that most laboratory rats will not voluntarily drink alcohol when it is presented to them.[157] In fact, rats only voluntarily drink alcohol after they have been force-fed it and developed a physical addiction.

In any case, my first drinks weren't all that good. I remember a lot of peer pressure. I was dating an older guy who hoped to lower my inhibitions. He bought me sugary wine coolers, but they didn't taste great. I longed for acceptance, so I worked to acquire a taste, although I would have preferred to drink something else. I was young, happy, and healthy. I didn't need the alcohol.

Disliking the taste of our first drinks helps us become stuck. If the first drink tasted amazing, we would be more cautious. Since those early drinks aren't very good, we throw caution to the wind. After all, how could we become addicted to something we don't like? I remember my first taste of vodka-infused orange juice. I was twelve years old, and my cousins and I had backpacked ten miles into the wilderness to a natural hot springs. A water bottle with what I now know to be filled with a screwdriver was passed around. When I had a sip I almost spit it out, asking, "Who ruined the orange juice?"

This is a great example of ignoring our instincts in favor of our intellect. If an animal drank something that tasted bad, instinct would kick in. They would not drink more because they would instinctively know the foul taste meant it was harmful. That would be the end of it.

Instead, we use our intellect, our reasoning abilities. We see everyone drinking. We have our first drinks and are surprised they don't taste all that great. We reason there must be something truly incredible about drinking. It must be a special treat if parents drink wine every night when it doesn't even taste good. We reason that there must be amazing benefits to drinking. Why else would everyone be doing it? This happens consciously, and, more dangerously, it happens unconsciously. So we work hard to develop a taste.

Suddenly, without realizing it, drinking has become part of our lives. We never make a conscious decision to drink as much as we now do. It just happens. Now we can't imagine dinner without wine or football without beer. Our tastes become accustomed to it. Over time we develop a tolerance. We experiment with stronger drinks and drink more often. Consuming this much was never a conscious decision.

My career contributed to my becoming dependent on alcohol. Early in my career I was promoted to senior roles, and at twenty-six I became the youngest VP in the company. I found myself traveling the country on business trips. Dinners out were characterized by heavy drinking, and of course, everyone could drink more than me.

I was called "kiddo" more often than I care to admit, and I had a chip on my shoulder to prove I deserved the promotions despite my age. I dedicated myself to building a tolerance in order to keep up with my colleagues. I had a routine: a glass of wine, a glass of water. This way I could drink more wine without feeling as tipsy, and it minimized the morning-after effects. It's pathetic to admit, but often I would sneak back to my hotel room, stick my finger down my throat to get the last glass or so out of my system. This allowed me to go on drinking. Or at the end of the night I would puke to get the last few glasses out before bed. I was on a mission to fit in, to prove myself, and sure enough I built a formidable tolerance.

Before I quit drinking, I, at 5'8", 140 pounds, could easily drink two bottles of wine in an evening. I often bragged about my ability to keep up with anyone in my company. Considering the company is headquartered in London, I felt this quite the accomplishment. I worked hard for my tolerance, for my unique ability to poison myself, and I was proud of it.

Not surprisingly, wine became part of every day, whether I was at work or not. I drank as much at home as I did at work and more when out with my friends. I can honestly say that in my last years of drinking I consumed more calories in alcohol than in food. It wasn't that there was always a reason to drink. It was just that there was never a reason not to.

When I was questioned about the amount I was drinking, I remember justifying it, saying that alcohol doesn't really affect me, that it wasn't hurting me. What else do we justify because it isn't hurting us? We don't rationally justify things this way. It's especially stupid when it's abundantly clear that alcohol was destroying my body.

I can't pinpoint exactly when things changed. If you haven't slid as far down as I had, take this as a warning—things do change. It sneaks up on you no matter how smart, successful, and in control you believe yourself to be.

I was often on international, overnight flights in business class. In business class the flight attendants seem on a mission to get the passengers drunk so they fall sound asleep for the journey. I would astound the flight attendant by how many times he had to fill up my glass. I would land in another country in the early morning hours, still tipsy. I inevitably had meetings first thing. So I would shower and change in the airport lounge before taking a taxi to the office. Soon I began to see things differently. I thought, "Hmmm, Annie, time isn't relevant anymore. You may be landing at 8 a.m., but it's 10 p.m. at home. Why not make yourself feel better and have one more when you land?" And it was easy to do. Alcohol flows freely at airport lounges twenty-four hours a day.

Hangovers caught up with me, either because I was drinking more or because I was so focused on the wine that I forgot the water. I'd heard that alcohol is the best cure for a hangover, so a beer or two at lunch (or earlier) began to sound like a good idea.

If you believe you are in control of your drinking, you are now thinking this could never happen to you. You may be right. You may have what I call "guardrails" in your brain where you have such a stigma against drinking in the morning that you would never let yourself fall that far. I hope you are right. In fact, I believed it would never happen to me. But my rationalizations became so powerful that I blinded myself to reality. I didn't see it as a problem, rather a temporary fix, all in the name of being more successful in my high-pressure, international role.

When you reach this point on the alcohol continuum, people around you start to see your problem before you do. You receive comments from family, friends, colleagues, or even your boss. You decide to prove you are indeed in control and determine to drink less. You've always said, "I can take it or leave it," and you have no doubt this is true.

You try to abstain completely on certain days or drink less per day. This is a critical change. Before this point you haven't questioned each and every drink. You drank what you wanted, when you wanted and didn't give it much thought. I definitely didn't think about how much I was drinking. I just drank.

Since alcohol has now caused an issue—enough of one for someone in your life to call you out on your drinking—it would seem you should want to drink less. Consciously you do. Unfortunately, your unconscious has not gotten the message, and it still desires alcohol, believing it is your key to enjoying social situations and relaxing.

You abstain and feel bored, annoyed, or grumpy. Everyone else is enjoying a drink after work, and part of you desperately wants one. You may give in, saying you will have only one or two. And you realize it's not fun to worry about how much you are drinking. After a few, it doesn't seem to matter anyway. You decide you will drink less tomorrow. Tomorrow comes, and you beat yourself up over your lack of willpower, wondering why you can't simply drink less. The fact that you are having a hard time keeping your commitments to cut back compounds the problem. You worry that alcohol must have power over you. Why else would it be so hard to drink less?

Before you decided to cut back, your drinking wasn't a problem; at least you didn't realize it was. You, like me, probably didn't give it much thought. Now every time alcohol is in the picture, you face a stressful dilemma. If you normally drink every day, this stress becomes a daily occurrence. I relied heavily on wine to help me relax and relieve stress. As soon as something stressful happened, I would reach for a bottle opener. When my beloved wine became the source of my stress, I found myself in a vicious cycle. This is a painful position to be in. You are simultaneously drinking too much and not drinking enough. I've heard it said, "One drink is too many and a thousand is not enough." This is truly a pickle—the part of your brain that sees alcohol as a problem is at odds with the part of your brain that wants a drink whenever you feel like it.

The struggle at this stage is palpable. You are incredibly stressed and end up drinking more than before. Eventually you realize, much to your horror, that you are not in control and probably need to stop drinking altogether.

This news, for many, is tragic. Mary, a former blackout drinker who found her freedom with *This Naked Mind*, described it like this: "I remember thinking, I think I just need to stop drinking. My entire body deflated as the words crossed my lips, overcome with sadness at the thought of giving it up forever and at the same time not believing I was capable. It felt so unfair. Why couldn't I just learn to drink like other people? Why did it have to come to this?"

The first few weeks and months of sobriety are described by some as the hardest thing they have ever done. My friend Beth, who quit drinking with A.A., said it was like losing her best friend. She mourned for alcohol and went through an intense grieving process. Quitting is a horrible experience for someone who believes that life will never be as sweet without alcohol.

No one plans to become an alcoholic, just like no one thinks they are capable of cheating on their spouse. We mentally segregate ourselves from "them," believing we would never allow these things to happen in our lives. The truth is they do happen. They happen all the time to people just like you and me. I was taught that a marriage is safest when you accept that you could cheat—that anyone could—and take precautions to protect your marriage. Alcoholism is no different. Alcohol is physically addictive, and a physical dependence on alcohol can occur in anyone.

Since I was high-functioning, it was easy for me to see alcoholics as separate from me; I couldn't possibly become one. It was easy to close my mind to the amount I was drinking because I was so successful in my family life and career. I even gave alcohol some of the credit for my success. I mean, how would I have had all those great ideas or done all that networking without booze? Now I know I'm much better at my job when I'm not drinking. One of the great things about the life you are about to lead is how much fun it is to disprove your false notions about alcohol. Realizing my ideas come from my brain, not from the bottle, is empowering. It feels great to know I don't need alcohol at all, for anything. I am strong, happy, and whole just as I am.

The Quest Begins

And so, once you realize alcohol controls your life, the quest to regain control begins. Sadly, many people avoid this journey, even though they dearly want freedom from alcohol's control, because they're afraid it will be impossible or result in lifelong pain. Remember the alcoholic living on the street in Las Vegas. Obviously he is no longer happy; alcohol is not giving him any real relief or enjoyment. In fact it's clear that alcohol is to blame for his tragic situation—sleeping on the sidewalk, hungry, filthy, begging for money, and being harassed by the police. Yet we observe his brown paper bag and wonder why, beyond all logic and reason, he continues to drink.

We might interpret his situation to mean that quitting must be an almost impossible feat. Why else would people allow their entire lives to be ruined? We are bombarded with statistics about how few people successfully stay sober. The task before us appears monumental. We start off with a feeling of apprehension and terror.

We hold on to the illogical hope that someday, if we can abstain for long enough, we will be miraculously released from our desire to drink. Why would that happen? All around you booze is still held up as the "elixir of life." Your friends are drinking and seeming to enjoy it. Nothing has changed, so why would you somehow, someday, be spontaneously freed?

When you stop drinking through sheer willpower, you start to see the benefits. You become healthier, and your situation in life improves. The reasons you quit begin to fade into the background. Inevitably you start to feel healthy and strong. You feel empowered because of the strength you have shown by quitting. You forget the reasons you quit to begin with. Humans have selective memory. We tend to remember the good things rather than the whole picture. You forget the fights with your spouse, the hangovers, or the stupid things you did and said. You forget your misery, and the reasons you quit no longer seem as important as they did before. You heal, and in healing the reasons to avoid drinking lose their immediacy.

You find an excuse for just one, and suddenly you are back in the mental misery of alcohol addiction. It makes no difference if you go straight to the blackout stage or if it's a gradual descent that takes years. You have not changed. Alcohol has not changed. Society has not changed. What would make this time any different than the last?

How will you know when you have succeeded? If you live waiting to see if you ever drink again, you won't know you are successful until you are dead. Living a life in recovery, yet never recovered, implies you have no greater expectation than for life to be OK. But when you completely change your mental (conscious and unconscious) perspective on alcohol, you begin to see the truth about drinking. When this happens, no willpower is required, and it becomes a joy not to drink. This is the mystery of spontaneous sobriety, which we will talk about after our next Liminal Point.

12.
LIMINAL POINT: I DRINK TO RELIEVE STRESS AND ANXIETY

"You cannot find peace by avoiding life."
—*Virginia Woolf*

You have **observed** people saying they need a drink after a long day. You have also poured yourself a drink to take the edge off, and your **experience** showed it did take the edge off your stress and anxiety. It was easy to **assume** alcohol was a stress reliever and quieted your anxiety. Eventually you came to the **conclusion** that alcohol was necessary to relieve stress and anxiety.

Let's consider reality:

Alcohol Relieves My Stress and Anxiety

I started as a social drinker, but during the last five years I used it to relax. Ironically, drinking made my life much more stressful. My health was affected. I compounded the natural stress of my job with the anxiety of wondering what stupid comment I'd made to whom during nights of drinking. Glass by glass I poured stress into my life, all the while deluding myself into believing alcohol helped me relax.

What is actual relaxation? You could say that being completely relaxed means having nothing to worry, irk, or annoy you either physically or mentally. How can alcohol do this for you? It does not fix the annoyances and stressors but temporarily dulls the symptoms. And guess what? As you build a tolerance, the actual effect of alcohol decreases, and your need for it increases. Soon the things that are making you upset are barely muted by alcohol, and you are addicted. Of course, addiction is a much bigger stressor than the stressors you drank to remove. You've created a mental craving for alcohol that did not exist before, one that you now have to either feed (with more alcohol) or deprive. Wanting something you shouldn't have does nothing to relax you; it creates a mental divide inside your mind, which is the very definition of frustration and agitation. It's the opposite of relaxation. Drinking to treat your problems ensures you will not address the true source of your discontent. It ensures you will remain stuck, treating the symptoms of stress rather than their causes. Things go from bad to worse when you add alcohol dependence to the mix.

A few years ago in Windsor, England, I stepped off the stage after speaking to about seventy people. I usually know I've nailed it, and this time I wasn't so sure. Something felt wrong. I knew I was not responding to the audience well, and they were not responding to me. Sure enough, a friend took me aside to ask what was wrong. He was, as good friends are, honest with me, saying I had lost my spark. I was not the animated, funny, and relatable communicator I used to be. I knew he was right and burst into tears. I didn't understand what was wrong, why I was so on edge. What I did know was I wanted a drink to calm my nerves. Alcohol caused the sharp decline in my speaking abilities. Yet in the moment I thought alcohol was the only solace I had.

I had that drink to "calm my nerves," but I was so stressed it didn't help. Heavy drinking and lack of sleep were why I had lost my spark.

When I reflect now on why I was such a mess, there was no real reason. While my career can be stressful, I thrive on a fast pace and constant change. I am in my element when I am responsible for large budgets and international teams. I was never in a life-or-death situation. All my stress came from my drive to improve and excel. Drinking to dull my stress made it worse. Now that I no longer administer myself a powerful poison on a regular basis, I can handle all sorts of situations, even the most daunting. Are they all easy? No. Do I feel stress? Of course. But the stress is never multiplied because I don't have the energy, self-confidence, or courage to deal with the issue at hand. Alcohol seemed to give me an easy way out. Have a drink, deaden my senses, and let stress seep from my mind. But it worsened every situation because I drank instead of facing the problems head-on.

I am writing this on a plane ride home, returning from a six-day, four-country business trip. I'll want to relax when I get home. At the end of a trip like this I inevitably feel wound up. I used to believe this was stress, and I needed alcohol to unwind. I admit, some of it is stress, but most of it is the responsibility of my role. I now see that I thrive when I am pushed. I crave speed with my job, my family, and the other projects I am involved in. I have been told, when I was especially on edge, to slow down, but slowing down does not make me happy. It's not the pace that is the problem; the problem is poisoning my body and mind so that I am physically unable to keep up with the life I want to live.

Imagine the intensity of sinking into a hot tub after a rigorous workout on a blistering summer day. A chilly and refreshing shower would feel better. However today, after twenty-nine hours of traveling, the hot tub sounds great. It will relax my muscles and help me sleep. Lying in bed with a good book is a treat for me. My son, at three, would find that very stressful. He is full of energy and can't yet read, so he would be frustrated by having to sit still. In order to relax, we need to figure out why we are not relaxed and address the problem.

If we are tired, we sleep. If we are cold, we start a fire or put on a sweater. If we itch, we scratch. You get the picture.

If I am stressed because I forgot to return an important phone call, I can either make the call or write myself a note to ensure I do it when I am able. This will relieve my stress. If I am experiencing stress because of a deadline, I can schedule time to work on the project or just get to work. The most thorough road to relaxation is removing the specific irritation that is causing you stress.

I have an executive mentor and coach. A few years ago we were discussing the fact that I was distracted by work over the weekends, and I couldn't unwind enough to relax and enjoy family time. This was when I was drinking, which further proves to me that a drink is not the magic relief button I once thought it to be. My coach gave me some great advice. He said there are really only three types of things that cause stress to creep into our minds outside of work. The first is something you forgot to do. In this instance, write it down and resolve to do it first thing Monday morning. The second is something you realized you'd messed up. In this case, decide if it's fixable. If yes, write it down, making a note to fix it as soon as possible. If not, you might need to make amends, but then you need to let it go. The third is a new idea, and if a new idea pops into your head, you should write it down and act on it once you are back in the office. This advice relieved my work-related stress more than any drink ever has.

You achieve relaxation by removing the source of discontent. Alcohol, by definition, cannot relax you. Now you may wonder about the numbing effects of alcohol. Surely alcohol would help numb pain. Yes, alcohol will numb your brain and your senses. It will numb you in such a fashion that, if you drink enough, it will render you unconscious. And unconsciousness will relieve your pain. But saying this is a good idea is like saying it's a good idea to go under the guillotine because you have a migraine. There are better solutions.

A 2012 study shows that alcohol makes you less capable of dealing with stress and anxiety. Researchers gave mice doses of alcohol for a month, then ran tests to compare the mice that had been drinking with normal mice. The mice were put in stressful situations to measure their reactions. Alcohol literally rewired the mice's brains to make them unable to deal with anxiety and stress.[158] Many find this shocking, but if you drink regularly you probably already know this is true.

Why do we believe alcohol helps stress and anxiety? Because it can make you oblivious to your stressors even when it's worsening them. You already know that when you sober up, unless you've done something to actually improve the situation, your stress remains.

On the beach with an excellent book, enjoying the sun and the breeze off the ocean, without a care in the world, I am fully relaxed. Alcohol can't improve that feeling. I was recently on the beach in Hawaii enjoying this very sensation, and I considered having a drink. I had always had a Mai Tai (or eight) while on the beach. When I thought about it, I realized a drink would make me tired and cranky. And since one would make me thirsty and awake my alcohol craving, I doubted I would stop at just one. Then instead of spending the next day sunning myself on the beach, I would spend it in bed, hung over. When I thought about it, I realized I didn't want a drink. Mental peace is having no distress. It is a feeling you can never achieve with a drug.

If you are truly happy and relaxed, you have no need or desire to change your state of mind. Looking back, I see that my constant need to drink to relax myself was really proof that alcohol was not relaxing me. If alcohol helped me achieve relaxation, wouldn't it follow that I wouldn't need as much of it? If alcohol cured my stress, wouldn't I need less, not more, of it over time? No, alcohol does not relax you. It does not fix the stress in your life. Rather, it inebriates you, which covers the pain for a short amount of time. As soon as it wears off, your stress returns and, over time, multiplies.

Being happy and stress free, dealing with the root cause of stress rather than numbing the symptoms is the only sure way to find relief.

Then you no longer need to cover the symptom with poison. I am heartbroken to know more than one person who has taken their own life. It's tragic that we deal with our unhappiness in this way, by rendering ourselves forever unconscious, believing the only cure to our depression or unhappiness is to erase ourselves altogether. Alcohol erases a bit of you every time you drink it. It can even erase entire nights when you are on a binge. Alcohol does not relieve stress; it erases your senses and your ability to think. Alcohol ultimately erases your self.

The Opposite of Relief: What Happens in Your Brain

So if alcohol doesn't relax you, what does it do? Quite simply, alcohol slows down your brain function. It does this by affecting two neurotransmitters (chemicals that transmit signals between brain cells): glutamate and GABA.[159] Glutamate is an excitatory neurotransmitter that increases brain activity levels and energy. Alcohol suppresses the release of glutamate, resulting in a slowdown along your brain's neural highways.[160] You literally think more slowly. GABA is an inhibitory neurotransmitter. Inhibitory neurotransmitters reduce energy and slow down activity. Alcohol increases GABA production in the brain, resulting in sedation, diminished thinking, reduced ability to reason, slowed speech, diminished reaction time, and slower movement.[161]

When drinking, science shows that you also alter brain chemicals that increase depression.[162] Your brain counteracts alcohol's artificial stimulation of your brain's pleasure centers, diminishing enjoyment until the illusion of pleasure no longer exists. At this stage the dopamine levels are high, which increases the craving for alcohol but without the illusory pleasure.[163] Neuroscience demonstrates that desire for alcohol can transition into a pathological craving that is associated with dependence.[164] Drinking creates a compulsive need for alcohol, but you don't actually receive any enjoyment from it. How long this takes is person-specific. In some people it can happen almost immediately, and in others it can take several weeks, months, or years of drinking.[165]

Alcohol affects your cerebral cortex, especially your prefrontal cortex. It depresses the behavioral inhibitory centers, making you less inhibited. This also inhibits the processing of information from your eyes and mouth[166] and further inhibits your thought processes, making it more difficult to think clearly.

In addition to slowing brain function, episodic drinking (defined as four drinks in two hours for women and five drinks in two hours for men)[167] can injure the brain by causing the death of neurons.[168] Finally, alcohol depresses nerve centers in the hypothalamus, which control sexual performance and arousal. Sexual urges may increase, but sexual performance and sensory pleasure decrease.[169]

To summarize many of the things we've been discussing about what alcohol actually does to you, I will use an excerpt from Jason Vale's book *Kick the Drink . . . Easily*:

"Alcohol has been proven to:

- Depress your entire nervous system.
- Undermine your courage, confidence, and self-respect.
- Destroy your brain cells.
- Break down the immune system, making you less resistant to all kinds of disease.
- Interfere with the body's ability to absorb calcium, resulting in bones that are weaker, softer, and more brittle.
- Distort eyesight, making it difficult to adjust to different light.
- Diminish your ability to distinguish between sounds and perceive their direction.
- Slur your speech.
- Dull your sense of taste and smell.
- Damage the lining of your throat.

- Weaken your muscles.
- Inhibit the production of white and red blood cells.
- Destroy the stomach lining.
- Cause obesity."[170]

Vale goes on to say, "When you stop putting a poison like alcohol in your body, it literally breathes a sigh of relief."[171]

13.
THE MYSTERY OF
SPONTANEOUS SOBRIETY

"No one saves us but ourselves. No one can and no one may.
We ourselves must walk the path."
—*Buddha*

Have you ever heard of spontaneous sobriety? It's a strange-sounding phrase, but it really just means recovering from alcohol dependency without any formal treatment. And the secret to spontaneous sobriety has everything to do with reconciling the internal conflict caused by your desire to quit drinking and your fear of missing out.

Sobriety Without Rehab

You may be surprised to know that in the U.S. people who spontaneously recover from alcohol dependence are between four and seven times more successful than participants in our main alcoholism treatment approach: A.A. According to a recent study by the NIAAA, more than one-third of individuals with alcohol dependence fully recovered without any treatment. They went from alcohol dependence, defined as demonstrating tolerance, withdrawal symptoms, and unsuccessful attempts to reduce or stop their consumption, to not drinking at all or drinking at levels that were no longer harmful and no longer characterized as dependence.[172] In comparison, Dr. Lance Dodes, a recently retired professor of psychiatry at Harvard Medical School, says, "Peer reviewed studies peg the success rate of A.A. somewhere between 5 and 10 percent, about one of every 15 people who enter these programs is able to become and stay sober."[173]

Not only are people who simply quit, without programs or outside help, more successful in maintaining a healthy relationship with alcohol, they appear to be more at peace with and happier about their decision. A significant portion of their time and energy is not dedicated to maintaining success. Instead of sobriety becoming a daily focus with meetings, readings, and devotionals, it fades into the background, allowing them to be truly free. Further research shows 75% of people who recover from alcohol dependence do so without seeking any kind of help, including specialty alcohol rehab programs and A.A.[174]

How can this be? It does not seem to make sense that simply quitting, without any assistance whatsoever, could be more effective than formal support programs. I found this incredible not only because of the success rates but also because the phenomenon of spontaneous sobriety is not publicized. If there is a way to quit or cut back without a lot of effort and without heartache, sign me up. I needed to understand what this phenomenon was and how it was done. I wanted to understand if there was something that happened inside these spontaneously sober people that I could replicate and teach.

Spontaneous Sobriety: Case Study

Fortunately, one of these spontaneously sober people is my dad. He smoked cigarettes for twenty years and drank heavily. One day he up and quit both, never looking back. My dad leads a unique life. After graduating college, he gave up a promising Manhattan-based future in film production to move into a tiny (twelve foot by twenty-four foot), one-room log cabin in the middle of the Rocky Mountains. There, my parents raised my brothers and me without running water or electricity. At that altitude, the roads are closed from November to May. We had to ski or snowmobile to get to the nearest town.

This is where I grew up—and where he still lives, forty-four years later. It is nestled in a basin at 10,500 feet above sea level, almost at the timberline, and the closest neighbor is miles away. In fact, I remember developing a fear of neighbors because I heard the term in school, and since we didn't have any neighbors I didn't realize what they were. In fact neighbors sounded quite terrifying, and I went home and asked my mom, "Do neighbors bite?"

I never knew my dad to drink, so I assumed he never had. In reality, he was known for his heavy drinking and drank as much or more than any other fraternity boy in the '60s. So why was his "recovery" nonexistent? When I asked him, he replied, "I realized it wasn't doing me any favors, so I decided to stop. I never looked back."

How is this possible when so many spend their lives in recovery, consumed by the fact that they no longer drink? How did my dad simply decide he didn't want to drink alcohol and never look back? My dad wasn't aware of the psychology or science behind why, when he made a firm decision to quit, he was able to stop without pain or longing. The answer is not immediately obvious, but it's actually very simple. I will explain with a story.

Cognitive Dissonance: Disagreeing with Yourself

My friend Chelsey is now happily married to an amazing man. Before meeting her husband, she traveled a long, bumpy road of suitors. One in particular rubbed me the wrong way. Many of the guys weren't good enough for her, but Jesse hit well below the mark. And she liked him, a lot.

My opinion created tension between us. We are close and have a hard time hiding anything from each other. I couldn't sugarcoat it. I didn't have a great reason why I so disliked him. I underestimated how much she liked him, and suddenly we were at odds about something that we couldn't easily reconcile. Usually, if we disagreed on something, we could chat for long enough and eventually see each other's point of view. With Jesse, I couldn't see why she liked him, and she couldn't understand why I didn't. While she dated him, it hung over us and affected how much she shared with me about her relationship.

The reverse happened a few years later when I was still deeply addicted. She did not approve, and though she wanted me to be honest with her about what I was going through, I couldn't. I couldn't explain what I was doing and how I didn't like myself because of it. So I didn't share with her as much as I should have. In both instances we had differences we couldn't reconcile, and we grew more distant than either of us wanted.

This is exactly what happens inside your brain when you realize you are drinking more than you should. In psychology this phenomenon has a fancy name—cognitive dissonance, defined as the mental stress or discomfort that is experienced by someone who holds two contradictory values, ideas, or beliefs at the same time.

Let me give you another example. It's Halloween, and the receptionist at your office brought in a bowl of candy. It sits on her desk, which you walk by every day. You want to eat some, but you've promised yourself that you're going to lose a few pounds, so candy is not allowed.

You have an internal struggle, which creates mental stress. You now have two contradictory trains of thought. You don't want to eat the candy because you don't want the sugar or the calories. Yet you crave the candy, believing it will provide pleasure and satisfaction. You give in and eat some. This is when problems with cognitive dissonance begin. You've done something you are not happy about, which creates discomfort.

This internal struggle has been studied in-depth. It is very difficult to be happy or at peace when we do something part of our brain doesn't agree with. We will go to incredible lengths to overcome the dissonance and restore internal peace. We do this both consciously and unconsciously. And because not all our attempts to remove the struggle are conscious, we can, unknowingly, lie to ourselves.

There are a few ways to overcome this division and restore our inner harmony:

1. We can change our behavior: "I won't eat any more candy."

2. Or we can justify our behavior by changing the conflicting idea or information: "I can cheat every once in a while. I deserve it."

3. We can justify our behavior by adding new behaviors: "It's OK. I will go to the gym later today."

4. Or we can delude ourselves by ignoring or denying the conflicting information: "Candy isn't that bad for my diet."

With addictive substances, we find more complications. You have a strong unconscious belief that alcohol relieves your stress and enhances your life. You have both a conscious and unconscious belief that cutting back or quitting is a legitimate sacrifice. You worry that quitting will be stressful. You don't have a substitute to take its place. In fact, life seems cheerless without it. And to make it all worse, everyone around you drinks!

You now have a strong, conscious belief that the amount you are drinking is harmful to your health, hurting your relationships, and negatively affecting other areas of your life. Since alcohol is an addictive substance, the conflict becomes physical as well as mental. You develop a tiny, almost imperceptible, physical craving for the addictive substance, which makes it more difficult to quit. With time, this craving grows powerful. This is a neurological fact—brain circuitry changes as a result of repeated exposure to an addictive substance, and over time cravings grow in strength through increased dopamine levels, which are the result of a learned chemical response in your brain.[175] Even when you're not drinking alcohol, the internal conflict rages because the craving is in constant disagreement with your desire not to drink. Add deteriorating health and relationships to the equation, and the internal conflict becomes increasingly more painful.

This phenomenon is the basis of addiction. All addicts lie to themselves and others. They do this to protect themselves and minimize the internal trauma caused by their conflict of wills. We become so good at making excuses, at blinding ourselves to the truth, that we believe our own lies. Being unable to trust yourself is terrifying and causes an incredible amount of pain. This is the pain of addiction. Contrary to popular belief, it's not the physical consumption that destroys our lives but the internal conflict and our determination to fix it while retaining an unconscious belief that the drug is somehow vital to our lifestyle.

With alcohol, we can rarely solve the conflict by simply changing our behavior. Since the unconscious mind has been conditioned to believe alcohol is our friend, that it helps us handle stress and improve our lives, we still desire to drink after we decide to quit or cut back. We need willpower to abstain. But, as scientists now know, willpower dries up.[176] And the few drinks we allow ourselves to have become coveted. We give in, drink, and then feel guilty. We are in the midst of cognitive dissonance, a divided mind, experiencing internal conflict.

When we realize we cannot stop drinking via willpower, the conflict in our brains increases. We have tried to change our behavior and found that difficult. We have tried to change our cognition, or thoughts, by reviewing lists of the horrible effects of drinking, and that too has failed. We try to justify our behavior by making excuses for drinking. We may not believe these rationalizations at first, but it's so much easier to tell myself that it's OK to have a drink at 8 a.m. because it's 10 p.m. at home than to experience internal conflict. Part of our brain realizes the excuses don't hold up, so we numb ourselves by drinking more. We try anything to overcome the conflict. We ignore and deny information that conflicts with our desire to drink. We are running out of options, and we don't understand why we can't overcome this. Then we start to blame ourselves.

You can see why scare tactics are rarely successful in overcoming an alcohol problem. We have known all our lives that alcohol is addictive and that it ruins people's lives, but we choose to ignore or deny such information, which compounds the conflict in our brains. Drinking becomes an illogical activity.

The belief that alcoholism only happens to other people, people with a physical or mental defect, gives us an easy way to address the conflict in our brains. It gives us a reason to believe we are in control even when we know we are not. It helps us deny our problem. You can observe how drinkers deal with cognitive dissonance by paying attention to the reasons people give for drinking. If you are honest with yourself about why you drink, I bet it will be difficult to find a reason that truly stands up to logical, critical examination.

Stopping the Internal War

So how did my dad overcome his cognitive dissonance? How did he achieve spontaneous sobriety? He chose the first way, to stop drinking once and forever. But when he made this decision, he had long since determined that alcohol was not doing anything positive in his life. He realized this with 100% of his mind, leaving no lingering doubt, no room to question his decision. He chose to stop drinking with all of his brain, and by doing this he ended the conflict, achieving peace. The personality characteristic that allowed him to do this, his decisive and definitive nature, is also a quality that contributed to his drinking. When he was a drinker, he drank with his entire mind. He didn't doubt or question every drink. If drinking a little was good, drinking a lot was better. This commitment is both what pushed him to become dependent on alcohol and what ultimately helped him find freedom.

I won't tell you what my dad did is easy to do. It's not. It takes a mind that is pliable enough and strong enough to change all of itself—both the conscious and the unconscious. *This Naked Mind* does that work for you. By reading this book, you are changing your unconscious mind, so you can easily and peacefully end the conflict inside your brain. You may have been living with division in your brain for years, even decades. Only you know how much pain and suffering this has caused.

Why is this division so painful? Conflict causes pain, which explains why we are, by nature, averse to conflict. It hurts to disagree with a close friend. We suffer pain when we don't see eye-to-eye with strangers or even when we witness conflict. How much more painful to fight with ourselves? If you've suffered from addiction, doing something you hate, you know the intense pain. I have not, in my life, experienced anything worse. There is nothing scarier. The conflict was so painful that I would "obliviate," rendering myself completely intoxicated in order to ignore the mess my life had become. In doing this, I lost my trust in myself. I did stuff I didn't want to do, and I didn't understand why I continued to do it. The misery was powerful and all-consuming. I no longer saw a familiar face in the mirror. I didn't know who I was; I lost myself. To find yourself again, and to restore your happiness, it is vital that you remove the disagreement inside your mind. And the first step is to examine the asserted benefits of alcohol, and prove, logically and rationally, with our Liminal Points that there are few benefits to drinking.

14.
LIMINAL POINT: I ENJOY DRINKING; IT MAKES ME HAPPY

"Addiction begins with the hope that something 'out there' can instantly fill up the emptiness inside."
—*Jean Kilbourne*

You have **observed** people "enjoying" alcohol in every conceivable manner for as long as you can remember. Advertisements promise alcohol will make us happy as we develop relationships, have sex, ignite the party, and enjoy our everyday activities. It's practically impossible in western society not to form the **assumption** that alcohol makes people happy. You determined to try alcohol, and over time your **experiences** confirmed this. Not necessarily because alcohol actually made you happy, but because once you built even the smallest tolerance you became slightly, almost imperceptibly, unhappy when you couldn't drink. In fact the **assumption** that alcohol makes you happy includes an unspoken **assumption** that not drinking will make you unhappy. And in this way your **experience** confirmed your assumptions, so you've **concluded** that yes, alcohol does in fact offer enjoyment and make you happy.

Let's consider reality:

Alcohol Makes Me Happy

Studies show that alcohol causes a lot of unhappiness in our society. It makes the drinkers unhappy, but it also makes the people around drinkers unhappy. It causes homelessness, joblessness, poverty, abuse, depression, pain, rape, misery, and death. There are support groups for victims of emotional, physical, and sexual abuse resulting from alcohol. Alcohol has devastated families, with 70% of alcohol-related violent incidents occurring in the home. Of these incidents twenty percent involve a weapon other than hands, fists, or feet.[177] Orphanages exist for children whose parents have died or can no longer take care of them because of alcohol. Alcohol causes arguments, fights, stabbings, murder, and unwanted pregnancies. In violent crimes, an offender is far more likely to have been drinking than under the influence of other drugs.[178] And people who drink regularly have a higher rate of death from injury or violence.[179]

Alcohol and the damage it causes in society is so rampant that I have yet to meet anyone who doesn't have a story of heartache, tragedy, pain, or regret. My beautiful cousin died the day after Christmas when she was twenty-three. She was crossing a street when she was hit by a drunk driver. Her face was barely recognizable. She made it to the hospital, where she died. We all have horror stories.

The effect of alcohol on children is the most heartbreaking. It is incredibly painful for children to see their parents—around whom their entire worlds revolve—stumbling, sick, arguing, or being mean to each other. My friend Julie's parents divorced when she was quite young, and her mother remarried a heavy drinker. I spent the night a few times, and her room lay directly beneath her parents'. I remember lying in bed, listening to alcohol-fueled fights and feeling so helpless. My friend pretended she was asleep. She must have been embarrassed. Her mom never drank, and the arguments seemed one-sided. We could only hear a male voice yelling while her mom cried. Yet in some ways Julie was lucky. Many children lie in bed or hide in closets while their mom is physically harmed. Often it's the children who are victims of abuse. It's terrifying to know more than half of all confirmed child abuse reports and 75% of child deaths from abuse involve alcohol.[180] Mothers convicted of child abuse are *three times* more likely to be alcoholics, and abusive fathers are *ten times* more likely to be alcoholics.[181] And the cycle continues because children of alcoholics are up to four times more likely to develop alcohol addiction later in life.[182]

Even without abuse, a drunken parent terrifies a child. They are either doting on you, constantly telling you they love you (which you realize is false, empty, and fueled by the drink), or they seem to disappear, and you no longer recognize your parent. They are no longer the person you know and trust. Although they may be physically present, you feel abandoned and afraid. You wish they would just go away. Being around them, even if they aren't violent, is painful. When a child can't communicate with their parents, it spawns hurt and neglect. Kids are also subject to morning-after abuse, when the hangover causes parents to snap at their kids, leaving them wondering why. Children hate to see their parents drunk; there are few things more upsetting.

You may argue these are extreme cases, and surely alcohol in moderate quantities helps you enjoy life. While you can see that on the whole it causes more misery than happiness, you are the exception. These horrible things happen to other people, but you find true joy in drinking. By some miracle, the substance that causes fathers to hurt their children, drivers to kill entire families, and drinkers to take their own lives makes you happy.

Perhaps I am not being fair. How can I dispute the euphoric tipsy feeling? I can't. You get a bit of a rush when alcohol first enters your system. That is a fact; it happens. Alcohol, unlike food, can be absorbed directly through the stomach lining. This means alcohol reaches your brain cells quickly. But have you noticed how quickly the feeling dissipates? Pay attention the next time you are drinking. It comes on quickly, but it's gone within twenty minutes. Some experts theorize that the "rush" is simply a boost in blood sugar as alcohol is made up of sugars and carbohydrates. To combat the rush of glucose and balance out your blood sugar, your body stimulates the production of insulin. The insulin causes your blood sugar to fall, resulting in lower blood sugar than when you began drinking. With low blood sugar you feel empty and tense. And perhaps another drink will relax you—for another few minutes—because it will give you the next rush of glucose.[183]

That feeling hooks you. Observe how you feel when drinking. After that initial tipsy feeling passes, it won't come back in quite the same way, no matter how much you drink. You drink more to chase the initial rush. After a few drinks, your senses are dulled, and your perceptions change. Life no longer feels quite real. You believe you are in control but can no longer gauge how drunk you are. You have lost your ability to moderate. This is why, despite warnings, danger, and the threat of a DUI, smart people get behind the wheel when they shouldn't.

Vale asks, "Each time you have had a drink, can you honestly say that you have been happy? Have you been uptight or argumentative when drinking? Have you ever been stressed out, felt depressed or cried during a drinking session? Have you become obnoxious or unreasonable when drinking?"[184]

He goes on to make the point that in theory, if alcohol made you happy, every time you drank you should be full of happiness. Let me ask you, from a purely physiological perspective, how could alcohol possibly make you happy? The effect of alcohol is to deaden all of your senses, to numb you, to inebriate you. If you are numb, how can you feel anything, happiness included? Surely you are not happy every time you drink.

None of us are proud of everything we have said or done while drinking. Yet in the moment we believe we are on top of the world, saying and doing anything we please, deluding ourselves into thinking it's making us happy. Are you happy when the room starts to spin, or your dinner comes back up? Is the drunk on the street in Vegas who has lost his home and his family to booze truly happy?

You might take issue with this and tell me that of course none of those things are enjoyable, but moderate drinking makes *you* happy. How is that logical? How does a substance that makes people act in ways they are ashamed of suddenly turn into joy juice when we drink a little of it? Wouldn't it make more sense that if a little alcohol made us a little happy, a lot of alcohol would make us a lot happy?

You may argue that you see drinkers all the time who are happy. They're drinking, joking, giggling, and enjoying themselves. I am willing to bet they are enjoying the situation, conversation, and time with their friends rather than the booze. You may argue that if the booze wasn't present, the situation would become somber. I agree—if the drinkers believed, as most drinkers do, that they couldn't enjoy themselves without alcohol. It's not that alcohol makes drinkers happy; it's that they are very unhappy without it.

It's hard to measure this because we have nothing to compare against. I don't remember attending a wedding, or for that matter a funeral, where alcohol wasn't provided. I certainly never went to a business dinner where drinking wasn't involved. I can't remember a single barbecue without booze. Looking back on my adult years, I don't remember any social occasions where alcohol wasn't available. We live near one of the world's best concert venues, and they serve alcohol but charge a lot for it. I was at my friend Laura's house, and we were in the kitchen. I noticed a loaf of bread with a piece broken off. I went closer and saw that a bottle was baked into the loaf of bread. Laura's husband is a whiskey fan, and they were planning to attend a concert. He didn't want to buy drinks and preferred his own brand, so Laura emptied the bottle and baked a loaf of bread around it. It was cooling, and then she was going to fill it back up. They planned to pack the bread as part of their picnic lunch in order to sneak the whiskey into the concert. You can bring as much food as you want, you just can't bring in booze, and they actively search your bags. As you can imagine, Laura was pleased with herself, and her husband was ecstatic.

My point is that when we are enjoying social occasions, which by their nature create true enjoyment, there is almost always alcohol present. Can you think of many social occasions where drinking was not an option? I don't mean that you were refraining or trying to drink less but that drinking simply wasn't part of the party? Even that statement sounds like an oxymoron. If you are part of a subculture that doesn't serve alcohol at every wedding or party, you have a better point of comparison than most of us. Think back to some of the most fun parties you've attended, with and without alcohol. You've been able to relax and enjoy yourself at both types of parties, haven't you? You've had a great time in social gatherings without booze. Doesn't this lead you to believe that maybe you had fun because you were talking and laughing with friends, rather than because you were drinking?

Now, instead of comparing myself to other drinkers at social gatherings, I can compare my non-drinking self against my former, drinking self. It's almost a joke how much more I enjoy my life. I actually know when I am having a good time, or a not-so-good time for that matter, but my emotions are one hundred percent mine. There are a million reasons why I am happier now, but above all I know myself. I feel comfortable and confident in my own skin. I love being alive, love being me. This is true happiness. After *This Naked Mind*, Mary describes it like this: "I don't drink anymore because all of these feelings are more euphoric and fulfilling than any experience alcohol has provided me."

It's hard to accept this when all your hipster friends are "enjoying" wine with dinner. It's the thing to do. Yet, deep down, we all sense that alcohol may be harmful. It's why we feel the need to justify how much, or how often, we drink. It's the black shadow hanging over the times you drink and the times you don't. We've convinced ourselves that we cannot enjoy life without booze, so we close our minds to the shadow. How is it possible that, at one time, we enjoyed life and found happiness before we ever drank? Happiness is feeling physically and mentally healthy, feeling great to be alive. How can anyone who is dependent on a drink that destroys their health and ensnares them be truly happy? Your mind is extremely powerful and what you believe will be true. If you believe you can't party or hang out with friends without a drink, you won't be able to.

If you are looking to turn off your brain, you can do this with alcohol. When you come out of your alcohol-induced stupor, your pain will still be there and quite often compounded. Will you magically be happy when you wake up from your night of drunken oblivion? Will your situation have somehow improved? Or will it be worse? You now feel both mentally and physically awful. Drinking has frayed your nerves, and you are less prepared to deal with the reason you started to drink to begin with.

A real sorrow or distress cannot be fixed by alcohol. You can't drown out things that are truly tragic. By drinking enough you can close your mind to them temporarily, but they will remain. The more you drink, the harder it is to deal with your problems when you finally sober up. When you wake, tragedy will still be there. Your loss will remain, seeming worse than before.

It's eye-opening to realize who is happy and who may not be. It's hard to be happy when we are obsessed with where our next drink comes from or how much alcohol we can put away in an evening. I often notice people who aren't drinking or are drinking so little you can tell it's for show. They are enjoying the atmosphere, laughing, and talking with friends. They are not controlled by alcohol—they seem at peace and truly happy. Make your own observations. Look around next time you are out to dinner or at a club. See who seems happy and relaxed. Then pay attention to whether they are heavily drinking. The results might surprise you.

If you feel you need alcohol to make you happy, relax you, or help you enjoy your evening, you are already in trouble. Just because your body is not yet falling apart and you have the means to feed your craving doesn't mean you aren't addicted. Maybe you have not reached the chronic stage where you are completely physically and mentally dependent on alcohol. But if you think you need alcohol to enjoy social occasions or to relieve the stress of the daily grind, you have already become emotionally dependent. The cumulative effect of alcohol, on any drinker, is unhappiness, not happiness.

Don't worry if you feel I am being unfair and painting too harsh a picture. The great news is that you don't have to take my word for it. Once you are free, you will prove these things to yourself over and over again. You will live your life to the fullest, attending dozens of social functions, happier than alcohol could ever make you.

15.
DEFINING ADDICTION: PART I

"Progress is impossible without change, and those who
cannot change their minds cannot change anything."
—*George Bernard Shaw*

Characteristics of Addiction: Abuse, Dependency, Craving

The term addiction is tossed around all the time. We can be addicted to chocolate, shopping, television, or really anything. The word has so many different meanings that psychiatrists prefer the term "Substance Use Disorder." Substance use disorders are classified based on certain characteristic features that fall into three categories: abuse, dependence, and craving.[185]

Abuse is characterized by significant negative consequences to the addicted. These can be health consequences, relational consequences, and consequences from no longer doing what you should be doing—like going to work in the morning.

Dependence happens when the addict depends on the drug psychologically and sometimes physically. Dependence is characterized by tolerance, when you need to consume more of the drug to get the same effect, and withdrawal, when you have unpleasant psychological or physical symptoms when you stop taking the drug.[186] Both occur when your body and brain have changed to compensate for the chronic presence of the drug.[187]

Craving is an extremely strong, illogical desire to use the drug. Cravings can contradict your feelings, meaning you may consciously desire to take the day off from drinking, but an intense craving for alcohol still exists. When an addict attempts to abstain, cravings can be so strong that the addict finds it hard to think about anything else.

For simplicity, let's define addiction this way: doing something on a regular basis that you do not want to be doing. Or doing something more often than you would like to be doing it, yet being unable to easily stop or cut back. Basically, it's having two competing priorities, wanting to do more and less of something at the same time. The addictive substance creates a psychological need for itself in your thoughts and a biological need in your gray matter. This need grows, and a cycle begins where the body tries to compensate for the presence of the substance, but it goes too far, creating a need for the drug.

Eventually the need—the craving and the desire for the addictive substance—is so all-consuming that choice is no longer involved. In studies of addiction, the subject will continue to self-administer the addictive substance ad infinitum at the exclusion of everything else in their lives, including taking care of their young or even feeding themselves. Rats in these experiments will starve themselves.[188]

When we reach that compulsive stage we must sever the cycle completely. We must starve the substance's need for itself.

We all have many addictions. In a way, we are an addictive species—we use the same skills to learn and adapt as we do to become addicted. Learning happens in the same part of the brain as addiction. Polk cites studies that confirm addiction is intrinsically tied to our brain's ability to learn. We will cover this in detail in the next chapter.

The Cycle of Addiction

This is one of the most important parts of this book. We must understand why we drink.

When crack addicts run out of crack, they freak out. They become anxious, irritated, and severely paranoid. They go to great lengths to get their next fix. Some people do things they could never have imagined before the addiction, even prostituting themselves for another hit. Their entire world revolves around the drug. They are miserable. When they find and smoke crack, they relax. It seems logical to conclude that crack is just the thing to alleviate misery, paranoia, and panic. Look at the evidence. One minute they are a wreck, and the next they seem happy and at peace. We know this is not true. In reality, the crack addict smokes crack not for the benefits of the drug, but to relieve the withdrawal the previous dose created.

It would seem that we only undergo withdrawals when we quit. In reality, every time we take the drug we experience withdrawal as it leaves our system. This is the reason we feel the need to take the drug again. We endure withdrawals constantly when we are repeatedly taking a drug or drinking alcohol. If the crack addict had never smoked crack, they would never suffer from the panic, the cold sweats, and the misery of a crack withdrawal. Isn't it clear that the drug creates rather than relieves these symptoms? We can see this from the outside, yet it's not clear to the person who is addicted.

Addictions vary from substance to substance, but the patterns are the same. The addict is conditioned to believe the substance will provide enjoyment or relief, that it will help them enjoy life more or ease their stress. The addict generally believes they are somehow incomplete and need something more than what their body can naturally provide. They may believe there is something missing inside of them, an empty space that can be filled with their substance of choice. These beliefs are not generally conscious.

Addicts usually take time to acclimate to the experience of using the drug. The first time I smoked marijuana, it wasn't pleasant; I felt paranoid, and I didn't like it. My friends told me that was normal, and the next time would be better, so I tried it again. Since the initial experience is less than ideal, whether it's the foul taste of your first beer or the paranoia of your first bowl, your fear of becoming addicted fades. How can we possibly become addicted to something that isn't all that great? According to Vale: "The irony is that the awful taste is part of what springs the alcohol trap."[189]

When we take a physically addictive substance, from caffeine to crack, we suffer withdrawal as it leaves our system. With some harder drugs it's intense, but with most addictive substances, like nicotine, sugar, caffeine, or alcohol, it can be a small, almost unnoticeable, feeling of discomfort. A vulnerable, anxious, empty feeling. The uneasy notion that something is not quite right, or missing, and that life is incomplete. Since alcohol can take days to leave the system, drinkers might experience this feeling almost constantly.

Since we don't suffer this feeling when we are taking the drug, we don't connect the feeling with the drug. The feeling of something being amiss is similar to stress or hunger, so we can't pinpoint it. When we drink another drink, we feel better. We have a drink and feel more relaxed, confident, and in control than we did just moments before. Since the relief is real, we start to believe the drink provides enjoyment. We are happier when we take a drink, not because drinking makes us happy, but because the drink relieves the withdrawal that drinking caused. This illusion confirms what we've been unconsciously conditioned to believe, that alcohol provides relief or pleasure.

We continue drinking to get rid of the empty, uneasy feeling that alcohol created. When we enjoy the "pleasure" of a drink, we restore the wholeness and peace of mind we knew our entire lives before we ever drank a drop. Since alcohol is harmful, we begin to build an immunity to it. We need more to achieve the same effect, more to relieve the empty, insecure feeling. Since addictive substances create the vulnerability to begin with, they cannot help us relax. They are the reason we feel tense, weak, and insecure. Vale says, "The beautiful truth is that you won't need to find different ways to relax as you will be far more relaxed as a non-drinker anyway. It is alcohol that causes you to feel un-relaxed in the first place."[190]

The immunity grows, and eventually you are unhappy, even when drinking. The drug destroys us mentally and physically. Our health falters, our nerves suffer, and the feeling of dependence becomes greater. We take more. The cycle continues. And suddenly we see how, without ever realizing it is happening, we have become dependent. We see how the drunken partier in Vegas becomes the homeless man clutching his paper bag.

As the cycle continues, the feeling of dependence becomes greater, and we begin to believe alcohol is the most important thing in our lives. Just as bad food would taste amazing if we were starving, our perception of booze is altered. Alcohol seems more valuable. Our loved ones see us slipping. By the time they say something, we have become so afraid of losing what now feels like our only solace that we unknowingly and unconsciously close our minds to what they are saying.

Eventually our tolerance is high and we are drinking so much that much of our mental and physical health has been stolen. The illusion of gratification is practically nonexistent. We start to listen to family and friends or pay attention to the small, cautionary voice inside our heads. We wonder if we should cut back or quit. Yet we've been unconsciously conditioned to believe cutting back or quitting is difficult, so we sadly begin to prepare for an uphill battle.

We try to abstain, but our unconscious mind still believes we are getting something positive from alcohol. Because of this we are tormented when we try to quit. We believe we are sacrificing something that has become important. Since everyone around us is "happily" drinking, we feel like we are missing out. Ultimately our actual experiences confirm our belief that it is hard, if not impossible, to stop drinking.

The longer we deprive ourselves, the greater the satisfaction when we finally give in. Why? Through abstinence, the feeling of misery has grown—and so has the relief. We translate this relief as pleasure when we finally give in and drink. In this cycle of addiction, both the misery of abstinence and the "pleasure" of surrender are real and intense.

Aftereffects of the Alcohol Cycle

I like how Allen Carr describes causation between alcohol consumption and the misery we suffer between drinks. These five points are his, but I've fleshed them out a bit for clarity's sake.[191]

First, we experience the immediate aftereffects from our previous bout of drinking. You are familiar with the general low mood, tiredness, hangover, headaches, and sluggishness.

Second, we have the mounting physical harms caused by ongoing drinking. These occur so slowly we don't notice they are happening.[192] Feeling sluggish, stressed, and chronically tired becomes the new normal. Ongoing drinking affects your mental well-being, with alcohol being a major cause of depression.[193] Drinking begins to affect our finances and relationships.

Third, we face the real stress in our lives. In *The Sober Revolution*, Lucy Rocca explains that since alcohol depresses the central nervous system, exacerbating depression and anxiety, a drinker often finds it difficult to cope with everyday stressors. Small, daily problems that shouldn't be much of an issue become an "ever-increasing mountain of the unachievable."[194] While the initial issues are not necessarily related to drinking, we would have dealt with them, improving upon or solving them rather than feeling overwhelmed, reaching for a drink, and putting them off until tomorrow. Without alcohol, we would be able to handle them as they arose rather than putting them off and making them worse.[195]

Fourth, we feel the empty, anxious, insecure feeling we only know as, "I want a drink." It's the imperceptible twinge that something's missing. These four factors combine to create the real reason we drink, an incredibly strong psychological craving.

It's obvious that the immediate aftereffects of drinking are caused by alcohol. The cumulative effects are harder to pinpoint, but they make up the fifth factor. We don't realize that our chronic exhaustion is related to continuously poisoning our bodies. We blame these feelings on life in general or on aging. We don't think about the actual stressors in life, things we've procrastinated on or blocked from our minds when drinking.[196] We don't consider the subtle, "A drink sounds nice" feeling because it is generally small, almost unnoticeable. All of these factors work together to create the fifth and final factor. This factor—the mental craving for alcohol—is much stronger than all the others put together. Alcohol, along with all addictive drugs, actually re-wires our brains, changing their function.[197] The craving becomes more than a mental illusion; it's a neural reality—a reality of dependence and withdrawal.[198]

The Itch to Drink

When you are between drinks, you crave a drink. This can happen either consciously or unconsciously. You want a drink, and you don't see a reason not to have one. If you can't have one in the moment (say you are driving), you look forward to drinking later.

When you decide not to satisfy your craving because you want to drink less, you become miserable. The little feeling of wanting a drink grows intolerable. Why? Any provocation can be small until you can't fix it. It's like getting a blister while hiking. The feeling is faint at first, almost unnoticeable. You could fix it by removing your shoe, but if you keep hiking, it will continue to rub, and the irritation will grow until you can't stand it.

A craving, when unsatisfied, becomes so strong you cannot concentrate on anything else. It's like the neighbor kid is playing the drums. The sound is in background, and you don't notice it. But eventually it seems like the drums are being played in your living room. Drum practice becomes overpowering, and you can't think, much less relax. Drumming dominates your mind until practice is over or you have a nervous breakdown and shove his drumsticks down the garbage disposal.

You drink to end the distress. The drink itself does not provide enjoyment, but you sincerely enjoy ending the nuisance of wanting a drink. The relief is so strong you feel happy, even giddy. You drink to get the feeling of peace that someone who is not dependent on alcohol always feels.

That's why the mental desire for alcohol is far stronger than all the aftereffects. When a drinker decides she needs a drink to satisfy her craving, she is unhappy until she consumes one. The longer the drumming continues, the more refreshing the silence. Similarly, the longer you crave alcohol, the greater the illusion of enjoyment or relief when you satisfy your desire.

You know the feeling—the misery of wanting a drink and not allowing yourself to have one. You know how real these feelings are, so real that you end up justifying the next drink in ways you never imagined. You also know how intense the relief is when your craving is satisfied.

The deception is the belief that alcohol itself provides the enjoyment and the relief. It does not. The misery you feel when you abstain is actually caused by drinking. It doesn't matter if you have just started drinking or are at the chronic stage, this is true. It's the reality of addiction, the reality of alcohol.

Claiming alcohol gives you pleasure is like saying it's enjoyable to create blisters for the relief of taking off your shoes. Alcohol doesn't satisfy your desire for alcohol; it is what created your desire for alcohol. Alcohol is the only reason you continue to crave alcohol and the only reason your cravings get worse over time.

When it was my turn to be the designated driver, I couldn't help feeling grumpy. I didn't think I would have as much fun without drinking. Since I believed it, it was true, and when I didn't have fun, my unconscious mind concluded that drinking was key to enjoying a party. I was duped into believing drinking made the difference. The deception is clear. It's not that alcohol is inherently enjoyable, but that because I was addicted, an evening without alcohol was miserable. The truth is that you don't need alcohol to enjoy yourself; you only think you do.[199]

The great news is that you are not stuck. Your life can be complete and whole again without alcohol. You don't have to continue to suffer.

The Ultimate Test

At the end of a long day, my mood used to change as soon as I ordered a glass of wine. I became upbeat and excited, and the cares of the day seemed to fade away. I couldn't have felt any of the physical effects of the drink just by ordering it or within seconds of my first sip. Yet my mood drastically improved. My mental craving was relieved. I would continue drinking, and the next three or four glasses wouldn't actually provide pleasure. My senses were numbed, and I became less sharp, less witty, and less interesting.

You can actually test this. I did. I wanted to see if alcohol provided me with honest enjoyment. Despite the fact that I drank every day, I couldn't accurately explain to you what it was about drinking that I enjoyed. I hoped to understand how alcohol made me feel. Was there, apart from the circumstances or the relief of ending my craving, any true enjoyment?

I did this at home, alone. It wouldn't be a fair test around friends who actually make me happy. And I couldn't be out at some sort of event that would have made me happy. I made a video of the experience so I could objectively view myself later. I opened a bottle of wine and drank it.

At first I had a tipsy, light-headed feeling, like blood rushing to my head. I was a little off balance. It didn't feel all that great but was the most pleasant part of the experience. This feeling came and went in less than twenty minutes. Eventually I got drunk and sat down to tell the camera exactly how I felt—out of it, like my vision was narrowing and the walls were closing in on me. I felt much less capable of doing the things I had planned for the evening, like reading or writing. Before the experiment I thought as soon as I got a buzz, I would want to do something fun, like go in the hot tub or play video games. I thought I would want to capitalize on and enjoy the feeling. I had no desire to do anything. I had zero energy, and nothing sounded like fun. It wasn't bad, but I couldn't say it was fun. It was more like everything got a bit soft around the edges, a bit less sharp, less real. I had a hard time putting my thoughts together and communicating.

I was horrified when I watched the video. I had slowly transformed from my generally energetic, confident, and happy self to a complete idiot. Alcohol stole my smarts. I sounded so dumb. I was shocked and embarrassed. I didn't expect it to be so bad. I knew talking to someone who has been drinking can be painful, but I had been so certain I was funnier, wittier, and more fun to be around when I was drunk. My perception was completely out of sync with reality. I thought I was making great jokes on camera. I wasn't.

And think about your own experiences. When you are talking to someone who has been drinking, you aren't envious of how they are feeling. Usually the last thing you want is to feel like they do. I don't remember ever talking to someone who was noticeably drunk and wishing I could have as much fun as they were having. Why? Because it was clear they were not having fun. They were no longer themselves. The real person had left the building. Only when you aren't drinking does this become crystal clear.

Drinking felt like tunnel vision. I was no longer aware of all my surroundings but only what was right in front of me, and even that took more effort and concentration than I had energy for. After an hour, the only thing that sounded good to me was sleep. Instead of staying up late to enjoy my night of drinking, I went to bed. My big party ended before 10 p.m. It was strange and disorienting. I certainly didn't feel happier.

As a marketer, I often ponder how I could sell something, a product or an experience. The experience of that night was something I would struggle to sell. I couldn't put the "amazing feeling" of alcohol into positive words. What is that feeling anyway? How is it possible, when we know all alcohol does is deaden our senses, to claim it gives us a truly amazing feeling that we enjoy? I consider myself an excellent marketer, yet from that night of experimental drinking, I could not find any benefit worth putting into an advertisement. I would have had to, as all alcohol advertising does, make it up.

Before the test I stopped drinking with *This Naked Mind* so I had no craving for alcohol. Without a craving, I experienced no relief. Alcohol creates an appetite for alcohol. It gets upset when you don't feed it, and you feel relieved when you do. The feeling of relief is a huge contributor to the illusion of happiness. As Jason Vale says, "The only reason a little alcohol appears to create happiness is because it removes natural fears and satisfies your psychological dependency on the drug."[200]

If you do try this test, it's important to minimize any external factors that make you authentically happy. Pick a day when you are not overly happy or overly sad. Don't watch TV, movies, or listen to music. It's important that you experience just the alcohol to see if you enjoy it. Be honest with yourself, and make it a true test. Ask yourself if you are happier than before. Ask yourself if you want to spend the rest of your life dumber, with your senses deadened, experiencing tunnel vision, and unable to concentrate on more than one thing at a time.

I made a big deal out of eliminating outside factors—friends, fun locations, even TV or music—because enjoying a situation that includes alcohol doesn't mean you're enjoying alcohol. Look at your life. You have enjoyed tons of occasions, but can you separate the drinking from the activity and realize you had fun because of the company or the event, rather than the "joy" of poisoning yourself and numbing your senses? Think back to before you drank, when you were perfectly capable of enjoying all sorts of things without drinking. That enjoyment is what's still present in social situations, only now it's clouded by alcohol.

What about when you didn't think much about drinking, so it was just something you did? Did you get excited about your night out because of how incredible the alcohol was going to be? Or can you entertain the idea that you don't actually enjoy drinking but feel deprived and unhappy without it? Can you see how ending a low, created by alcohol, is not the same as experiencing a true high? Do you realize that a fun evening with friends is fun for every reason except alcohol? In fact, during most of your drinking life, when you took alcohol for granted, the illusion of enjoyment was barely noticeable.

And what about the other times? Was the boozy moms' group really fun when you realized you're back home but have no memory of how you got there? That's called a blackout, and though they are rarely discussed, they happen more frequently than we realize. In fact, a 2002 study published in the *Journal of American College Health* found that more than 50% of drinkers at Duke University had experienced blackouts.[201] If you can't remember it, how can it be fun? And don't forget all the times you said something stupid, went home with someone you didn't want to, or puked for hours on end. Don't forget when your speech became slurred, or when you got in trouble with your spouse because she found the bottles you'd been hiding in the closet. Or perhaps your trouble was with the law when they pulled you over for swerving and served you with a DUI.

The irony is that the times you're drinking are no better than the times of misery between drinks. It provides no enjoyment. It provides no relief.

One of the first times I got drunk, I remember feeling out of control, like the room was spinning. It was horrible. This feeling ended in terrible sickness, which I now know was my body's ingenious survival mechanisms at work. My body saved my life by purging the alcohol that could have killed me. My first time was long ago, but the feeling hasn't changed. At the end of my drinking days it just took me a lot more booze to get to that stage. In fact, I had built such a tolerance that I didn't feel that way after two bottles of wine. I didn't actually feel much of anything. When I was drinking, though I never consciously thought about it, I believed I was drinking because I liked it and because I chose to. Now I see I was drinking so much because I was addicted. If drinking made me giggly, it was never the same as true, fulfilling happiness. Laughing gas also makes me giggly, but it certainly does not make me happy.

16.
LIMINAL POINT: IS ALCOHOL VITAL TO SOCIAL LIFE?

"Dear alcohol, we had a deal where you would make me funnier, smarter, and a better dancer . . . I saw the video . . . we need to talk."
—*Anonymous*

Before you ever drank a drop you did not need alcohol to enjoy yourself socially, yet as you grew older, you **observed** everyone around you drinking in social situations. In fact, you almost never **observed** social situations without alcohol. You **assumed** alcohol was a key ingredient for a good party. You began to drink socially, and initially you probably still didn't find alcohol vital to socializing. Since alcohol is part of practically every social situation, soon you only **experience** social situations with alcohol. Eventually you developed a small dependence, and you missed alcohol if it wasn't available. Your **experience** confirmed your observations. You didn't have quite as much fun if you didn't drink. You **concluded**, yes, alcohol is vital to social life.

Let's consider reality:

I Drink for Social Reasons

Clearly drinking is a social pastime. At many occasions, alcohol turns a great event into a mess. At our wedding we only offered beer and wine to guests. We knew providing certain guests with liquor would mean trouble. We all have stories of the uncle or friend who gets drunk and ruins the wedding. And that doesn't only happen at weddings. There are plenty of nights out at the club or the bar where social drinking quickly turns antisocial.

I knew a girl whose boyfriend would get drunk and pass out so hard he repeatedly wet the bed. He was thirty years old. His problem was well-hidden, as most are. At the party he was the happy-go-lucky drinker, yet bed-wetting was a nightly occurrence. You cannot tell me this is a social activity.

My brother, a non-drinker, is a second-degree black belt, something he would not have had the discipline to achieve in his drinking days. We relish competition, experiencing new things, and meeting new people. We enjoy these things because our senses are engaged. It's part of our nature as human beings to pursue the company of other humans. According to research by Johann Hari, social activities can help prevent addiction. If rats are put in cages alone with both drug-laced and clean water, the rats quickly become addicted to the drug. But if rats are in cages with lots of friends and social activities—Hari says to imagine a rat park—they ignore the drugs and prefer plain water. And before you think rats might not be a good representation of human nature, you should know their genetic, biological, and behavioral characteristics closely resemble those of humans, making them excellent test subjects.[202] Hari believes the antidote to addiction is actually companionship.[203]

With my personal experience, I can't help but agree. Addiction turned me into a loner. I had secrets and couldn't connect with others as well as before. My cravings drove me to a point where I valued the drug more than people. This is hard to admit, but it's true. When drinking we become insular, we lose ourselves, and we miss out on true opportunities for companionship. It's not the drinking that makes these activities fun; we enjoy them because we are with friends and doing something we like. When was the last time you came home from a football game and raved about the quality of the beer instead of talking about the amazing touchdown pass?

We have become accustomed to drinking on these occasions. We didn't need alcohol to enjoy them before, but now we have developed a habit of drinking. We have intertwined, within our minds, the alcohol and the joy we feel from the occasion. This is for a few reasons:

- The idea that drinking enhances experiences has been ingrained in our conscious and unconscious minds through advertisements.

- We reconfirm this when we develop an almost unnoticeable physical dependence on alcohol. Alcohol can take ten days to fully leave your system, and your body physically craves a drink. You probably don't even notice this, or you just notice the feeling as, "A drink sounds good." The relief of feeding this craving makes alcohol seem as if it is contributing to your enjoyment of the occasion.

- The mental belief that drinking enhances the occasion creates a placebo effect. This makes two things happen.

  1. Since you believe alcohol is helping you have fun, it does. Your mind is incredibly powerful.

  2. If you skip a drink, you feel deprived. You believe you are not enjoying yourself as much as you would with a drink in your hand. You come to believe that you won't have fun without a drink.

- This cycle continues, and as drinking is addictive, you eventually create a physical addiction. At this stage, once you are addicted, you will feel tormented when you do not allow yourself to drink.

How can you know this is true? You don't have to look further than people who don't drink at all to realize it's not the alcohol that makes social occasions amazing. Think about a school dance. There was no alcohol, yet it was fun and exciting. You scoped out girls or guys, enjoyed looking at everyone's outfits, and spent social time with friends with no parents allowed.

As Rocca says, "Alcohol stifles your creative mind, dulls your senses and turns you into something of a slave to its every whim, the real world shrinks drastically until it is nothing more than a cycle of hangovers, booze and falseness."[204] Alcohol homogenizes life, meaning you experience the same deadened sense of drunken reality at a hockey game as you feel at a fancy dinner. And you won't remember much of either. Instead of enjoying the wide variety of social activities available to us, drinking makes them all blend together. Rocca describes it as life becoming small, a boozy Groundhog Day in which you become ensnared. You don't realize you are caught fast in your small life until you crawl out of it and re-enter the land of the living.[205] Drinking ensures social events become unmemorable and monotonous. After all, drunkenness feels the same no matter what you are doing.

You dumb down every experience. Instead of making sharp, crisp, lifelong memories, you recall social occasions through a haze or not at all. You know the saying—"It must have been fun; I don't remember it."

I now have more fun than when I was drinking. I no longer worry about what I will drink next, where it will come from, or how much I will have. I can't wait for you to experience this. At a restaurant or sporting event, you will be amazed at how much you're enjoying yourself and truly happy you no longer drink. When you stop believing you need to drink to have fun, you won't need to. You'll realize that alcohol can actually hinder your fun.

What about Hindu weddings? Talk about a party! The joy is palpable, and the dancing goes on until dawn. Everyone is laughing, eating, talking, and celebrating. These parties go on for days. No joke, literally days on end of amusement and joy. And guess what? Generally, Hindus don't drink. It's definitely not the alcohol that make these occasions fun. If everyone was drinking, the party couldn't go on for days on end. The second day would be full of hangovers and headaches.

You may worry that you'll only want to spend time with others who don't drink. You don't want to give up your friends or avoid situations where alcohol is present. I don't blame you. I don't want to limit my social activities either. But don't worry. When your unconscious desire to drink is gone, you won't be pining for a drink. You won't feel that you are giving something up. The bar will be a reminder of the freedom you have gained, not of what you feel you've lost. No, once your mental, unconscious, desire goes, your cravings are purely physical, and they last only as long as you are healing from the drug. In fact, you'll feel completely different. When you see alcohol as your mortal enemy instead of your best friend, you will love going out and not drinking. It will give you pleasure. Instead of hiding in the shadows, you will dance on your enemy's grave.

I remember pressuring my friends to drink. I would tell them they weren't being any fun as a ploy to get them to drink with me. Now when I order a non-alcoholic drink people call me boring. Why do we do that? Probably because we don't want to question our own drinking. Why do you think drug addicts and heavy drinkers hang out together? Could it be because no one makes them feel guilty about how much they are consuming? I found it easier to drink as much as I wanted in the company of other heavy drinkers. It seems OK to poison ourselves if everyone else is doing it—our dependence is masked. It eases our guilt and our misery.

High school hallways are filled with laughter, shouts, and jokes, and there is no alcohol. The locker room after a winning game has a buoyant, joyful atmosphere, again with no drinking. Is it so hard to accept that what you enjoy about social activities are your friends and the experiences? Do you remember how great the beer tasted? Of course not. You remember how much your friend made you laugh or the good-looking girl who kept smiling at you.

You may think alcohol helps people get over their initial shyness, encouraging a party atmosphere. Alcohol—by deadening your natural senses, including apprehension—removes the filters between your brain and your mouth. This gives us the illusion that the party is starting to kick off. Everyone is getting chatty, and conversation is starting in earnest. In truth, people take a bit of time to warm up. Even as kids, everyone is unsure of how they fit in. Give it a few minutes, and they are off and running, having a great time. It's a good thing to be cautious at first. It helps you understand your surroundings and take the time to get to know the people you are with. Our initial shyness not only protects us but also ensures we don't do or say something we will regret. You might even like being the person breaking the ice, introducing yourself and asking questions. Everyone else feels just as nervous, and all it takes is one person to start the conversation. Taking a little time and asking a few questions is much better than breaking out the booze and then sending everyone home in their cars. Already one in ten drivers during the night and weekend hours are drunk.[206] Let's take the time to get to know each other, break the ice naturally, and make our streets safer.

Isn't it strange that, in studies, the most popular reason we give for drinking is that it's a social thing to do? Especially when we know drinking is harmful and addictive. Aren't we actually saying we don't know why we do it? We don't have a truly good reason? We might even be saying that we don't actually enjoy it. And if we don't enjoy it, why do we drink? We drink because we are addicted to a drug.

17.
DEFINING ADDICTION: PART II

"There is no greater misery than false joys."
—Bernard of Clairvaux

The Lowdown on Alcohol-Induced Lows

You may feel there is something wrong with you, that you have no choice but to desire alcohol. The truth is we only want something we think provides a benefit. Addicts crave drugs because they are deceived into thinking drugs will enhance their lives. Once you see the drug for what it is, the cause of your misery and cravings that gives you nothing in return, the desire for the drug dies.

It's easier to see this with cigarettes. As a society, our entire perspective has changed regarding smoking. It is no longer socially acceptable. Social cues strongly influence your unconscious mind. Through numerous messages, both overt and subliminal, we are now conditioned to believe that there are few benefits to smoking. In Australia the government mandates all cigarettes to be sold in packages that visually depict the harms of smoking. When someone pulls out their pack of smokes, they see gruesome images: holes in tongues from mouth cancer, feet with toes missing from vascular disease, gray and black teeth. The images are disgusting and hard to look at. You can Google them if you want to see for yourself.

Further, nicotine acts quickly. In an hour it has left your body, so the craving for a cigarette happens almost immediately. This leads to chain smoking and panic when a smoker doesn't have cigarettes. Alcohol, however, takes between 72 and 240 hours to leave your body.[207] It can take up to ten days to recover from the lows of drinking. A heavy drinker starts to regard these lows as normal. The lows are created when your brain releases a chemical called dynorphin, which counteracts the "pleasure" from alcohol in an attempt to maintain homeostasis. Again, you know this phenomenon as tolerance. Dynorphin not only dampens the effect of alcohol, it also turns down the natural pleasure you get from everyday activities.

According to Polk, the drinker's body becomes used to the presence of alcohol in such a way that eventually the chronic drinker will need alcohol just to feel normal. And at some point no matter how much you drink you will be unable to feel anything but misery. Yet because of your brain's conditioned response to the drug, you will crave alcohol constantly.[208] The descent can be long or short, depending on your individual chemistry and the amount and frequency of your drinking. The following graph is a visual demonstration of the peaks and troughs that alcohol causes, and how it can impact your ability to enjoy everyday pleasures.

The time it takes for a drinker to move through the stages of alcoholism, from imbibing their first drink to needing vodka before breakfast, varies. But because alcohol is addictive, consuming it changes the way your brain works, meaning that no matter how slow you descend, everyone is moving the same direction—down. The descent happens faster when you drink to combat stress. Social drinking is limited to certain circumstances, which slows your

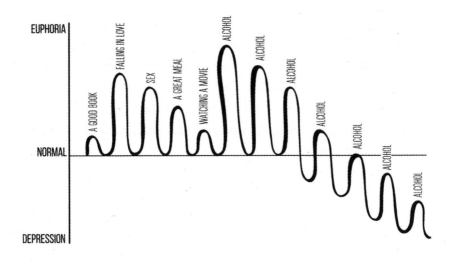

inevitable descent. If you are drinking to hide from life, to block stress, you can always find a reason to drink. The more you drink, the more stressful your life becomes. Soon there are good reasons to drink at lunch or to have a screwdriver with breakfast. You drink to dull your problems, but drinking never solves your problems. It compounds them. At some level you know this, and it bothers you. The easy solution is to take another drink, pushing this from your mind.

After a hard day I would kick off my shoes, pour myself a glass of wine, and sit down to relax. I would feel happy and calm after the first sip, well before the alcohol took effect. It was not the alcohol helping me unwind. If alcohol truly helped us relax, we would encourage drinking before a job interview or college exams. If someone was aggressive and violent, we would give them a drink to calm them down.

What is important now is to realize that alcohol does pick you up, but only from how far it kicked you down, never up to where you were before you started drinking. Since alcohol takes up to ten days to leave your body, the lows can be ever-present for regular drinkers. It is not that the alcohol makes you happy. It's that as a drinker, you are unhappy when you are unable to drink. Scratching an itch is pleasurable, but you would never purposely sit in poison ivy just to scratch your ass. This is a key to all drug addiction—the drug creates the low and then deceives its victims into believing that, by ending the low, it is providing a high.

That's how drugs work, and the further they take you down, the greater your perceived need becomes. With alcohol it can be so gradual you barely notice you are falling. As you drink, your tolerance grows, and soon you need to drink more to get the same effect. It can happen quickly, but often it happens slowly, over a lifetime.

At some point you realize you are drinking more than before, more than you ever wanted to, but life is so stressful. The stress mounts, and there's never a good time to cut back. You decide to put it off until your life becomes manageable again. You see the difficulty—as long as your intake increases, your life becomes less manageable. You started drinking to hide from stress, but you've only worsened it.

The Science of Addiction

The neurological and physiological evidence to back this up is overwhelming. I will do my best to explain. Let's start with dopamine. Dopamine is a neurotransmitter, which means it is a chemical produced in the brain that transmits signals from one neuron (brain cell) to another. Dopamine plays a central role in addiction and is commonly known as the addiction molecule. This is in part because alcohol and other addictive drugs chemically release dopamine in the brain.[209] Until recently, scientists believed dopamine was linked to pleasure. We now see that while higher levels of dopamine give us increased motivation to seek reward, the dopamine itself does not provide an actual reward or any pleasure. Scientists now believe dopamine is responsible for cravings. If you have experienced intense cravings, you know that the craving itself is not pleasurable, and craving something is very different from liking it.

In one study, scientists genetically modified rats by breeding brothers and sisters for twenty generations so that their genes were similar. They bred rats that were dopamine-rich, meaning they had more dopamine at all times, and dopamine-poor, meaning they had less. The dopamine-rich rats were more motivated to seek out any type of reward—food, companionship, or sex—but did not demonstrate any greater level of pleasure when enjoying the reward. The dopamine-poor rats were unmotivated to seek rewards. In fact, they were so unmotivated they would starve rather than make the effort to walk to the food dish. Yet when they were nursed, they demonstrated the same levels of pleasure in eating as any other rat.[210]

It's important to understand the difference between wanting and liking. When I was in the deepest levels of my addiction, the cravings were overwhelming to the point where I felt I was no longer in control. Yet the pleasure I got from drinking was practically nonexistent. I remember drinking all night long, coming back to the hotel room, and thinking about how much I'd consumed and how I didn't feel it at all. My tolerance was so high that it was hard to drink enough to get drunk. My craving was increasing, yet my enjoyment was decreasing. I thought this strange; however, studies of the brain make sense of it.

While dopamine does not trigger pleasure, it does motivate us. Dopamine is key to learning and is vital to our survival. Say you live in the caveman era and are exploring a new area in search of food. You find a thicket of raspberry bushes. This discovery causes a rush of pleasure. The pleasure occurs in another part of your brain, the nucleus accumbens, or pleasure center of the brain. Dopamine is also released, which signals that something important has happened. The beauty of dopamine is that it helps your brain process environmental cues, including cues from before you discovered the raspberries. You subconsciously learn how to best find raspberries. You will not be consciously aware, but your mind is remembering the vegetation around the bush, the amount of shade nearby, and the texture of the soil. Soon you are finding raspberry bushes more frequently without realizing how or why. We are amazing creatures with an incredible capacity for learning. Unfortunately, when addictive drugs chemically release dopamine in the brain, you are learning addiction.[211]

The ventral tegmental area of the brain, or the VTA, stimulates dopamine release.[212] The VTA is one of three parts of the brain involved in processing reward. We briefly mentioned the nucleus accumbens, and the third area in the reward circuit is the prefrontal cortex. Liking and enjoyment happen in the nucleus accumbens. James Oldes and Peter Millner of McGill University inserted electrodes directly into this region of the brain in rats. When the subjects were allowed to self-stimulate the region by pushing a lever, they continued to push it thousands of times to the exclusion of anything else. They neglected their young and forwent sex and food, even to the point of starvation, to continue stimulating this part of the brain. They even endured severe pain in order to push the lever. Pain they would not endure in order to get food, even when they were starving.[213] This has been demonstrated in humans as well. Robert Heath performed controversial experiments on humans where he observed the same repeated and seemingly uncontrollable self-stimulation.[214]

You won't be surprised to learn that addictive substances stimulate this area much more effectively than everyday rewards. While watching a movie or eating a good meal will stimulate it, drugs stimulate it more directly, producing activity levels well beyond the normal range. This sounds great on the surface—a way to stimulate the part of the brain that causes us the most pleasure. But really, it's terrifying because, in an effort to maintain homeostasis and protect itself, your brain will decrease the stimulation it is receiving. When alcohol overstimulates your nucleus accumbens, your brain produces CREB, which allows for the production of dynorphin, a natural painkiller.

The dynorphin inhibits the stimulation of the nucleus accumbens in an attempt to maintain internal equilibrium. You, in turn, feel less pleasure from drinking. You know this feeling as your tolerance increasing. You will need more alcohol to get the same effect, and eventually you will become physically dependent. Your brain will have compensated so much for the chronic ethanol exposure that you will need to drink to feel normal. Worse, you become less sensitive to all types of natural stimulation. Pleasures such as eating a delicious meal or spending time with friends no longer activate your pleasure center in the same way. The nucleus accumbens becomes numbed.[215]

The final change in your brain occurs within your prefrontal cortex. This is the part of your brain responsible for decision-making. It allows you to make well-thought-out decisions, exhibit self-control, and prevent the more reptilian parts of your brain from running the show. Alcohol damages your prefrontal cortex, resulting in a decreased capacity to make good decisions.

To summarize, three changes happen in your brain as a result of drinking:

- First, alcohol increases cravings (but not pleasure) by releasing dopamine.
- Second, alcohol artificially activates the pleasure center of your brain, the nucleus accumbens. Your brain tries to compensate for this overstimulation, leading to tolerance and the eventual numbing of your pleasure center.
- Finally, alcohol damages your prefrontal cortex, decreasing your ability to exercise self-control and making it more difficult to abstain.

You are caught in the horrible cycle of addiction—more cravings, little to no pleasure, and an impaired ability to break out of it.

As we've learned, it's difficult to control how much you drink because, over time, drinking will actually alter your brain. You have no way of knowing when that change will happen or to what degree. And just as dieting makes food more attractive psychologically, trying to control your intake increases temptation. The good news is that by overcoming the mental desire to drink, you can more easily resist the physical craving. When you stop drinking, your brain will stop compensating and repair itself. You can again find pleasure in simply living—as you could before you ever started drinking.

18.
LIMINAL POINT: IT'S CULTURAL.
I NEED TO DRINK TO FIT IN.

"Whenever you find yourself on the side of the majority,
it's time to pause and reflect."
—*Mark Twain*

You **observe** everyone drinking all the time. In fact, at almost every occasion, from grade school fundraisers to "wine and women" church groups, and even the finish lines of marathons. You **experience** all manner of conversations about alcohol—at work, after work, at home, on the weekends, and in the media. You **assume** our culture is so intertwined with alcohol that living a life without it will be next to impossible. You **conclude** that our culture dictates, even mandates, drinking, and you will find it too difficult and lonely to live without drinking.

Let's consider reality:

We Live in an Alcohol-Centric Culture

This is our last Liminal Point, and it is the most difficult to combat because it's closer to reality than any of the others we've explored. Our culture is alcohol-centric. In the last few decades we have collectively thrown caution to the wind, even deluding ourselves into believing that drinking is a healthy and vital part of life. But although this is true today, it doesn't have to be true tomorrow. We can educate ourselves and our children and work toward labeling and promoting alcohol the way cigarettes are now labeled and advertised. Although we can work for a better tomorrow, tomorrow is not yet here, so we need to explore some things about today.

Those Who Defend Alcohol the Loudest Are Often the Most Worried About How Much They Drink

More than seven thousand people volunteered to read this book, providing feedback before it was published, and many readers believed they were unique in their struggle, believing that everyone around them was perfectly happy with and in control of their drinking habits. I have discovered this is just not true! If you regret last night's bender, so do the people you were out with. If you sometimes worry about drinking every day, chances are so does your partner. If you wish you could stop after just a few, odds are so does your best friend. Alcohol addiction is so insidious because of how well we hide it, even from ourselves. We are ashamed to question our drinking. We worry that by asking a question we may be forced to quit drinking and live marginalized from society. We keep our fears to ourselves. Our questions hidden. Because no one is talking about the problem that so many have, we allow it to grow.

Since I stopped drinking, dozens of people have confided in me that they too want to cut back. Remember how my career contributed to my descent? Many of my colleagues read the book, and it turns out we were all trying to keep up with each other! While everyone worried about how much they drank, no one wanted to say it. One of my former bosses read the book and told me, "Annie, it's like your book has lifted a burden. I felt drinking was practically mandatory. There was so much social pressure that I didn't feel like saying no was an option. I now realize I can simply say no. That is empowering, thank you."

We Think the "Cool" People Drink (a.k.a. People Who Don't Drink Are Lame)

I am guilty of this one! I remember looking down my nose at people who weren't drinking as much as I was. I felt proud of my drinking lifestyle and how much "fun" I was having. I imagined that people who didn't drink must be downright boring! It is common to hear people say, "I don't trust someone who doesn't drink." The truth is that the cool people are cool if they drink or not. The funny people are funny if they drink or not, and the lame people are lame if they drink or not. Now I will add a caveat that if you feel you are making a sacrifice by not drinking when you are out with friends, of course you aren't going to be (or have) any fun. The beauty of *This Naked Mind* is that you will not feel that way. So your coolness is not going anywhere. I love being the life of the party and making people laugh. This is still true! In fact, since my wits aren't dulled, my jokes are much funnier than they were in my drinking days, and we all laugh harder.

I can't tell you how much it surprises people when I am the life of the party without a drink in my hand. I have a friend who can't get over it. He just stares at me; I think he is trying to figure out if I'm putting on an act. Why is it so surprising? Because we truly believe that alcohol is the fuel to our fire, and we are gobsmacked when that is not true. I offer one warning: You will be ready to have fun before your friends. I show up to the party ready to crack jokes, but everyone else thinks they need a few drinks in them before it's OK to "let loose." This is not because the alcohol is the key to their enjoyment but because they believe it is. Thinking something is true often makes it so.

How Will My Partner React?

One of my readers has had a boozy relationship with her partner of more than two decades. He has no interest in changing, and she is fearful their relationship will weaken. Another reader drank wine with his wife every night. When he decided to stop drinking, she thought it was a phase that wouldn't last. As the weeks went by and he kept declining wine at dinner, it began to bother her. She would say things like, "So you are still on this kick, huh? I thought it would have blown over by now." She even began to pressure him to drink with her.

These are not pleasant outcomes. When readers shared them with me, I worried about the unintended consequences of change. The truth is that any change, no matter how positive, disrupts the synergy of a relationship. Even if your partner is happy about your decision, it will change the dynamic of your relationship. Be conscious of the fact that a change for you will mean a change for them. Be aware and treat them, whether they continue to drink or not, with respect. Don't force a change on them or feed them advice. Do share as much as possible about your journey, how you are feeling, and what you are thinking. Honest and compassionate communication is key.

How Can I Keep My Friends or Make New Ones?

Making friends, especially if you believed people who don't drink are boring, might be a real concern. What will people think about you? How will you navigate ordering a tonic without making them feel awkward for ordering a gin? First, let's explore your perception of people who don't drink. Do you truly know any? If the answer is yes, and you still feel they were boring, was it because they didn't drink or were they not that interesting of a person anyway? But it doesn't really matter because perception is reality, so if you thought they were boring it was true to you. How do you overcome this perception when so many people feel exactly the same way?

The best way is through experience. First you need to know without a doubt that you are the same person (even better!) without a drink in your hand. This will take time. You will need to experience many different events without alcohol for your anxiety to fully go away. You will probably be anxious before every experience without alcohol. The exciting news is that each experience will show you how much fun you can have without drinking. It's a process. This is a change that will affect every aspect of your life. You will need to be patient as you adjust, but I believe that each experience will bring you closer to knowing, without a doubt, that you are the same person (even better!) than you were when you were drinking.

It's true that some people will write you off before getting to know you. You can deal with this however you see fit. In the days when my confidence was low, and I was adjusting to not drinking, I dealt with it in all sorts of ways. You can pretend to be drinking: Order a gin and tonic, then get up to use the restroom, find the waitress, and ask her to hold the gin, or order a beer in a dark bottle, pour it out, and fill it back up with water. Readers have also contributed some things they say to avoid drinking without having to declare themselves the dreaded non-drinker:

- I can't tonight; I'm driving.
- I overdid it last night, so I'm taking the night off.
- I'm on a detox that doesn't allow alcohol.
- I'm watching my weight.
- I'm trying to cut back.
- I'm doing an alcohol-free challenge.
- I don't feel like it tonight.

- I have an important meeting tomorrow, so I want to keep a clear head.

Dating is another concern. How will you meet people without drinking? How will they react when you tell them? You must realize if a hundred people are drinking heavily, eighty of them wish they were able to enjoy themselves while drinking less. You might be surprised to know that, when looking for a partner, people find minimal alcohol consumption attractive. It's partially subconscious but true. We respect the non-drinker, admiring their character and self-discipline. We even feel they will ultimately make a better partner and parent. The bottom line: Not drinking is sexy!

Telling Your Friends Without Losing Your Friends

I made these mistakes so you don't have to. I am an excitable person, and when I was discovering *This Naked Mind*, I was vocal with my friends. I would say things like, "You'll never believe it! Just one drink causes cancer; there is no way I'm putting that shit in my body," or "You don't need alcohol to have a good time! It's crazy, but we've all been deluded by media and society."

As you can imagine, I was annoying. A friend even told my husband, "Yikes, I can't imagine what it's like living with the anti-alcohol evangelist." It wasn't pretty. Drinkers are fearful of having to quit. Without the reverse conditioning that *This Naked Mind* provides, they still believe that alcohol is vital, and not drinking (or feeling like they are being judged for drinking) creates stress. If they have developed a psychological, physical, or emotional dependence on alcohol (practically everyone I know), reminders of the harms of alcohol create stress. This needs to be a positive experience. When they see you enjoying yourself, it will give them hope rather than fear.

Often when someone stops drinking, they wish they were able to drink "normally" and are jealous of people who are still drinking.

Drinkers know this and have pity on the non-drinker. They separate themselves, believing that the non-drinker has a problem to which they are not susceptible. With this dynamic, there is little to no tension between the parties. The drinkers are, in fact, very accommodating, even ordering mocktails for the non-drinker to support them in overcoming their "problem."

A different dynamic occurs when you stop drinking with *This Naked Mind.* Rather than admitting to a problem, you have been educated and enlightened. You will no longer want to drink. Drinkers may have a hard time with this. How can you not want to drink? It won't seem possible. You may even feel smug that you no longer need alcohol when everyone around you does. Since drinkers are unable to pity you, it's possible that they will begin to feel sorry for themselves. They may feel judged when you decline a drink. You are now holding yourself to a higher standard. You are demonstrating you care more about what you put in your body and how it affects you. This is great, but not everyone will see it that way.

So how do you deal with this? How can you gracefully tell people about your decision without alienating your friends? I think the answer is relatively simple. It's not about pleasing everyone all the time. You did this for you, and by making this decision, even though you may cause tension at first, you will soon become a beacon of hope that they too can change.

In terms of specific phrasing, you will need to figure out what works for you. Try a few things. Make sure you are truly without judgment; speak truthfully about you, your decisions, and your story without imposing your beliefs on others. And try not to condemn their drinking habits, as your friends undoubtedly see alcohol as you once did—a companion, comfort, and friend. These are some phrases that have worked for me: "I realized I'm happier when I don't drink," "I'm on a health kick and giving up booze is part of it," "I decided drinking was no longer doing me any favors, so I quit," and "I feel better when I don't drink."

19.
THE DESCENT: WHY SOME
DESCEND FASTER THAN OTHERS

"Genius is more often found in a cracked pot than in a whole one."
—E.B. White

My husband blamed my compulsive nature on an "addictive personality." This always rubbed me the wrong way. So I asked him to define what exactly he meant by "addictive personality." He named people he thinks have an addictive personality and others who don't. The common trait among the addictive set was that we were, or had been, addicted to something. His definition never satisfied me. You can imagine my vindication when I discovered that scientists and doctors now agree that there is no such thing as an addictive personality. Despite trying for years to define what personality traits make someone prone to addiction, the scientific community has been unable to do so with any degree of certainty.[216] In fact, attempts to identify an addictive personality by linking a specific configuration of personality traits to addictive behaviors has been largely abandoned.[217]

But wait. Isn't it common knowledge that some people are more prone to addiction than others? As you've probably realized by now, common knowledge about alcohol and addiction is more likely myth than fact. So let's look at why some people fall into the addiction cycle faster than others, and why some people never seem to become dependent.

To review, addiction is doing something on a regular basis that you don't want to be doing, or that you want to be doing but find yourself unable to easily stop or cut back on. In the previous chapter, we explored how the cycle of alcohol-induced lows pushes us into a state of addiction where our desires (to drink and not to drink) are at war with each other.

We've also established that addicts go to great lengths to protect their drug of choice. They are loath to blame the substance for any ills they experience when using it. If they blame the substance, the next logical step is to eliminate it from their lives—which seems terrifying. Since the majority of Americans drink, it's not a stretch to assume that we have an addicted society: a society that protects alcohol by portraying alcoholism as a personality defect.

We take the existence of an addictive personality for granted. It's an inescapable prop of mainstream conversations about alcohol. We protect alcohol by blaming addiction on a person's personality rather than on the addictive nature of alcohol.

Am I saying that personality doesn't affect how quickly we become addicted? Not at all. Many factors impact the speed at which we slide into addiction—environmental and social factors, genetic factors, and, yes, personality factors. Just as personality affects every other aspect of your life, it must factor into how quickly you become dependent on alcohol.

So if I believe personality can play a role in addiction, why am I taking issue with the term "addictive personality?" I think it's negative and misleading. The same personality traits that caused me to drink more, like commitment, decisiveness, and a strong will, are primarily positive attributes. In fact, these "addictive" attributes played a vital role in finding my freedom.

The nebulous idea of an addictive personality allows us to protect our precious alcohol. We focus on the addictive personality, which makes alcohol dangerous for them but not for us. We protect the alcohol and blame the individual. This takes hope away from the alcoholic, encouraging them to believe they are powerless against their personality. The concept of addictive personality lets us close our minds to the fact that alcohol is addictive, period. If there is an addictive personality, and we don't feel we have one, we no longer need to exercise caution with alcohol.

"Addictive" Personality Traits

While I want to point out the fallacies in the broad brush and ill-defined concept of an addictive personality, it is worth noting that personality traits are potentially linked to problematic alcohol involvement. Interestingly, while some of these traits can be viewed as negative (including being more independent and less agreeable) most are neutral—or even positive—including extraversion and openness to experience.[218]

The negative concept of an "addictive personality" leads us to feel there is something wrong with us and implies that traits having some link to addiction are wholly negative and harmful. Not so. Some traits can, in fact, be desirable and positively influence a person's character and experiences. Other linked traits include experience seeking, decisiveness, impulsiveness, and nonconformity. As you can see, every personality trait that may contribute to a person's slide into addiction has both negative and positive sides. A collection of traits, which can have positive or negative implications for someone's life, should not be stigmatized and labeled as "addictive."

Let's look at my father again. He is a person who makes up his mind and sticks with it. Once he decided to stop drinking, he had no internal struggle and no pain because his decision was definite and permanent. He uses this decisive quality in other aspects of his life. He realized at the age of thirty-seven that he needed daily exercise to enjoy a full life. He found mountain biking and skiing most agreeable, so for the last thirty years he has biked sixty to a hundred miles every week and skis forty to eighty times per winter. He determines something is good, and he goes for it. He's also a nonconformist, not generally influenced by what other people think or say.

I believe his decisiveness, consistency, and nonconformity may be the same personality traits that led him to drink heavily. He determined he was receiving some pleasure from a little alcohol and concluded he would receive more pleasure from a lot. So he drank whenever he wanted with no qualms. Since all drug addiction escalates, he drank more and more. When he realized that alcohol was not providing any true pleasure, it was his decisive, consistent, and independent personality that made it easy for him to quit.

Here is another scenario. At a restaurant, a friend of mine, who is conscious of what others think of her, was the first to order and ordered a beer. After everyone else ordered, she realized that no one else in the group ordered alcohol, so she changed her mind and asked for water instead. She obviously wanted the beer, but in her mind, the stigma of drinking alone outweighed her desire for a beer. My bet is that her descent, so long as she continues to spend time with people who rarely drink, will be slow. Alternatively, if she spends time with heavy drinkers, this same personality trait may push her into drinking more than she wants.

Millions of factors contribute to the pace at which you become alcohol dependent. Perhaps you're someone who paces yourself, never jumping into anything. It stands to reason that you wouldn't jump head-first into drinking. On the other hand, if you are like me and get passionate about everything, including drinking, it makes sense that you would drink more, crave more, and fall faster.

Our finances can affect how fast we descend. I have a friend who tells me she loves to drink and would be an alcoholic if alcohol wasn't so expensive. Another friend truly enjoys dessert, and since she is on a tight budget, she weighs an alcoholic drink against dessert. Though she would like both, the dessert wins every time. In both cases, my friends desire to drink more, but either finances or a sweet tooth prevent them. This slows their descent.

Our surroundings also play into how quickly we descend. For me, moderate drinking evolved into heavy drinking when we moved from Colorado to New York City. When we lived in Colorado, we hiked, skied, camped, and enjoyed the diverse activities available there. In the big city, drinking was the main social pastime. Social life in Manhattan, London, and most of the other large cities I visit revolves around drinking.

And don't forget the effect of family opinion. A friend of mine was raised in a household where drinking was "of the devil." Though she does drink, the stigma she grew up with ensures that she limits her intake to limit her guilt.

No One Is Immune to Addiction

Countless motives, personality traits, and circumstances contribute to the speed at which someone falls into alcohol addiction. It is true that most drinkers will drink until they die, never suspecting drinking is taking years off their life, never feeling out of control, never suspecting they have a problem. But not realizing they have a problem does not mean they don't have one.

No one is immune from addiction to alcohol. The more you drink, the more you will want to drink. When a stressful life event occurs, the most moderate drinker can slide into either physical or emotional alcohol dependence. Even when the fall is nearly imperceptible, it is still happening. Barring a hindering circumstance, do the people you know drink more than they did a few years ago? Do you? Everyone who drinks now drinks more than they used to; I know this is true because at one time they didn't drink at all. You and the drinkers you know will be drinking more in five years than you are today—that is how alcohol works.

It's terrifying how fast you start to sink when you begin to suspect a problem. You have become dependent on an addictive substance. It is a vital part of your life, and you cannot imagine dealing with stress or enjoying social situations without it. Drinking more than you want creates panic and stress. You are accustomed to drinking when stressed, so you drink more of what is causing your stress. The cycle spirals out of control. Whether you feel life would be incomplete without your weekly beer or your daily bottle of vodka, the problem is the same.

We spend a lot of time trying to categorize drinkers: moderate, heavy, problematic, regular, alcoholic. We spend even more time trying to figure out what category we are in. This makes the entire topic of addiction more confusing, and if we are honest, it's a silly conversation. Perhaps we are all in the same dire predicament: all caught. As Lucy Rocca says, you have "positioned yourself at the top of a very slippery slope and with each drink you consume you're sliding ever quicker toward the bottom."[219]

Why is it so hard to believe that when you are in high school and start to experiment with alcohol, you are the bee drawn to the pitcher plant? Can you see the bee struggling on the sticky slope as the drinker trying to cut back or quit? Is it still hard to believe that your favorite beverage is a highly addictive drug? Why else would our society continue to consume it despite the epidemic alcoholism has become?

Why is it so hard to see the obvious truth? If alcoholism was due to a physical or mental flaw or a defect in my personality, I would have been incurable. How do you explain the fact that I have been cured, completely and painlessly, of this incurable disease?

There is no inexplicable defect in our personalities, no elusive flaw in our bodies. Alcohol is simply a highly addictive drug.

There is a logic principle called Occam's Razor. It states that, all else being equal, the simplest explanation is most likely correct. The explanation that alcohol is an addictive substance is far simpler than the convoluted theories (none of which we can prove or satisfactorily explain) around personality and physical and mental defects leading to alcoholism.

We find it hard to accept that we are all drinking the same addictive poison. Doing so means we must accept that the difference between the alcoholic and the moderate drinker is only how addicted they have become and how quickly. How far they have progressed on the alcohol addiction continuum. We must accept that alcohol cannot change in nature if it's consumed by an alcoholic or a moderate drinker. It is the same substance, with the same poisonous qualities.

Over time, drinking provides no honest enjoyment. When you reach the point of dependence, this truth is inescapable because, at the chronic stage, even the illusions of pleasure disappear. Alcohol is a physical depressant that poisons your body and ensnares your brain. It destroys you physically and mentally. It deadens your senses, thereby deadening all your survival instincts. It takes the happiness of this beautiful life with it.

Yet what message does our drinking generation send to our children? When I was drinking, my kids often asked if they could have a sip. I didn't realize it, but they saw alcohol as a coveted, adult treat that they couldn't wait to try. This now fills me with dread; I never want them to experience addiction. I have never felt more worthless than when I was addicted. Alcohol addiction is so scary that contemplation of suicide is 120 times more likely among adult alcoholics,[220] with alcohol involved in a third of all suicides in the U.S.[221]

Debating alcohol's inherent addictive nature with moderate drinkers is not generally useful for you or them. I've made that mistake. The new information you provide creates internal conflict, which is painful. They will do everything they can to convince you and themselves that they are enjoying their drink, remain fully in control, and can stop whenever they want to. You can't undo decades of unconscious conditioning with a quick conversation. As John A. Bargh, a professor of psychology at Yale, put it, "Unconscious systems are continually furnishing suggestions about what to do next and the brain is acting on those, all before conscious awareness. Sometimes those goals are in line with our conscious intentions and purposes and sometimes they're not."[222] They may consciously see your point of view, but their unconscious attachment to alcohol is strong and controlling.

If you do want to convince a friend or loved one, let them see how free and happy you have become, and let them ask you how you did it. Then go slowly and carefully. It is rewarding to help others, but trying before they want help will be frustrating for both of you. And give yourself a high-five. Consider how far ahead you are of the "take it or leave it" group. Why? Because you cannot fix an issue you don't know exists.

Time for a Self-Check

So am I saying that anyone who drinks any alcohol at all is addicted? No, that is clearly not true. I think anyone who illogically or unconsciously desires alcohol is addicted whether or not they are consciously aware. Anyone who feels fear at the thought of never drinking again is already emotionally dependent. If someone told me I could never eat another apple because they will eventually kill me, I would stop eating apples. It would be a logical decision, and it wouldn't fill me with dread. While I may be a bit bummed, I would also feel relieved that I was no longer going to die early and thankful that the truth about apples and my health had come out. I would certainly quit eating apples as soon as I was presented with the evidence. If you only drink on occasion and can "take it or leave it," why not leave it?

Take a moment and make a list of everything you get from drinking. This is important because you need to clearly understand that alcohol does you no favors. If you feel afraid, just realize that your fear is proof of what I am telling you. If I was lecturing on the harms of red meat, you might feel disappointed, since you like a good steak, but you wouldn't feel dread in the pit of your stomach. That feeling of dread is the manifestation of addiction—fear that is created by drinking.

Is ignorance bliss? If I thought I was getting pleasure from drinking, isn't that basically the same as getting actual pleasure? Wouldn't I rather go through my life with the perceived pleasure than nothing at all?

It's a valid concern, but ignorance is only bliss if nothing can be done to make things better. In this case, through knowledge and education you achieve freedom. You are about to be free. You will experience so much more pleasure being whole, healthy, and happy than you ever did from drinking. You will no longer see quitting as "I never get to drink" but "I never have to drink." So let's move on toward finding your freedom.

20.
LIVING A NAKED LIFE IN OUR SOCIETY

"Yesterday I was clever, so I wanted to change the world.
Today I am wise, so I am changing myself."
—Rumi

Freedom at Last

Once you've finished this book and freed yourself, you have some important lifestyle choices to consider. Deciding not to drink will be a pleasure, so you will not suffer by being out at a bar or around your friends who are still drinking, and you won't need to avoid situations that you enjoy. You don't have to change anything about your lifestyle. But we should talk about a few exceptions. Be honest with yourself. Are there activities in your life that are only reasons to drink, and which will no longer give you any pleasure?

You may find once-desirable activities to be nothing more than a waste of time. Some people may have only been fun because alcohol slowed down your brain enough to make them so. I'm not talking about spending time out at the bar with your real friends or doing anything you actually enjoy where others are drinking. But you may discover that you were choosing activities that aren't actually fun and are with people you don't truly care for, just to have somewhere to drink. These activities now feel like a waste of your time.

After I stopped drinking, I went to Las Vegas. The trip had been planned before I quit. Before *This Naked Mind*, the idea of a trip to Vegas without drinking would have been unbearable. I would have canceled the trip. Once I quit, the idea of going to Vegas without drinking was not a concern. I was looking forward to the trip with the absolute certainty that drinking is not needed to have a good time. That's exactly what happened. I have never had more fun in Las Vegas. I was with my closest friends, enjoying engaging and hilarious conversations. I laughed until I cried. I didn't suffer a single hangover, and there was no black shadow hanging over me. I reveled in my freedom. I had no worries or cares and woke up each day with tons of energy. Every meal seemed to taste better than the last. Interestingly, alcohol deadens your ability to taste,[223] so food really did taste better.[224] Without drinking I was better able to experience one of life's greatest pleasures: eating.

During this trip drinking occupied zero percent of my brain space. I was more present and engaged than I could ever have been while drinking. And I secretly reveled at breakfast when all my friends had headaches, wearing their sunglasses and ordering mimosas to try to rid themselves of massive hangovers. I felt great, headache-free with no nausea, full of energy to meet the day, and I couldn't help smiling to myself about how far I'd come.

I ended up leaving Vegas a day early to go abroad for a work trip. As you know, my career, with its heavy drinking dinners, was a big factor in my descent. This trip was no different and included plenty of nights out for drinks. I was out four nights in a row with different colleagues, vendors, and clients. I enjoyed the dinners and conversations. It was my first business trip without drinking, and I was determined to do everything I used to do, including going out for more drinks after dinner. That's when things got weird. I didn't understand why I wasn't having fun. I had done this so many times before and always seemed to enjoy myself (though I admit I don't remember a lot of specifics). I must have enjoyed myself, since I did it every night, often staying out well into the next morning.

When I got back to the U.S., I was a bit panicked. I worried that I was no longer having fun without alcohol and couldn't think of a good reason why. I discussed this with my husband, who immediately knew the answer. It was simple, and I have been on many business trips since without any problem. Late-night drinks after dinner with colleagues or vendors with whom I don't have any real relationship are not actually fun. We weren't close friends enjoying each other's company and conversation; in fact, if we left the company, we'd probably never see each other again. We were only getting together to drink. The conversations were repetitive and centered around office gossip, which is never very nice. The reality is that the situation, without my senses thoroughly deadened, is not that pleasant. I now go out and enjoy great dinners in exotic places and then retire to my hotel room. There, I read, write, or, most fun (if the time zones allow), Skype with my kids. In the mornings I no longer drag myself out of bed fifteen minutes before my first meeting. Now I often wake up early and explore the city before I go into the office.

Last night I was at a London train station, Charing Cross. I was with my UK-based marketing team, having coffee and a chat. Next to us, lone commuters also enjoyed a quick drink before their commute home. Everything about the situation looked sexy. The beer was in a proper pint glass, very British. The British accents lent sophistication to the scene. The act of enjoying a pint, in a busy train station, while transitioning from the grind of work to the relaxation of home, was glamorous.

Before my experience with *This Naked Mind* it would have been almost impossible for me to resist ordering a beer. I would have bought into the societal cues, the ambiance, and the experience.

Yesterday I had no desire to drink a beer. I saw the situation for what it was. I was saddened to see a smart, healthy group of people unwittingly sinking into a deadly pit. The pitcher plant is a beautiful but lethal flower. The experience was freeing because I was not tempted. I could see the truth.

As a reaction to the damage alcohol is doing to British society, public health organizations have introduced Dry January and Stoptober (Stop October). In Australia they have Dry July. These are months when people are encouraged to experience life without drinking. This year I was in London during Dry January. You could tell who some of the participants were because they walked around with a holier-than-thou attitude. They seemed to feel superior to those who had not manned up enough to give up booze. At first I didn't understand the bravado, but soon I realized it was a defense mechanism. In order to maintain sobriety, they needed to minimize their desire for a drink. So they looked down on drinkers. Nothing says addicted more than trying to prove we're not.

You are about to have a completely different perspective. Instead of feeling a desire to drink and needing to avoid places where people are drinking, you will feel freedom. Actually, being around drinkers is one of the best reminders of your freedom. You'll see the irrational reasons people give for drinking. If I'd asked the guy at the train station why he was drinking, he probably would have told me he likes the taste. He ordered and drank the beer in less than two minutes so he could make his train. He didn't have time to savor the taste. I was drinking fresh-squeezed orange juice and taking it very slowly. England has amazing juice, and I wanted to enjoy every sip.

You can easily investigate these collective reasons for drinking. Look around and observe why others are drinking. You will see they are not making rational decisions. In fact, the reasons they give for drinking are simply excuses. They don't understand why they are drinking. These "regular" drinkers, rather than tempting you, become a powerful reminder of how lucky you are to be free.

Not only will you watch regular drinkers without resentment, but you will start to recognize drinkers on the slow (or fast) descent into the abyss of addiction. Most drinkers are unwittingly drinking more over time, perhaps more than they ever wanted.

It can become confusing because drinking is so prevalent in our society. We build bars like shrines to booze, and some are beautiful, even striking. Your unconscious mind is vulnerable, and although you are freeing your emotional desires from alcohol through the education in this book, you will need to ensure you don't allow the garbage back in. If day after day you see people happily drinking alcohol, you may trick yourself into believing there is something special about drinking after all. The most important tool is to use your brain. Drinkers don't yet know what you know, and as a society we collectively close our minds to the risks of drinking. When I tell people that alcohol is a known carcinogen, a fact that was scientifically proven in 1988, they are surprised. Not so long ago I was shocked to discover that my dear wine was not the life-affirming drink I believed it to be. The key is to think. Be mindful and aware of the constant barrage of messages you are subject to every day. When you start to question, remind yourself of the truth about alcohol and consciously undo these influences as soon as possible. Your unconscious mind is susceptible to the influences that tell you alcohol is key to life. You must be on your guard, not allowing your mind to be a guesthouse or storage area for junk. Take out the trash as soon as you realize it is coming in.

Take control of your mind and fight to see the truth. You will probably find this fun and empowering. I was eating at a restaurant with a beautiful bar in another London train station, King's Cross. It has huge brick walls with ceilings at least four stories high. This bar was truly a sexy and incredible shrine to alcohol, with shiny glass bottles full of rich, amber liquid stretching up all four stories. In reality, the architecture and design were beautiful. Marketers have done specific studies on how much more alcohol they sell—up to 40%

more—when the liquor bottles are properly displayed and lit. It's amazing how much influence beautiful presentation has on our minds. I took a minute to admire the architecture, but instead of wishing I was part of something with so much apparent beauty, I made a conscious decision to see the amber liquid for what it was: a substance that would destroy my brain and body. A drink that would render me tired, insensible, and hung over.

I know a consultant for bars and restaurants. His main job is to help bars become more profitable, which means selling more alcohol. He told me that pubs should always be set up with clear pathways to the bar. The bar should, if possible, have multiple access points. Bottles should be displayed up high so that customers can see them over the heads of other customers, and these bottles should always be lit from below. He says that if a bar provides water with every drink, the customers will not get drunk as quickly, and the bar will sell more booze. There's even a correlation between bathroom accessibility and noise levels to encourage the most alcohol consumption. That day at the spectacular alcohol shrine at King's Cross, I smiled to myself and smugly ordered my tonic and lime, knowing without a doubt that the beauty of the alcohol display only ran skin deep.

Don't believe you're immune to the constant assault of pro-alcohol messages. No one is. We must recognize the lies and put them in their place. Realize how powerful the bombardment must be to convince the majority of adults to regularly drink poison. If the majority boarded a ship that hit an iceberg and was sinking, would you envy them? You, hopefully, would feel compelled to reach out and lend a hand to help others escape from the sinking ship.

Is Moderation an Option?

While I've presented you with analogies, facts, and scenarios that favor leaving alcohol completely behind, I have not given you definitive direction to stop drinking altogether. I have a hard time with rules. If there is a rule I must follow, my every instinct is to break it.

A definitive statement to answer this question is difficult. I don't want to write a rule and have the rebels, like myself, feel that they are bound. I would much rather present you with all the facts, allowing you to come to the decision that is best for you.

Moderation with any addictive substance is difficult, and for some it becomes impossible. Brain changes from drinking can be permanent. Theoretically, when someone develops a strong physical dependence, their brain and body may have altered to such an extent that they can't function without alcohol. Let me explain.

We spoke about the changes that happen in your brain as a result of drinking. We've discussed how alcohol increases cravings but not pleasure by releasing dopamine. I want to expand on the dopamine relationship to explain why some people are unable to stop at just one drink.

To review, addictive drugs, from nicotine to heroin, release artificially high levels of dopamine in the brain. While scientists used to believe dopamine was linked to feeling good, they now believe that dopamine is linked to learning, and learning includes wanting, expecting, and craving.[225] Rather than giving us pleasure, dopamine teaches us how to get pleasure. It helps us learn the most effective ways to stimulate the brain's pleasure center.

We know that alcohol artificially stimulates the brain's pleasure centers. We also know that to maintain homeostasis and protect itself, the brain turns down the pleasure received from alcohol over time.[226] This is tolerance. This is why at the end of my drinking career I was desperate to drink, yet I received little to no actual pleasure even after two or more bottles of wine. The explanation is clear: My brain was repeatedly, artificially overstimulated by alcohol, so it built a tolerance and produced a counter-chemical, dynorphin, which turned down the stimulation. Over time it took more and more alcohol to feel any stimulation. And everyday pleasures wouldn't even register because of the high levels of dynorphin my brain was producing. This is why neuroscientist and professor Polk says:

"Consider what happens in a drug addict when they repeatedly over-stimulate the brain with their drug of choice. The brain will continue to turn down the overstimulation, and over time the addict will feel less pleasure from the drug. The high won't be as rewarding, and the addict will require more and more stimulation to get the same level of reward. And of course that is exactly what drug addicts report, they need more and more of the drug to feel the same high: And eventually they need to take the drug just to feel normal."[227]

Let's dive deeper into the role of dopamine in addiction to under-stand why some people become unable to stop at just one. Basically, dopamine's role in learning is to ensure pleasure can be found again. Wolfram Schultz says, "An adaptive organism must be able to predict future events such as the presence of mates, food and danger . . . predictions give an animal time to prepare behavioral reactions and can be used to improve the choices an animal makes in the future."[228] Dopamine plays a central role in how adaptive species, including hu-mans, are able to anticipate and be motivated to pursue a reward.

Terry Robinson and Kent Berridge formulated a theory for the neural basis of drug craving called the incentive-sensitization theory of addiction.[229] The theory states that repeated use of addictive drugs makes the brain's dopamine center hypersensitive to that specific drug. This will happen differently in different people. Some people have higher natural levels of dopamine and some naturally lower lev-els. However, as I understand it, it is possible for this hypersensitivity to a specific drug (in this case alcohol) to happen in anyone over time with repeated use.

According to Robinson and Berridge: "The repeated uses of ad-dictive drugs produces incremental neuroadaptations in this neural system, rendering it increasingly and perhaps permanently hypersen-sitive to the drug." This hypersensitive dopamine system creates a crav-ing for the drug that can occur separately from liking the drug. And this can produce "addictive behavior (compulsive drug seeking and drug taking) even if the expectations of the drug's pleasure is diminished . . . and even in the face of strong disincentives, including the loss of reputation, job, home and family."[230]

Did you catch that? This means if you drink enough alcohol, over time you can change the response of your brain to alcohol. And once the change has occurred, it may never return to normal. This explains why someone can be sober for thirty years, drink a single beer and be thrown back to drinking past the point of throwing up, until they are unconscious. This means that one drink, even after prolonged abstinence, can stimulate craving for alcohol so that you will continue to drink no matter the consequences and worse, that *you won't even enjoy it.*

This is how we explain the alcoholic whose spouse threatens to leave if they don't stop, yet remains powerless against the pull of alcohol. This is how we explain the illogical and irrational behavior of alcohol and other drug usage. After enough dopamine is repeatedly released, your brain responds to alcohol in a completely different way.[231]

I would like to note here that if you have altered your brain to this extent, there is hope. Once you have broken the cycle, your cravings will go away. You will never be back in the misery of addiction if you never drink that one drink. Even though the dopamine hypersensitivity to alcohol will exist, it will remain dormant as long as you introduce no alcohol into your body.

For me, craving something I no longer enjoyed felt like someone had moved into my brain and was calling the shots. It was like being held captive by an adversary who was constantly growing stronger as I grew weaker. An enemy that would kill me if I didn't kill him first. Lucy Rocca describes it this way: "The monster wants to be fed . . . alcohol keeps people pushed down . . . alcohol makes people powerless and turns them into slaves of drinking."[232]

It is interesting to note that more dopamine is released by alcohol in men's brains than in women's,[233] which may be a reason why, on the whole, more men drink alcohol and develop alcohol addictions than women. In fact, men made up 70% of all alcohol-related deaths in the U.S. (88,000) in 2014.[234]

I would also like to say that if you have already reached the point where you cannot resist a drink, if you are unable to stay sober long enough to read this book, you need to go somewhere for help: a place that will prevent you from drinking and make alcohol unavailable to you as you detox. The good news is that once the alcohol is out of your system, and your mentality has changed, meaning you see that you no longer need alcohol, you can regain control.

> *"Trying to have 'just one drink of alcohol' is like trying to knock just one domino down in a huge line of them."* —Craig Beck

The Stress of Decision-Making

Did you know that making decisions causes stress and expends our brain's resources? Studies show that little decisions appear to take as much neural energy as big ones.[235] And brain energy, like any other type of energy, gets depleted. When you use your brain's energy on tons of little decisions (should I drink today? how many will I allow myself to have tonight?), you deplete your decision-making abilities. Not to mention that the alcohol itself, once it enters your brain, negatively affects your ability to make sound decisions. Don't forget that over time alcohol chemically damages your prefrontal cortex.[236] This is the part of your brain that is vital to making sound, long-term decisions. The prefrontal cortex balances out the pleasure-seeking, animal regions of your brain, and when it is damaged by alcohol abuse, its effectiveness is decreased. You make worse decisions, and temptation is harder to resist because the animal regions of the brain, the parts that seek pleasure without considering consequences, become stronger than the more measured areas of the brain.[237]

For me it was a cycle of insanity. I would make myself promises about moderation, which I would keep at first. Success gave me a profound sense of satisfaction, of control. I felt proud, invincible. I could enjoy the nectar and then fly away. Then I would stumble upon more reasons, seemingly legitimate reasons, to drink more or to give in to temptation. Eventually it became clear that moderation was not working, that I had crossed the line, but at that point I could not stop. In the cycle of addiction, the funhouse, nothing is as it appears. I felt let down, ashamed of myself. I didn't understand why I continued to do what I had come to hate, and it terrified me. I felt alone and began to isolate myself from those close to me, who I knew would be disappointed. I became a miserable shell of myself. Sometimes I was so deceived that I was not aware of how far I had fallen. How dependent I had again become. My tolerance would build, and within days, weeks, or months, I'd return to the chronic stage.

Before addiction, I had a typical capacity for reward. When I was addicted, I no longer enjoyed normally rewarding experiences. In a situation like this, you start to fear you can only find joy with the assistance of the drug. This fear keeps you in the clutches of addiction. Experience confirms that you only get pleasure from drinking. What you don't realize is that drinking "pleasure" is not true pleasure, and everyday pleasure will return as soon as you stop drinking and allow your brain and body to heal.

You will recognize the deception and realize you don't need alcohol to relax or to enjoy yourself—you were duped into believing you did. In order to reach that place you must defeat your mortal enemy.

At the beginning of the book we broke down our problem into two areas: the drinker and the drink. On the surface it seems that you, the drinker, should be able to control yourself. But the reality of addiction, once it's taken hold and changed your brain, is that you can't. Addiction takes control away from the drinker. The good news is that you can control the drink. You can—now that the unconscious conditioning has been reversed—make a conscious, logical, and rational decision about drinking. You can control alcohol so it does not control you. While being fully in control will mean different things for different people, for me it means staying away from booze. The great news is that I no longer have any desire to drink an addictive poison that does nothing for me. Miraculously, as a result of this process, I am thrilled that I no longer drink. Few things have made me happier than gaining my total and complete freedom from the clutches of alcohol.

It is important that you not make the mistake of clinging to any former illusions about alcohol. If you retain the desire to drink, you will spend the rest of your life wondering when it will be a good time to have that next drink.

Don't underestimate the power of your mind. I was contemplating the power of the human mind on a recent flight. There I was, 35,000 feet in the air, and if something happened to the pilot, the plane would have been able to fly and practically land itself. Humans built this technology. We built global positioning systems that broadcast the plane's exact location. We have the intelligence to understand gravity and space; we launch satellites into orbit so GPS can work. We are powerful.

My first conscious experience of my mind's power was when my back was healed through mental education and understanding. Through Dr. Sarno's work, I realized my mind was more powerful and influential in my physical body and emotions than I could have possibly imagined. I now know, without a doubt, that if I choose to believe I will be miserable without alcohol in my life, I will be; if I choose to believe I can't relax without a drink, I won't be able to. I also know that if I choose to see alcohol as it really is, a toxic and addictive drug that should be treated with caution and doesn't deserve a role in my life, I will have no desire for it. The choice is mine.

Now that you know the naked truth about alcohol and what it has been doing to you, your body, and your mind, you'll be able to act. Your unconscious mind is changing, and drinking is again becoming a fully conscious decision. You can use your powerful mind to find freedom from alcohol.

When you see the truth, you realize you are able to let go of your desire to have an occasional drink. You realize one drink can create the physical addiction, which in turn creates the mental addiction. The cycle will continue. If you retain your desire to drink, it will be difficult, if not impossible, to find freedom.

Alcohol is addictive, and if you have been presented with all the facts and continue to desire alcohol, it's difficult for me to believe you are fully in control. Just because people seem to be in control of their drinking doesn't mean they are. There are a few things you can observe to see if someone is really as in control as they think they are:

- Do they willingly offer a fair conversation about alcohol? Can they comfortably discuss both the pros and cons of drinking?
- Do they make a big show of explaining why they drink in a way that they would not do with other things they choose to do (for example, drinking soda)?
- Is drinking daily and habitual, done without any real or conscious thought as part of their everyday life?
- Do they feel uncomfortable around you if you are not drinking? This is a definite sign that they're not making choices they are fully comfortable with.
- Do they feel the need to justify their drinking to you? Especially when you haven't asked?
- Do they seem unable to have a good time if they are unable to drink?

Again, be gentle. Even if someone is controlled by alcohol, they may be unaware, and we humans hate it when our self-control is questioned. You may need to smile and nod, realizing that everything you have read is true and that you are no longer caught up in the alcohol cycle—a cycle that only leads one way: downward.

Recently on a ski vacation, everyone was sitting around drinking while I enjoyed my soda, cranberry, and lime (which is an excellent drink!). My friends were discussing plastic bottles and how the plastic can leach into your drinking water and poison you. Everyone at the table was intelligent and seemed very in control of their drinking, yet there they were, drinking a known poison in massive quantities and speculating about the possibility of plastic leaching into their drinking water. It was a startling demonstration that even when we know the research and understand everyday pollutants, alcohol gets a free pass.

Moderation is a dangerous game. It's like saying you want to jump a little way out of a plane or lose your virginity but just a little bit. Alcohol tricks us because drinkers hide how much drinking affects their lives. Many don't outwardly hit rock bottom. Millions worry they may be in danger, but asking for help means enduring the stigma. Instead, they spend years worrying, wondering if they actually have a problem.

Let's End It Now

My goal with *This Naked Mind* is to help people before they reach a stage where alcohol has such a hold on them that their lives are unmanageable. I hope to give people freedom before they slide so far down into alcohol addiction that their brains are forever altered by the drug. To make them aware of the dangers of alcohol before they become slaves to it. Surely we should focus on arresting alcohol abuse well before the disease has progressed to full-blown alcoholism and begins ruining lives.

Alcoholics, because of the stigma, usually sink low, often harming themselves and others, before they ask for help. It's not OK. We place this stigma on people who have done nothing more than become addicted to an addictive substance, like the bee in the pitcher plant. The stigma and the diagnosis of an incurable disease conspire to ensure we don't ask for help at the early stages when we can still avoid deeply hurting ourselves.

Let's change it. Let's lose the stigma and admit that when it comes to alcohol and drugs, none of us are in control. In fact, let's stop calling it "alcohol and drugs" and acknowledge that alcohol is a drug—the most dangerous drug on the planet.[238] Addiction blocks your mind from the drug's harms and deceives you into believing you are in control, despite the irrationality of your decisions. All alcoholics started with one drink. The only difference between drinkers who feel they are in control and those who admit they are not is what stage the disease has progressed to. How much their bodies, their situations, and their wallets can cope with how much they drink. They are not in control. You were not in control, and if you decide to drink again, you will give up control.

Don't envy people who seem to control their drink. Just because alcohol seems to enhance a pleasurable occasion does not mean it actually does. I, as the non-drinker, feel amazing at occasions I would once have drank at. I am free. I have all my wits around me, and as a result, I laugh a lot more. I am funnier and smarter without drinking than I ever was while deadening my senses. I still have bad days, of course, but even then I realize that self-medicating with alcohol is a horrible idea. My friend Mary puts it this way: "The bottom line is, if I am unable to find joy in a situation, it's most definitely not the lack of alcohol to blame." If you struggle with depression or anxiety, it's time to get help. Continuing to self-medicate with booze will only make things worse. I say this from experience.

Placebo Effect

> *"Man is what he believes."* —Anton Chekhov

The placebo effect demonstrates the incredible power of our brains. Basically, the placebo effect occurs when someone is given a substance they believe will cure them. Even though the substance lacks the active ingredient, the person still experiences the anticipated cure or result. A study by Slavenka Kam-Hansen in the journal *Science Translational Medicine* showed that, for some drugs, more than half the impact of the drug is due to the placebo effect. People improve while taking them not because of anything in the substance but because of the staggering power of human belief.

I was eating alone in Paris, and the table next to me filled. They sat down, clearly in a funk from a long day of work. There wasn't a ton of conversation. The wine came, and they became instantly happy. They started laughing and talking excitedly about the wine. Someone said it was not his favorite kind, but "it does the job," which is apparently a French saying. It struck me that they began to have a great time as soon as the wine came. Without any drinking, the mood transitioned from slightly weary, just off work, to buoyancy and giggling. The fact that the mood changed before they drank a drop proved to me that the wine itself did not create happiness. No, this was clearly the placebo effect. It was the promise of wine that changed the mood. If someone took the bottle away, surely the long-day-at-the-office misery would have returned.

Can you see how addiction, until you drink enough to change your brain, is mostly mental? Relief was coming, and that was enough to change the mood even before anyone drank a drop. I had an early morning, so I didn't stay to watch the dinner play out. However, I have been the lone sober person at many of these occasions. Here's what happens. The wine comes, and the mood changes, so the conversation is intelligent, quick-witted, and full of life. Fast-forward two or three glasses, and conversation grows a bit dull, even among some of the most intelligent people. The wine does exactly what it is supposed to; it slows your brain function and dulls your senses.

Drinking does not make dull people fun. Alcohol makes smart and engaging people dumb and boring. Its very nature slows your brain function and dulls your wit and senses. People rendering themselves senseless are not entertained. What could be more boring than the monotony of experiencing life with only part of your senses? It is no fun to be controlled by a poison.

Remember the relief that the group of diners demonstrated when the wine arrived? The relief that a craving would soon be assuaged? The beauty of being a non-drinker is that I live in the place of relief, or rather freedom, from craving. I never again have to endure that painful, anxious craving. I don't experience withdrawal symptoms. I am ready for a good laugh and to enjoy whatever's next. I love the fact I don't need to stop at the liquor store to enjoy my evening. And while everyone has bad days, mine have become fewer and easier to deal with. I no longer make one bad day into two by getting drunk and spending the day after with a hangover. It's time for you to find that same freedom.

21.
THIS NAKED MIND

"Knowledge itself is power."
—Francis Bacon

You are close. With every word you have read, every idea you have contemplated, you have been undoing the lifelong conditioning of your unconscious mind. You have used Liminal Thinking to dive deep into the foundation of the obvious, examining your observations, experiences, and assumptions. You have slowly but surely been regaining the perspective of someone who has never had a drink, who has never been addicted to alcohol.

And now you have the advantage. You've experienced alcohol addiction, and you know how vile and insidious it is. I have perspective that the non-drinker doesn't have—I've seen the evils firsthand. Survival deserves a medal, not a stigma. I am stronger than before. I now have a shield of experiential armor against the horrors of alcohol. I feel strong enough to stand up and fight. My mission, the mission of *This Naked Mind*, is to change how our society views alcohol, to expose the truth and to provide tools to change our direction.

In writing this, my research has brought me to tears on numerous occasions. Why? I hurt for all of us. The most destructive part of this, the most rampant of all drug addictions, is how it steals our ability to respect and care for ourselves. Without self-respect, everything else falls apart. We are blinded, naively destroying our loved ones and ourselves. We unknowingly contribute to our children's future struggles. A recent study shows that kids who are allowed sips of alcohol are more prone to abuse alcohol as adults, and kids with alcoholic parents are four times more likely to have problems with drinking in adulthood.[239] At school, kids receive a message of caution against alcohol, but at home, our kids receive another, much stronger, message from the ever-present bottle of wine.

Alcohol is society's most dangerous addiction, causing four times as many deaths as prescription and illegal drug overdoses combined.[240] And it's growing. Death by alcohol consumption is increasing every year, and it has now surpassed AIDS as the world's number one killer of men aged 15–59.[241] More people are addicted to alcohol than any other drug on the planet.

Yet we've stigmatized not drinking. I experience this all the time. Refusing a drink invites criticism and judgment. The assumption when someone doesn't drink is that they must be recovering from a serious problem. Not only is it insulting, but it encourages this rampant and most destructive of all addictions to thrive unchecked.

If we don't change, we are on a terrible trajectory. In every category, misery from alcohol increases. We spend more money advertising alcohol than ever before, and more teenagers are trying alcohol, more college students binge drink, and the suicide rate among students is higher than ever. We're seeing more deaths from alcohol than ever before. Yet we continue to embrace alcohol as the "elixir of life." Our generation perpetuates this; I know I did. We are consuming so much wine that the latest trends are wine clubs and boxed wines. Our children see alcohol as vital to life's enjoyment. It is up to us. It is our responsibility to change this and expose alcohol. Once your eyes have been opened, it is clear. You see our entire society trapped in the pitcher plant, sliding downward, and it is terrifying.

Alcohol causes poverty, homelessness, domestic violence, child abuse, homicide, rape, death, and destruction. Alcohol doesn't just affect the drinker but everyone around them. We have an obligation to ourselves and the generations to come to expose this hideous disease for what it is. And we have a choice. We are doing this to ourselves. We can be the change. We can stop the cycle. We've put tobacco in its place. Why can't we do the same for alcohol?

At the beginning of this book, I assumed the thought of never drinking again filled you with apprehension, possibly panic. I dreaded the idea of spending my life without alcohol. By now alcohol's grip on you should be starting to loosen. The idea of not having to drink is exciting and welcome.

If the idea of giving alcohol up forever still makes you apprehensive, that's OK. For many, the proof that life can and will be enjoyable comes in living free from the insidious clutches of alcohol. Only then do you experience the joy of knowing you never have to drink again.

No matter where you are mentally, it's important to consider all the facts as you make a decision about alcohol in your life. Again, it truly doesn't matter if you are still attached to alcohol and feel afraid of life without it.

It's important to make a decision, a commitment, even if it's just a commitment to try an alcohol-free life for a period. This is for two reasons. First, the effort it takes to make one decision is the same amount of effort it takes to make each of a thousand decisions. Allow yourself to feel the freedom that comes with a single commitment, a single definitive choice—it is intoxicating. Second, without a decision you won't know when you are free. Our society is filled with conditioning; it's all around us. We got together with some other couples and their kids for St. Patrick's Day, and everyone was drinking. It's hard when you see people you know, love, and respect drinking alcohol as if it were the elixir of life. It's hard not because you want to pour poison down your throat, but because you know that truth. You have a perspective they don't, and you are grateful to know you are free.

But it is hard for the same reason cognitive dissonance is hard. You know something is true, yet the evidence in front of your eyes, in the form of your close friends casually drinking, telling you they can "take it or leave it," creates disagreement. Not because you think they are correct, but because you can't understand why they cannot see what you can. Remember their unconscious minds that control their desires and emotions still believe that alcohol is necessary to having fun at social occasions. Their nonchalant manner toward drinking is contrary to all of the truths you now know. These experiences don't make you question your commitment or point of view, but they create difficulty because it is hard to have different opinions than the people you care about.

Humans like to belong. You won't feel tempted to drink for the sake of drinking; in fact, at home, drinking won't even cross your mind. But in a social situation, you may be tempted because of a desire to fit in or to relieve the division you now feel between you and your friends. It's not easy to be different. Remember in grade school, when everyone got into certain brands and you begged your parents to buy you the same clothing your classmates had? It's human nature to want to be part of a group, to fit in.

While it's not easy to be different, it is good. And you are strong. It is a testament to the addictive nature of alcohol that your quitting evokes such emotional reactions from those around you. When I stopped eating eggs, no one got emotional or offended or questioned if our friendship would be as close as it was before. As much as your friends care about you, no matter how graceful you are about your decision, a divide will likely spring up between you and them. If they worry that they may have a problem, your not drinking will increase their anxiety, yet they will still feel all the emotional and mental attachment to alcohol as you did before you began reading this book. This is another important reason to make a commitment to yourself: When you are committed, it will be easier to prepare for these situations.

It's OK if it's not always easy. Nothing worth doing is completely easy. By being different you are making a strong statement. I laughed a lot at the St. Patrick's Day celebration. Your friends see you laughing and enjoying the evening sans booze, and it has an impact. And at some point, if you go gently and don't adopt a "holier-than-thou" attitude, they may ask you for your secret. They may open the door for a conversation about their struggles with alcohol.

Let's look again at Beth, a recovering alcoholic who is in A.A. and has been sober for five years. She knows I am writing this book and asked me if I could teach her to drink in moderation. I asked her if she wanted me to teach her how to drink motor oil in moderation. She looked at me as if I were crazy—why in the world would she want to do that? That's exactly the point. If you see alcohol as it truly is, nothing but an awful tasting poison that is destroying our society, our families, our relationships, and our bodies, why would you want to drink it? Even on occasion?

As part of my research into moderation, I read some forums about an approach called moderation management. The participants check in on online platforms and report on how many drinks they consume in a week. They count each drink, trying to obtain a target number of drinks per week. They are consumed every day by when they will drink, how much they will drink, and if they will keep their drinking goals. Instead of finding freedom from alcohol, they've become consumed by it. It is like our friend the bumblebee. She enters the plant trying hard to avoid slipping in while still drinking the nectar—nectar made from decay and rot. If she makes one misstep, she gets stuck, slides down, and becomes the nectar.

If you have no desire to drink, why would you try a single drink and give your enemy power again? As Carr says, once you see the truth about drinking, the fear of never being able to drink again is replaced by the excitement of never *having* to drink again. The experience is euphoric. You see your entire life, long and healthy, stretch out before you. You are proud. You have done something amazing. You are excited to enjoy this remarkable life and all of the many, wonderful human experiences it holds.

I drank for so long I forgot how beautiful life could be. I forgot how it feels to wake up energized about what the day can bring. Drinking drags you down. When you drink, you're inviting your mortal enemy to move back in. It's the alcohol monster who only feeds on more alcohol and destroys you in the process of feeding himself. His thirst is always growing and never satisfied. Of course, one drink will partially relieve the craving. It may quiet the monster for a little while. Yet it's this temporary solace that deceives us. Soon, you can see the bottom of your empty glass. I clearly remember thinking about my next drink before I had finished the drink in my hand. It's the same with all addictive substances—they all create an insatiable thirst for themselves.

Imagine that you arrive at an open house. The realtor has opened the home for prospective buyers, and you are one of many on the tour. You walk in and start to explore. The realtor has baked cookies so that the house smells wonderful. You are offered these fresh-baked cookies. You eat. You explore for a while, but then you realize there is something wrong about the home. It is certainly not the home you thought it was from the outside, and it's not for you. You decide to leave, and upon trying to walk out the front door, you find you have become lost. You wander through long, dark hallways, past eerie doorways, up and down stairs until you no longer recognize where you are or how you came to be there. The house has turned into a frightening maze. You realize the cookies are making you ill, but they're the only food available so you are compelled to eat them. It's a chilling experience. You see other prospective buyers, still walking around and enjoying the cookies. They haven't realized the cookies are poison or that the house is a deadly maze. Just because they don't find the house alarming yet doesn't mean they are any less stuck or that the cookies are less poisonous. The reality is terrifying whether they understand it or not.

A comparative risk assessment of drugs including alcohol and tobacco was done using the margin of exposure (MOE) approach. MOE is the ratio between intake and toxicology. A MOE of less than 10 is categorized as "high-risk," an MOE between 10 and 100 falls into a "risk" category. Cocaine, alcohol, nicotine, and heroin were the only drugs to fall into the high-risk (less than 10) category. When the population was taken into account, only alcohol fell into the high-risk category. All other drugs (with the exception of cannabis, which had an MOE of more than 10,000) fell into the "risk" category.[242] These are facts; they are not up for debate. Our society insists that alcohol is somehow separate from drugs; we even say "drugs and alcohol" rather than accepting that alcohol is the most dangerous drug of all.[243]

You will need to be on your guard because it's easy to believe drinkers who say they have no problem with alcohol and can take it or leave it. We have no reason not to believe them. We trust our friends. And they are not deceiving you on purpose; they believe what they say. They still seem to be enjoying the tour of the house. Often the main reason they believe they can take it or leave it is that they have never tried to leave it.

Imagine if I told you I could sometimes go a day without chewing gum. Wouldn't you immediately think I was obsessed with gum? Or consider smokers. It would seem that someone who smokes three packs a day enjoys smoking more than someone who smokes a single pack per day. If you ask the person who smokes three packs, they will tell you that they wish they could only smoke one. They envy the person who smokes less.[244] Why don't they just cut back? If they aren't enjoying all the cigarettes they are smoking, why smoke at all? Like drinking it is because they are tortured when they try to moderate or quit. A chain smoker no longer believes they are getting honest pleasure from smoking; in fact, they hate smoking but don't feel they can deal with life without cigarettes. This is not control; this is addiction.

Perhaps you feel you can, equipped with this new knowledge, drink only at a moderate stage again and stay there. Maybe you can; if alcohol hasn't yet changed your brain, moderation might be possible for a while. I have no desire to spend effort trying to moderate because alcohol no longer holds any allure. If I decided to moderate, it would be to fit in rather than because I desire to drink. I am aware that is a stupid reason to poison myself. I wouldn't take Advil if I didn't need to in order to be part of the crowd, and drinking is so much more dangerous.

I didn't mean to slip from "enjoying" a glass of wine with dinner to "enjoying" a bottle. Alcohol builds a tolerance, an immunity, which is simply our body trying to protect us from the poison we are consuming. We are compelled to drink more and more. When did I decide to drink more? I didn't. Slowly the wine wolf moved in and developed an insatiable thirst. I fed that thirst and it grew. Once I was poisoning myself every day, life became truly stressful. The subtle, "I need a drink" feeling was constant. Since life was stressful, I drank to deal with the stress. I cannot express how grateful I am to be out of that horrible nightmare. Alcohol is just not worth the risk of re-entering addiction's cycle of misery.

Look back at your drinking career. How many times did you have a few too many and throw up? What about a hangover? Or a headache? How many nights are fuzzy or completely erased? What about saying and doing things you regretted later? Maybe you said unnecessarily mean things to your friends or family. Are you starting to see how lucky you are? Can you start to see the delight of never, ever having to experience any of those things again?

A Brief Review

Perhaps you already feel the wonder of never having to make yourself stupid, hung over, or miserable again. The wonder of never *having* to drink again. If you haven't had that experience yet, don't worry. You may not experience it for weeks or months after you stop drinking. Your body will need to heal. You may need to actually experience life without alcohol to realize the truth of what I am telling you. That's OK. Since your unconscious mind is changing, it will be easier to abstain, to allow yourself to heal and to experience an alcohol-free life. You will now recognize the lies society feeds you. If you're still feeling specific doubts, go back and re-read the chapter that addressed those questions.

You started reading this book because you felt like alcohol was a problem in your life, and you wanted to regain control. However when you tried to cut back, you discovered that controlling alcohol intake was practically impossible, and the thought of not drinking again was terrifying. This reaction was different than what happened when you tried to control other food intakes in your life. Consider this example.

I became allergic to eggs after my second son was born. I liked eggs, and at first I would absentmindedly eat eggs, forgetting about my allergy. I would get a brutal allergic reaction. After a few of these painful reminders, I completely removed egg from my diet. It was not all that difficult, and it certainly wasn't emotional. I don't spend my life thinking about the fact that I no longer eat eggs. I barely give it any thought unless someone offers me an egg, and then I easily decline. Although eggs are delicious and nutritious, I do not mourn them. I feel no pain because I no longer eat eggs. When my doctor ran tests and initially diagnosed me with this allergy, I knew it would be a lifestyle adjustment, but I did not feel any dread; there was no emotional dependence. Instead, I was thankful that I finally understood the source of my painful allergic reactions.

By comparing these two experiences, you can recognize that we deceive ourselves when we believe we can control alcohol just like any other food. Alcohol's not just another food; it's an addictive drug. But we deny our dependence on it and say we can take it or leave it. This is because of the divide between your conscious mind and your unconscious mind. Once you see that drinking is creating problems for you, you consciously want to drink less. However, evidence clearly demonstrates that routine and customary decision-making processes (like regular drinking) do not occur fully within your conscious mind. According to Dr. Chris Firth, a professor of neuropsychology at the University College of London, there is a "bottoms-up" decision-making process, in which the unconscious parts of your brain weigh the rewards, make a decision, and interact with your conscious regions later, if at all.[245] Your unconscious mind controls your desires and your emotions. The unconscious runs on known programs, which exist from years of environmental conditioning.[246] It is in your unconscious mind that your beliefs, habits, and behaviors are formed and reinforced over time.[247]

The divide between what you consciously decide (to drink less) and what you unconsciously feel (you want a drink) creates heartache. Internal division, or cognitive dissonance, results in anguish and sorrow. You choose to obey your conscious mind and feel deprived when not drinking. Or you choose to give in to your deep cravings and drink. When you drink but don't consciously want to, you cannot understand why you've lost control. You feel weak and unable to stick to decisions or commitments.

You drank, your body became immune to drinking, and you drank more. You were in the habit of listening to that small voice saying, "A drink sounds good," so you drank anytime you wanted to. This is your baseline. Your baseline increases over time because your tolerance increases.

At the end I was drinking two bottles of wine a night. Moderating my drinking meant spending a lot of time and energy denying my cravings. This caused stress because my brain was split, my inner self divided. Soon life was dominated by when I would allow myself my next glass and how many glasses I would have. I may have been drinking in moderation, but I was far from free. I was more controlled by alcohol than I had ever been.

We only decide to cut back when our drinking starts to cause issues in our lives. Although we are duped into believing drinking provides pleasure or stress relief, alcohol wasn't that important when we did it all the time. We didn't think about it before it became a problem. We can't remember it that well. It certainly seems we took it for granted. It was simply part of our lifestyle.

Spending your life wanting something you can't have is not freedom. When you spend your day waiting for five o'clock, you don't enjoy the day. Five o'clock comes, the waiting is over, and you are duped into believing that the drink was the magic bullet—in reality it was relieving a craving. Ending the wanting.

Initially, when your resolve was strong, it seemed you could drink less. As a result you felt more in control and better about yourself. You suddenly had more money, and your health improved. These improvements actually conspired against you, making you forget why you quit. Like how food becomes more precious when you diet, alcohol becomes more precious when you abstain. Moderation is like an alcohol diet that will continue for the rest of your life. The longer you crave a drink, the greater the illusion of enjoyment when you give in.

And willpower is a finite and exhaustible resource, much like a muscle, that can be fatigued. Mark Muraven, a PhD candidate at Case Western Reserve University, wanted to understand why, if willpower was a skill (like riding a bicycle), he seemed to have it sometimes but was missing it at other times. He conducted an experiment to prove that willpower was more effective when conserved and that, when taxed, it could run out. Subjects, under the guise that they were participating in a taste-based experiment, were placed in a room with two bowls on the table: a bowl of fresh-baked cookies and a bowl of radishes. Half of the subjects were told to eat the cookies and ignore the radishes and half were told to eat the radishes and ignore the cookies. After five minutes they were given a puzzle that appeared easy but did not actually have a solution. Because the puzzle was impossible, continuing to work on it required willpower. The subjects who had previously exercised willpower by ignoring the cookies worked on the puzzle for 60% less time than the subjects who had not used any of their willpower reserves. Furthermore, the contrast in attitude between the subjects forced to eat radishes and those allowed to eat the cookies was drastic. The radish-eaters were surly, frustrated, and some even snapped at the researchers.[248]

It's easy to see how exercising and fatiguing our willpower to avoid alcohol, day after day, can make us bitter and unhappy. Willpower runs out, and you drink. This drink provides illusory relief, the forbidden fruit syndrome. The "pleasure" of relief is intensified because you've abstained. You regret the drink almost as soon as you consume it, and you deal with this regret by pouring another. The more dependent you are on alcohol, the more you convince yourself that you cannot enjoy life or cope with stress without it, and the quicker it eats at you. Your life becomes less fulfilling. You develop or reinforce a physical dependence, which ensures you stop receiving pleasure or stimulation in your nucleus accumbens from the activities you used to enjoy. This experience is like opening the front door of your mind and inviting depression in to live. You need to remember this: Alcohol physically alters your brain to remove your ability to enjoy normal things.[249]

Clearly, willpower is not the answer. The answer is simple. We must become aware that alcohol is creating our problems. Once the lifelong unconscious conditioning has been reversed, the unconscious mind, which is responsible for desires and emotions, will no longer desire a drink. Now drinking, or not, becomes a fully conscious decision. You only struggled to make rational decisions about alcohol because your unconscious mind had been conditioned to believe lies about alcohol and because alcohol's addictive nature physically affected you. The key is to make a conscious decision to see alcohol in its true form. To allow yourself to see what it really is and smugly decide that it is the last thing you would ever want to put in your amazing body. You will need to make a conscious and continuous effort to see alcohol as it really is from now on. What is so clear now may not be obvious in the future. Why? Because nothing has changed in our society. The media, your friends, and even family will continue to bombard your unconscious mind with the benefits of alcohol. Your unconscious mind will continue to be susceptible to all types of conditioning. The key is to realize this so you can make a deliberate and conscious effort to combat it. You fight the unwanted conditioning by being aware that it is happening. When a desire for a drink creeps back in you must immediately realize that you are being conditioned. You then can consciously question where that desire is really coming from. Examine it and understand if it is a solid, rational reason for drinking or if you have unknowingly allowed false truths to creep back in. As long as you are aware of what is happening, the conditioning will be easy to undo, and over time you will build solid armor against it. You can resist societal conditioning by being aware of it and taking immediate action to reverse it by recalling the truths you now know.

The new perspective you have gained cannot easily be unlearned. It is like an optical illusion—you see one thing until you gain a new perspective and see another. Once you see the new, it is difficult to go back to what you originally saw. I once believed the lie that drinking a liquid that systematically poisoned me and stole my confidence and my health was a good thing. How much easier it is to believe the truth that alcohol is an addictive poison. That all I have to do to be free forever is to stop drinking.

Once I was educated about the science of addiction and what alcohol was doing to my body and my brain it was easy to stop. Every day that goes by I am more, not less, sure of my decision. My eyes have been opened to the plight of others, and as a result my life is filled with gratitude for my freedom.

Again, it isn't easy to be different from the majority, especially my friends, but I am happy to be standing for something I know is right. As a result, self-loathing and a lack of self-respect have been replaced with confidence. I like who I am when I go to bed at night and when I wake up in the morning. My mind has more time and space, now that addiction doesn't dominate my thoughts. Time to spend with my family, to take care of myself, to progress my career, to write this book, to think about how to help others. Time to think about how to start a revolution in our society to wake people up to the danger we face.

It was strange at first. When I was drinking, my nights faded into oblivion. Now I am fully aware and alert from the moment I wake up until the moment I go to bed. What a gift. I make a conscious decision about when to sleep, based on feeling tired, not on how much I've drunk. My memories are not fuzzy, and I have no regrets. It's incredible to live a life where you don't need to hide anything, where you can be honest with yourself.

It takes a lot of courage to be different, to go against the majority. Courage I wouldn't have if I were still drinking and hating myself for it. I am no longer controlled by something I hate. There is true pleasure in leaving shame and misery behind. I find joy in the challenges before me—breaking the sober stigma and helping to eliminate the shame for all who choose to live free from the groupthink of alcohol by choosing a different path.

22.
THE SECRET TO HAPPILY AND EASILY DRINKING LESS

"The first step toward change is awareness. The second step is acceptance."
—*Nathaniel Branden*

Special note: Reading this chapter before the rest of the book won't work. I know it's tempting, and I'm glad you share my eagerness, but the answers you seek are in the journey, not the destination. If you haven't read or understood the rest of the book, your unconscious, which is slow to change, will not have caught up with your conscious mind. You will still unconsciously believe that alcohol is your friend. Applying the approach, while this division of both wanting to drink and not wanting to drink exists inside you, may make things worse.

We've covered a lot of ground together, and you are now ready to embrace your new understanding and change. Congratulations! You've realized by now that I believe you are happiest when you are not drinking at all. When I talk about drinking less, I mean much less—in fact, I mean nothing. This idea may provoke some anxiety, and if you are still apprehensive, that's OK. You may need to experience the joy of life without alcohol to realize the truth of what you have read. That's no problem. This is new territory, and you don't know what to expect. You don't want to make a commitment you're not sure you can keep.

What is important is that you are wary, for all the reasons we've discussed, of moderation. There is no halfway once you are addicted. Your brain physically and chemically changes, which makes moderation next to impossible. If your brain hasn't suffered chemical changes, they can happen at any time. It is the accumulation of alcohol in your body, no matter how little you drink each time, that creates pathways of addiction in your brain. The problem with alcohol is that the brain doesn't simply forget it. Dopamine is the learning molecule, and your brain has learned to crave alcohol. You can abstain, and these cravings will disappear, but if you drink again your brain immediately remembers. A conditioned response usually stays.[250]

This is why a single drink can land you back into the painful cycle of addiction. You go directly from the enjoyment of one drink to the lowest point of your descent. The key through every cycle is to remember you are strong. In order to be strong enough to choose freedom, you must forgive yourself for each failure. Forgiveness and gentleness with yourself, no matter how long your personal journey takes, are vital and central to finding your freedom.

The beauty of making a decision is that once that decision is made, you will see alcohol as a villainous traitor instead of an alluring seductress. One overarching choice frees you from all the little daily choices that alcoholics suffer for a lifetime. Instead of deciding to forgo every beer presented to you for the rest of your life, you decide once and forevermore to see the truth about alcohol. This single choice means freedom and is much easier on your psyche than daily decisions. A single choice can be made in conscious knowledge, whereas daily decisions rely on constant willpower.

The true difference is that this single choice decides not whether to drink the one drink in front of you, but the amount of space you will give alcohol in your life. A single choice is like a breakup, or better yet, like a marriage to a new, healthier life. Once you are married you no longer have to decide every day that you won't flirt with the handsome man on the airplane. That decision is already made. You are married. At first, when someone flirts with you, it takes practice to consciously think of your husband and how lucky you are to have him. Likewise, it takes practice to remind yourself of the amber death that is in the bottles in the beautiful bar. You will need to make a conscious effort to protect your unconscious mind.

Once a firm commitment is made, you face no decision. When the handsome man smiles at you, there is no willpower required to remain faithful. You simply remember that you are married, for better or worse. At the bar, again there is no wondering if now is the time to have that one drink—after all, this beautiful display of alcohol is so tempting. You simply remember your decision and remind yourself of the truths you now know. A single, strong choice made with all of your brain liberates you from willpower. It frees you from the hundreds of decisions you would have to make if you decided to take it one drink at a time.

And don't forget. If you do give in and have that one drink, your enemy, addiction, can immediately move back in. He plants himself in your brain and starts exactly where he left off. The pathways of addiction are still there. You will not notice him when he is starved and weak, but once he is fed, he grows strong. Why? Because your brain remembers. This enemy is physical dependence. Irrational cravings. Inexplicable behaviors. If you let him in by feeding him, his thirst for booze can be stronger than anything in your arsenal. You are easily overcome by your cravings. Remember that wanting is not enjoying.

The addiction adversary does not just attack a certain defective segment of our population called alcoholics. Sure, he might move in at a different pace depending on how your brain is wired. And sure, there are different physical reactions in each of us that make the artificial high alcohol provides more or less powerful inside our minds. The point is that you cannot become addicted to alcohol if you don't drink.[251] And no matter who you are, if you drink enough, you will become addicted. No one is safe; everyone needs to approach alcohol with caution.

Even if you drink moderately, it is vital to be aware that your drinking is most likely increasing, not decreasing, over time. There are some exceptions. Let's take my friend Todd. He approaches alcohol with extreme caution, and for this reason he allows himself a single beer on Friday and a single beer on Saturday. He never drinks more than one, and he doesn't drink on other occasions. He is strict with these rules, and it is his way of ensuring addiction does not take over. He will probably, as long as he maintains this same level of staunch self-control, go his entire life without developing a physical dependence. That being said, Todd's body is building a tolerance to even those single beers, and the actual effect he believes them to have is probably nonexistent.

While it's great to have that level of self-control, the majority of us are not like Todd. His commitment to this moderate drinking is a result of his religion and his commitment to his faith. Yet even in this situation, I wonder, why drink at all? Over time the beers cease to have any effect whatsoever, so why even drink them? In my mind, this behavior is like smoking two cigarettes a week. Perhaps there is some placebo effect of self-indulgence, but personally I just don't see the point. And further, if Todd really desires the beer, surely he wants more than just one. Surely every Friday and Saturday night he feels some sort of sadness when this single beer has been drunk. "Oh well, that's it then. I'll enjoy another one next week."

It is important to realize that even in Todd's extreme case we can't assume that he will be able to keep his two-beers-a-week limit forever. The very fact he drinks those two beers means he enjoys drinking beer. If something was to change in his life, who's to say he wouldn't use this coveted beverage to self-medicate? And even if he limits himself forever to these two beers, who's to say it won't become an obsession where he spends his week looking forward to his weekend beer? No one can predict when we will slide from drinking without physical dependence to drinking with physical dependence. With some alcoholics it happens within the first few drinks. With others it may never happen during their lifetime. There are a million reasons for this. It is impossible to predict.

It is important to realize when it happened to you, or to accept the fact that if you have not yet reached a point of physical dependence on alcohol, you have no way of knowing what drink will push you across that line. With every glass, you are one drink closer to a physical alcohol addiction.

"When you can stop you don't want to,
and when you want to stop, you can't . . ."
—Luke Davies

Your enemy becomes strong when fed, and he will push you around. You may have kicked him out of your house, but he is waiting outside, plotting. Imagine moderating a cocaine or heroin habit. If you want your mind to be free, and you want complete control back, remember that moderation is not control or freedom. Unless you want to be consumed by an addictive poison that will do nothing for you except eventually kill you, you need to make a commitment to fly away from the pitcher plant, starve your mortal enemy, and revel in your freedom.

So what's the secret? It's simple, and it has two parts: awareness and acceptance.

First, be aware that you have become emotionally and/or physically dependent on alcohol. You cannot fix an issue that you don't realize is there. You are in the grasp of your adversary: alcohol.

You may still think that stopping will be hard, that you won't be able to resist social pressures, and you will feel deprived. The truth is that if you decide in your heart and mind that you never again want to be a slave to alcohol, you have removed any indecision. You have ended your cognitive dissonance. You have ended the internal conflict.

I won't lie to you, depending on how much alcohol you have consumed and for how long, you may have some physical withdrawal symptoms. But when your mind is in the right place, the physical symptoms are greatly diminished because you know why they exist, and you know they will end. They may not be comfortable, but with each physical discomfort, remember alcohol is creating the discomfort. If you are fearful of withdrawal symptoms because of your level of dependence, please seek medical attention to assist you in the process. Think of it this way: You are in a battle, and withdrawal symptoms mean you are winning. You are killing off your mortal enemy. There may be some trauma in the fight, but once he is dead, you are free. You can start to live a happier, healthier life than you ever imagined possible.

You are strong, and by making your commitment you have already won. The fight may not be fun, but it won't last forever—hopefully no more than a few weeks, with the worst part over by the end of the first week. You can do this, and each day will get easier. You are fighting for your life, and victory is yours. I know you can, and deep inside you, you know you can too.

It may be easier than you think. It was for me. Why? Because it is the mental craving that makes it hard to stop. In the Vietnam War, many American soldiers began using heroin with alarming regularity. The government was sure they were going to have an entire generation of heroin addicts on their hands when the war was over, and they tracked these soldiers carefully once they returned to the states. Yet once the soldiers were home and reunited with their families, they quit heroin, easily, with almost no withdrawal symptoms or relapses. This demonstrates how much addiction is in your mind and how freedom comes with a clear decision. The soldiers were not willing to use heroin at home, so they decided not to.[252] There is a good chance you won't experience any withdrawals, and if you do they will be minimal. Who wouldn't be ill for a few weeks to cure themselves from an incurable disease? Don't forget, every symptom you feel was caused by alcohol. You will never, ever have to feel it again.

What to expect? It depends on how long and how heavily you have been drinking. I suffered anxiety and a lack of concentration. I had night sweats; I think that was my body ridding itself of the toxins I had consumed. Some describe the experience like a mild flu. I didn't mind my symptoms because they spelled victory. I knew a drink would make things worse, not better. I was overcome with happiness and the euphoria of knowing my life had forever changed, which made the physical discomfort minimal. It felt like my desire to drink had been surgically removed from my brain, and the result was giddiness. This far outweighed any physical discomfort.

> *"You are in the midst of transition and . . . sickness is the means by which an organism frees itself from what is alien; so one must simply help it to be sick, to have its whole sickness and to break out with it, since that is the way it gets better."*
> —*Rainer Maria Rilke*

Something else happens after you stop. You start to look back at your drinking career in a different light, through the lens of self-acceptance and honesty. It's not easy to face all of the things you did and said, perhaps all of the people you hurt. It can be very hard to forgive yourself. You need to let it go, apologize to people if you feel compelled to, but most importantly forgive yourself. Realize that you were captive, a prisoner of your adversary, in the prison of addiction. There is no reason to waste your bright and exciting future dwelling on past mistakes, though now and again you may revisit your past and remember the horrors of addiction. Addiction takes a considerate, honest person and tears them down until they're doing the most horrible things. Also, remember it was not your fault. Alcohol physically changed how your brain works. You were deceived. You are healing, and you don't have to be sick again.

When a former alcoholic continues to crave alcohol months or years after reaching sobriety, it's not because of the addictive nature of the drug—that craving is physical and relatively easy to deal with once the alcohol is purged from the body. The physical addiction will go away when the alcohol is completely out of your system. If you are a chronic drinker and drink to the point that you are ill yet keep drinking, you may have altered your brain to such a degree that you need to be isolated from alcohol while it leaves your system. You may need professional help in the form of a rehabilitation center, and I encourage you to get that type of help. For most others, you will easily be able to overcome the physical cravings because you know the cure. You know you are on your way to being happy and whole. The mental craving, which is generally stronger, only comes when you feel you are making a sacrifice, giving up something desirable. Once you see there is nothing worth desiring, your mental cravings will be gone. You will crave alcohol as much as you crave drinking motor oil.

The beauty of *This Naked Mind* is that once you understand the scientific basis for your inexplicable behaviors and the truth about what alcohol does to your body and mind you are not likely to fall victim to addiction again. Even if it takes you a few cycles of relapse to fully grasp the truth, you will be aware, educated, and knowledgeable. That is vital to your permanent freedom. You will no longer suffer the mental division caused by one side of your brain wanting a drink and the other side feeling like you should cut back. Both sides of that struggle are driven by fear. Fear that you will be unhappy without drinking, and fear that you are harming yourself by drinking. You are about to end that struggle. You didn't suffer from it before your first drink, nor will you after your last.

> *"The more you depend on alcohol, the more convinced you*
> *are that you cannot cope or enjoy yourself without it and*
> *the quicker you die inside. Then your life is less fulfilling*
> *and when this happens, the more you rely on alcohol to*
> *fill that gap. This is why I was so afraid of stopping."*
> —*Jason Vale*

Second, you must accept the truth about alcohol. Decide to let go of your attachment to alcohol by accepting that it does nothing for you. When you stop drinking, you are killing your mortal enemy. He has stolen or will steal more from you than you can imagine. He steals more than 2.4 million hours of life (just in the U.S.) every year.[253]

You now know that you are gaining everything rather than giving anything up. You are killing your enemy, not losing your friend. You can be free the easy way, by accepting the truth about alcohol or you can make it difficult for yourself by retaining some of the unconscious conditioning and seeing alcohol as desirable. If you retain a desire to drink you will have to deprive yourself every time you decide not to drink, for the rest of your life. Why not make it easy for yourself? Why not allow yourself the freedom you deserve? All the pain you have been in, all the pain you have caused, was because of alcohol. You may feel excited, or apprehensive, or not quite prepared. That's OK. It's natural to feel a bit afraid. You're venturing into the unknown, which can cause apprehension. Don't worry. Sometimes you need to go ahead and jump, and let the joy of living without alcohol demonstrate how much better your life has become. Start the journey with joy—you are about to accomplish something truly awesome.

Start Now!

The first secret to happily and easily stopping drinking is deciding you want to be free. Have a good talk with yourself, with those close to you, those who will hold you accountable as you make this decision. There has never been a better time than now.

If you have lingering doubts or still believe that alcohol provides enjoyment or relief, re-read the Liminal Points or join thisnakedmind-community.com for community and support. Believing that you will get enjoyment from a drink is different than having a few cravings. Cravings are normal and relatively easy to deal with. You are changing your entire life, and it may take some getting used to. You might crave a drink in the next few days, months, or even years, but the craving will be small and entirely conscious. The understanding you've gained from this book will allow you to approach the craving rationally, making a fact-based decision. Remind yourself of the principles in this book, and the cravings will die. Since you will not suffer from an unconscious and unexplainable desire to drink, you can easily put any cravings in their place by remembering the truth about alcohol and by seeing that there is nothing to crave.

You may find that your brain has been conditioned to believe it wants a beer at a sports game; you will need to change that. You've been drinking for a long time, and this is a big change. It will take some getting used to. If you let yourself continue to crave a drink or wonder if drinking is pleasant, you will start reconditioning your unconscious to believe all the same old lies. Don't do that; there is no need. Look honestly at the feeling, identify where it is coming from (most likely it will be because everyone around you is doing it and you feel out of place), and realize how stupid it is to drink bad-tasting poison just to fit in. Take a stand for yourself, realizing you want nothing to do with the groupthink of alcohol. Be brave and be different.

Make a choice to let go of your desire for alcohol. Choose to see alcohol in her true form. Society paints alcohol as beautiful, but look beyond all the enticing social cues that conceal the danger. Our conditioning draws us to her like moths to a flame, like a bee into the pitcher plant. But the beauty is an illusion. You now see beyond the surface, and there is nothing but death.

> *"Every time you wake up after drinking, you are physically, mentally, emotionally, socially and financially worse off than if you had not taken the drug in the first place."*
> —*Jason Vale*

Once you realize you want to be free there is only one thing left to do. Deliver the fatal blow to your adversary. Cut off his food supply:

Stop Drinking

Allow yourself to see alcohol in its true form, eliminate your desire to drink, and free yourself completely from the misery of addiction.

Sometimes it is a good idea to have a final drink. This marks the occasion, letting you know you are truly free. Don't make it your favorite drink—use some kind of hard alcohol. You can make it a ritual, a commitment to your new life. Concentrate on how bad it really tastes and wonder how you ever let this toxic liquid control you and why you ever paid for the privilege (heavy drinkers can spend about $400,000 on alcohol during their lives, which makes your last drink akin to winning the lottery!).[254]

Whether you decide to have a final drink or not doesn't matter. What's important is to know, *without a doubt*, that you are free. Free to enjoy this beautiful life. The reminders below will help you navigate this new, abundant life.

Reminders for the Journey

"If you really want to remove a cloud from your life, you do not make a big production of it, you just relax and remove it from your thinking."
—*Richard Bach*

This Naked Mind speaks to both your conscious and unconscious mind by reversing the conditioning you have received from the media, friends, family, and society. You must not forget you are still surrounded by these messages, and you will still be bombarded with them every day. It is difficult not to be influenced. Each one is targeted to deceive you into believing that you are missing out by not drinking. For me, revisiting the principles of the program quickly reverses any unintended conditioning. You can do this by joining us in community at thisnakedmindcommunity.com. Journaling, blogging, and community have been shown useful in this process. Our community site allows you to have your own blog where you can give and receive encouragement and support. If you want, you can join under a pseudonym, making it anonymous. It can be useful just to hear about other people's journeys or to bounce around ideas.

You can re-read part or all of this book. One of my early readers read the book four times in her first sixteen days of becoming alcohol-free. She is still happily free but the conditioning in her life was such that she needed to ensure the information stuck. That's OK. Do what you need to do to make sure you fully understand the truth both now and in the future.

Here are a few tips that have helped me:

Don't put off the day you decide to stop drinking. Why not make it today? There will always be an excuse. Isn't there a wedding coming up? Or a football game? Perhaps there is stress in your life that you need to deal with. Don't fall for that. That is what you've been doing your entire life, and it hasn't worked. Drinking just pours more stress into your life. There is no need to wait and no need to be frightened. The instant you decide to be free, you will be free. You won't need to avoid your friends or social situations. In fact, you will enjoy them much more.

Today can be the first day of the rest of your life. Make it a celebration—you have done something incredible. Celebrate however you choose, but do something special and commemorative. Declare your freedom. Your entire life is about to start. Relish the moment. Going back to a naked mind is no small thing. You are already free. Own it. Make a commitment to yourself, and if you want, declare your freedom to your family and friends. The moment I knew I was free, I sent an overly-excited group email. Cheesy, I know, but it made me feel great. You deserve to feel great. Well done and congratulations!

You may have already experienced the incredible realization that your whole life has changed, and you are free. I remember it vividly; I was in awe. It is one of the happiest moments of my life. If this hasn't happened for you, it's OK. For some it happens by the end of the book, and for others it happens a few weeks or months after stopping, when you realize that it's all true—that life is amazing without alcohol. Importantly, don't try to force it. It will come. It might be after an occasion you never imagined you could enjoy without drinking, like a tailgate party, a BBQ, or a nightclub. You suddenly realize you had a great time and drinking alcohol didn't cross your mind. Just let the moment come. Go and be surprised when it suddenly dawns on you that you are free.

For the first few days to a week, your body will be going through detox. It takes ten or more days for alcohol to fully leave your system. Since you have altered your dopamine levels, you may experience cravings. This is a reality, and you have to starve those cravings, allow them to die. They will die. When the psychological desire to drink is eliminated, the physical aspects are manageable. Since your mind is free, killing these cravings can be an enjoyable experience. You are starving your mortal enemy. Your cravings may take some time to go away. That's normal. Think of it as your dopamine monster, a monster you want to make smaller and smaller until it shuts up and leaves. And it will. You are now in control, not your cravings. Don't forget that. And take care of yourself. Do things that make you feel good; you deserve it.

Feel free to think about the fact that you no longer drink, but think in terms of "I don't have to drink" rather than "I don't get to drink." It's true. You are free. You never have to experience another hangover, embarrassment, or headache related to drinking. Best of all, you won't experience the mental stress of wondering how much is too much or the black shadow that comes when you know you are drinking more than you should. You never have to drink again. No one will force you. You are again in control of your destiny. This is great news.

Remember, this new life will be an adjustment. You have reached for a drink for every conceivable reason for years, maybe decades. It's understandable that habits can linger. But if you pinpoint why you actually want the drink, you'll soon find that your craving will disappear again. You will realize the reason is just an excuse, and you don't actually want a drink. It's just your mind playing tricks on you. If your craving continues, re-read sections of the book or visit this nakedmindcommunity.com where you will find additional tools to support this amazing adjustment you are making.

Having just one drink causes the vicious cycle to begin, but you might be stubborn and need to find that out for yourself. If at some point you do, don't beat yourself up. Learn. And love yourself. Remember you are only human. But be on your guard. Society will continue to tell you how amazing alcohol is, and a voice may creep in suggesting that you are missing out. It's all lies. The further I get from my drinking past, the better my life becomes.

The "just one" game will cloud your judgment and cause you pain. Nothing has changed, alcohol is still addictive, and the danger is still present. You've realized there is no true pleasure in drinking. You understand you don't need to drink; you only thought you needed to. When you start to play the "just a few" game, you allow yourself to be duped again. You allow yourself to be deceived into believing there is pleasure in drinking. You have been fighting this mental battle long enough. Remind yourself of alcohol's true nature, that all it actually does is deaden your senses to the point of oblivion . . . oh, and fuel your car. Remind yourself that life with alcohol is homogenous and that with each drink you are not only losing years of your life, but also precious memories of the only life you have.

Sometimes when society all around me is lauding booze as the "elixir of life," it's hard to see the harm in just one drink. But when I start to entertain the idea of "just one," I become very uncomfortable. It's clear why. Indecision creates mental division, which causes pain. As soon as I realize what is happening, I remind myself that alcohol was never my friend but an enemy in disguise. I remember the pain of addiction and how thankful I am to be free. I also realize that I don't get any real joy from drinking; it just makes me tired and grumpy. The pain evaporates. Just remember, you are stronger than any craving. You are in control. And try not to worry about it. It's OK. It will pass. Your brain can crave anything, and if it starts to shout at you that you need a drink, just remember who is boss— you are.

Your change won't be easy for the drinkers you spend time with. They may mourn it. It's easy to understand why. If you are in a room full of people all taking the same drug, it is easier to not think about it. They are unknowingly deceiving themselves, telling lies and believing them.

If you forget you no longer drink, that's OK. I was drinking tonic and lime, and the waitress asked if I wanted another one. I said, "Yes, gin and tonic please," then caught and corrected myself. It was embarrassing. I'm sure she thought I was jonesing for some gin. The truth was that I wasn't thinking about not drinking, and habitual words just slipped out. If you've ever tried to stop cussing (a serious vice of mine), you know how words can just come out. This is actually great news; it means you are not thinking about alcohol. When you are consciously trying not to drink and exercising willpower, you don't make that type of mistake. Alcohol was so far from my mind that I didn't remember I didn't drink. Talk about being free.

This is life, real life. You will have good days, great days, bad days, and horrible days. That's OK. Remember, if drinking made you happy, you would never have been unhappy as a drinker. Alcohol doesn't make you happy, but we know it can make you very unhappy. It's OK to live this life as it is, in all its raw, naked beauty. It's OK to cry, to scream, to be frustrated, and to feel. This is your life, and it's the only one you get. Accept it and accept yourself. You are an incredible human being, and you have so much to give. If you have a great day—live it up. If you have a shit day—remember it will pass. And if for some reason it doesn't pass, if ceasing to self-medicate through alcohol reveals that you are indeed struggling with depression or anxiety, please get help. Remember, alcohol was never helping. It was hiding a real issue that needs to be fixed. It is important to find the right treatment. Depression is not a weakness; it is a disease. You can find help that will actually improve your life rather than steal it like alcohol does. Please do so.

There are a few things that, contrary to popular belief, you should do. First, with the *Naked Mind* approach, it's OK to think about the fact that you no longer drink. There is no reason not to. You got here by questioning everything, examining everything, and allowing yourself to see stuff differently. Don't stop thinking critically now. Finding your truth, in all areas of life, is a beautiful thing.

Many people report dreaming about drinking after they have stopped. That's OK; it's natural. It's happened to me plenty of times.

I would realize I was halfway through a pint (in my dream) and panic (in my dream), worried that I was again caught in the tangled web of alcohol addiction. Waking up reminds me how grateful I am to be free. If you dream-drink and enjoy it, that's OK too. You've been drinking for years. It's understandable that your dream self will need a bit of time to catch up. It doesn't mean you are sliding back or that you have a sincere desire to drink. There is no need to worry about it. Most likely you will be like me, waking up with relief that you are free and that drinking is in your rearview mirror.

Second, there is no need to avoid your drinking friends or places you used to go to drink. You are free to do whatever you want. But be kind to yourself, and only go if you truly enjoy the activity and the company. There is no point in wasting this beautiful life doing things or spending time with people that don't bring you authentic pleasure. You are free. Enjoy it. The more you remind yourself of the fact that you are free from alcohol, the happier you will be.

I was not prepared for how strong the reactions would be when I stopped drinking. Drinkers are very curious when someone suddenly stops drinking. It's assumed that you lost control and are an alcoholic. Ironically, you are the one who no longer drinks, but you're supposed to be the one with the problem. They are still drinking while asking if I have a drinking problem.

People can be aggressive in demanding my reasons. Then after I explain, everyone starts to tell me all the reasons they drink. Unprompted, they all start to tell me why they don't have a problem with booze. Funny, right? When I told people I was no longer eating eggs, no one started to tell me all their justifications for eating eggs or insisting that they didn't have an egg-eating problem.

Be prepared for mixed reactions. It's OK. You didn't do this for anyone else; you did it for you. They may now be jealous of you. They are wondering how you're still enjoying yourself, how you're still happy and relaxed. They will wonder how in the world you did it; they will be baffled by your strength.

Remember, ignorance isn't bliss. Even if someone is completely unaware of being stuck, they are not experiencing bliss. Alcohol doesn't change; it is still harming their health, stealing their money, robbing them of energy, and fraying their nerves. They are building a tolerance to it, and there is no doubt that they will be drinking more a year from now or five years from now than they are today. With alcohol, ignorance is not bliss.

You have so much to look forward to. It was such delight for me to realize it was the company of the people I enjoyed, not the alcohol, that I loved. Enjoy doing all sorts of things for the first time. Start today. And with every experience marvel at the fact that it's life, not alcohol, that makes things worthwhile. Before *This Naked Mind*, you thought quitting drinking would be miserable, that life would be such a bore. The opposite is true, and it's glorious. You can have an amazing time without inebriating and poisoning yourself. This is great news.

Now that you are free, make sure to guard your freedom by guarding your mind. All decisions are yours, but when making them please remember that alcohol does not change; it will trick and deceive you. It will create a need for itself, and when you become physically addicted (which may happen after a night of drinking or just a few drinks), your mind will no longer be entirely yours. You will start to believe the tricks your mind will play on you. These tricks get you to feed the physical aspect of alcohol addiction, to feed alcohol's need for itself. You will feel divided again, and you will do things to end that division. You might justify your behavior or close your mind to the truths you know now. It is a slippery slope and alcohol itself will not change. Alcohol is addictive, and when you attempt moderation, you end up spending excessive time and effort, not on living but on moderating, determining when to and when not to drink. There is an easy way out, but you need to decide to take it. Today your unconscious mind, your entire mind, no longer craves alcohol like it once did. Take this opportunity to free yourself.

Some drinkers think quitting is like losing a best friend. You know the truth: This friend is actually a backstabbing fiend who wants to slowly kill you by destroying your body and your mind. This friend is your mortal enemy—who, if given the chance, will keep you engaged in a horrible, confusing battle until your death. Don't let him. Kill him now and forever. Enjoy his death, dance on his grave, and remember there is absolutely nothing to mourn.

Revisit the truths in this book and visit the forum at thisnaked mindcommunity.com for stories and encouragement. It is difficult to live in this world where we are constantly assaulted with hundreds of pro-drinking messages every day. You will need to be on your guard, or you will again fall victim to your mortal enemy, and he will slowly, cunningly steal your life.

Finally, be happy. You can now see that quitting does not have to be tragic. When you see the truth you can't help but feel joy at your newfound freedom. There is nothing to mourn, you have killed your enemy, not lost a friend. You have just added precious hours to your life and put a significant amount of money back in your pocket. Spend your time and money doing things that bring you true happiness. It can be fun to make a list of what types of things you enjoy and are looking forward to. Then do them. And enjoy your wonderful *Naked Life*!

23.
THE JOURNEY: "RELAPSE"

"It's better not to give in to it. It takes ten times longer to put yourself back together than it does to fall apart."
—*The Hunger Games: Mockingjay*

This Naked Mind is about being aware, stripping away that which is false and finding truth. Your life will be so much better when alcohol is a small and irrelevant part of it. I believe your best chance at peace in your relationship with alcohol is by starving the alcohol monster and letting him rot.

I don't like the word relapse. It seems to impose unspoken rules and judgments, reeking of stigma. But we cannot ignore it. Your alcohol monster may reawaken, maybe more than once, during your journey to his final death. You must know that even with the best intentions and the strongest commitments, you may, someday, allow alcohol back into your life. We must face this reality. We cannot hide from it. Our intelligence allows us to protect ourselves, avoiding traps by understanding how they work. Awareness of risk diminishes it.

Drinking again may not be a big deal. But more likely it will become incredibly painful. The alcohol monster will awaken stronger than before. You may find yourself deeper in the pit than ever. Your loved ones have seen you healing. Even if you never verbalized commitments, they have been made through your actions. Drinking will mean breaking those commitments, not only to those you love but, even harder, to yourself. You may lose trust in your own judgment, resolve, and strength. This is not a reason to avoid commitments. Your strong decisions are a vital part of destroying your thirst for alcohol. But if you do fall prey, you may find yourself deep in a pit of self-loathing, addiction, and despair. So deep that freedom appears impossible.

Addiction is a war with the highest stakes imaginable. For me, the most terrifying thing about relapse is how easy it is to believe that, by relapsing, we have lost the war. Society tells us that if we are unable to stick to our decisions, we are weak. If we break promises, we cannot be trusted. It's easy to believe that making mistakes makes us useless. We figure that if we "fall off the wagon" we might as well "go all the way" because "it's too late now." We feel beyond repair, no longer worth fixing. We pile up internal guilt, convinced we deserve the hatred of those we love. So we punish ourselves, often by drinking more—even to the point where we are sick. We drink to oblivion, binging to numb ourselves to the horror of our failure. Hating ourselves more each time. Falling further and feeling lower than ever before.

It is a mistake to believe that by losing a battle we have lost the war. The truth is that each battle makes us stronger as long as we remain committed to a better tomorrow. We must fight this battle with compassion and forgiveness. We must allow that lost battle to be a reminder of all the reasons we quit rather than an unforgivable mistake. We must remember: Losing a battle does not mean we have lost the war.

Drinking will remind you why you stopped. You will remember how much effort it took to moderate. How painful hangovers are. You will remember the internal struggle, the recrimination, and deception. It may come after that first drink or down the road after a time of successful moderation when your willpower runs out. Let your mistakes become powerful reminders of your freedom. Let them tell the story of how far you've come. Let them be a stepping stone on your journey.

Examine why you drank. Perhaps, as you heal, your reasons for not drinking alcohol seem less important. The pain fades, and you wonder: Is alcohol really as bad as I imagined? Am I missing out? Can I now, with enough distance, moderate?

Maybe you feel socially isolated and desire connection. You wonder if you would fit in better and have more friends if you had an occasional drink. If you struggle from loneliness, you must find connections. But alcohol will never heal your loneliness or provide friendship.

If you are struggling with depression or anxiety, you may begin to wonder if a drink would take the edge off and provide relief. Remember, drinking is like turning off your check engine light. It may temporarily numb your symptoms, but it can never heal you.

You may drink to fill a void in your life. Societal conditioning convinces you that alcohol is key to filling the holes inside you. This will never happen; alcohol can only tear you further apart.

And again, if you have a strong physical addiction, freedom may not be easy or even possible without others to fight alongside you. You may need a rehabilitation center or an ongoing support group. You may need to call for backup. Call for backup now. Discuss this possibility with those close to you; ensure they are prepared to fight with you when the battle comes. Get whatever help you need. Asking for help does not make you weak; it makes you strong.

You will overcome this. Let each temptation, each battle bring you closer to winning the war. Learn from each fight, discovering your truth about alcohol and its role in your life. Alcohol does not define you. It does not give you worth. It is not who you are. It will not fix your problems, solve your loneliness, or provide any of the answers you seek.

This is a journey, not a destination. It is a road that no one can walk but you. These are choices that no one can make but you. But know that by committing to a different future, no matter how many battles you have ahead of you, the war has already been won.

24.
PAY IT FORWARD

"Don't spend your precious time asking 'Why isn't the world a better place?' The question to ask is 'How can I make it better?' To that there is an answer."
—*Leo F. Buscaglia*

Life is an incredible journey. It can be hard to understand why we are here and what it all means. I am convinced that our responsibility, as humans, is to take care of and respect each other and this planet, our home. But in order to do that we must first take care of and respect ourselves. You are one of the brave. You will pioneer this change, helping save our children, our society, and our future.

We must love ourselves first, take care of ourselves, change our habits and behaviors, and then we can change the world. How do we have a chance of overcoming war or hunger or saving our beautiful Mother Earth if we don't first love ourselves? How can we become enlightened, open-minded enough to accept other humans with love and respect, when we don't respect our own decisions?

I can't begin to tell you how much you will accomplish when you are mentally and physically healthy. When you combine your health with a true sense of self-acceptance, self-respect, and self-love there is nothing you can't do. This is the way to change our world; it's cliché, but it truly starts within. By solving our own problems with alcohol, we will have the mental capacity, the internal love, and the drive to solve the world's problems. They say peace begins at home, and your truest home is inside yourself.

Take your time; adjust to your new life. Enjoy breaking all of the associations. It's a game for me, doing something I couldn't have imagined without a drink and enjoying it more than before. It reinforces my resolve and fills me with gratitude.

> *"Life is a series of natural and spontaneous changes. Don't resist them; that only creates sorrow. Let reality be reality. Let things flow naturally forward in whatever way they like."*
> —*Lao Tzu*

Your body and mind will soon heal from the trauma of drinking and hating yourself for it. Your body is incredible; it will quickly purge itself of the poison. Your mind may take a bit longer. You may have doubts, lingering cravings, or times of disbelief. That's all OK; don't worry. And don't try not to think about it. A 1987 study from Harvard confirmed that when you try to repress certain thoughts, you think about them more.[255] It's OK to think about what comes naturally into your head; just think—that's the important part.

Take care of yourself; you deserve it. One day, in the very near future, when you feel at peace and whole, perhaps your gratitude will overflow. There is incredible power in giving to someone else the gift you have been given, in helping someone become free. It is an amazing and life-affirming thing to help another person. Either individually or by joining me in this movement, let's ensure we and our children exercise the right level of caution with alcohol. There is so much to be done, from simply helping one person to getting in touch and spreading the word.

Helping other people is one of life's great secrets of happiness. Compassion is actually quite selfish. The Dalai Lama said in a TV interview on ABC News, "The practice of compassion is ultimately to benefit you. So I usually say: We are selfish, but be wise selfish (helping others) rather than foolish selfish (only helping yourself)."[256] In fact, exercising compassion and helping other people is incredibly satisfying. Brain scans show that acts of kindness register in our brain's pleasure centers much like eating chocolate. The same pleasure centers in the brain light up when we get a gift as when we donate to charity.[257] Helping others ultimately helps you. It is an amazing and completely natural high. Over and over it has been shown that service to others is a vital part of our happiness as humans.

Do it. Pay it forward. Go gently and remember never to judge. Change starts here, change starts now, and you are the most important part of this change. The world needs you to be your best. The world needs you to help save it, one person at a time. At the end of the day, *This Naked Mind* is about a mind that comes to care for and respect itself, just as it is, just as it came into this world—simply naked. Remove the pollutants you struggle with. When we do that, we save ourselves and prepare this amazing planet and all its incredible inhabitants for the next generation, for our children.

Pay it forward; it's your turn.

Dear Reader,

If you feel inspired to pay it forward, there is one simple and power-ful action you can take immediately. Share your story. You might worry that your story isn't relevant, or that no one can relate. Alcohol addiction does not discriminate; it touches people from every walk of life. No matter your story, someone will be touched and inspired by what you have to say. Your story will provide hope; it may change someone's life.

Perhaps you are thinking, "Wait, I'm not ready to commit to give up drinking." That is not important. *This Naked Mind* is not about rules. It's about knowledge and awareness. It's about ending internal struggle and finding peace with yourself—no matter what that means for you.

What will inspire people is how your perspective has changed. If you have taken small actions, like choosing not to drink on a single occasion and realizing you enjoyed yourself, that is powerful! That is worth sharing. Together we can break down the societal condition-ing that constantly tells us alcohol is a vital part of life.

Your voice is important. It can be just as significant to give some-one hope that they could enjoy a dinner out without wine than to tell them you've sworn off booze forever. Tell *your* story, as raw and real and true as it is. If there is hope, write about it. Peace? Write about it. Fear? Write about it! Struggle? Write about it! Just tell it honestly and from the heart.

Alcohol addiction remains a hidden and stigmatic problem marked by denial and fear. There are millions suffering alone, afraid to ask the question, "Am I drinking too much?" We worry others will think we have a problem or that we will have to admit to having an incurable illness. So we tell ourselves, and everyone around us, that we are fine, saving our concerns for midnight Google searches with our private browsers turned on. This is where your story, anonymous or not, will greet others just like you. This is where your story will make a difference, sparking hope for someone. We must be brave and vulnerable, letting those who still suffer know they are not alone in their struggle. We must force these questions and answers out into the open. We must let people know that there is hope and that life truly is much better when alcohol is a small and irrelevant part of it.

If you are considering it but are stuck on what to write, I recommend starting at the beginning. When did you start to drink, and how did you feel about it? Talk about your drinking life and how it progressed. Share some of the more poignant moments in your journey. Describe when you realized you needed to change and why. What has that journey looked like? Conclude with how you feel today, in this moment. Do you feel a glimmer of hope for the first time in a long time? Share that. Are you planning to give up drinking? Share that. Again, the only requirement is that you are heartfelt and honest. And you might be surprised—writing your story may prove a powerful step in your own journey. You may find writing to be freeing and healing.

There are many ways to share your story. I would be honored to feature your story on my blog (thisnakedmind.com/blog/). You can email me at hello@thisnakedmind.com. Alternatively, you can set up a independent personal blog or join my social blogging site at this nakedmindcommunity.com, where people blog about their journey and help others who are looking for support and inspiration.

Thank you for considering sharing your story, and no matter what you decide I wish you the best in your journey.

You are amazing—never forget it.

"You are very powerful, provided you know how powerful you are."
—Yogi Bhajan

Love,
Annie Grace

P.S. If you are looking for more support in your journey visit this nakedmind.com for additional resources and next steps or sign up for my weekly newsletter at thisnakedmind.com/reader.

Maybe you need a practical way to get started. Why not simply commit to thirty-days alcohol free? Join me for a thirty-day "Alcohol Experiment" at alcoholexperiment.com.

ENDNOTES

1 Bergland, Christopher, "New Clues on the Inner Workings of the Unconscious Mind," *Psychology Today*, March 20, 2014, psychologytoday.com/blog/the-athletes-way/201403/new-clues-the-inner-workings-the-unconscious-mind.

2 Carey, Benedict, "Who's Minding the Mind?," *The New York Times*, July 31, 2007, nytimes.com/2007/07/31/health/psychology/31subl.html?pagewanted=all&_r=0.

3 Bergland.

4 Ibid.

5 Polk, Thad A., *The Addictive Brain*, The Great Courses, 2015.

6 "The Conscious, Subconscious, and Unconscious Mind–How Does It All Work?," The Mind Unleashed, March 13, 2014, themindunleashed.org/2014/03/conscious-subconscious-unconscious-mind-work.html.

7 Siedle, Edward, "America's Best Doctor and His Miracle Cures: Dr. John E. Sarno," *Forbes*, September 26, 2012, forbes.com/sites/edwardsiedle/2012/09/26/americans-best-doctor-and-his-miracle-cures-dr-john-e-sarno/.

8 Sarno, John, "The Manifestations of TMS," in *Healing Back Pain: The Mind-Body Connection*, New York: Warner Books (1991), 16.

9 Hoyt, Terence, "Carl Jung on the Shadow," Practical Philosophy, practicalphilosophy.net/?page_id=952.

10 Ozanich, Steven Ray, "The Mind's Eyewitnesses," in *The Great Pain Deception; Faulty Medical Advice Is Making Us Worse*, Warren, OH: Silver Cord Records (2011): 145–151.

11 Anando, "It's now a proven fact—Your unconscious mind is running your life!," *Lifetrainings*, lifetrainings.com/Your-unconscious-mind-is-running-you-life.html.

12 Ibid.

13 Gray, Dave, "Liminal thinking The pyramid of belief," YouTube, youtube.com/watch?v=2G_h4mnAMJg.

14 Gray, Dave, *Liminal Thinking: Create the Change You Want by Changing the Way You Think*, Two Waves Books, 2016.

15 Gray "Liminal thinking."

16 Ibid.

17 "The Conscious, Subconscious, and Unconscious Mind."

18 Weller, Lawrence, "How to Easily Harness the Power of Your Subconscious Mind," Binaural Beats Freak, binauralbeatsfreak.com/spirituality/how-to-easily-harness-the-power-of-your -subconscious-mind.

19 Gray, "Liminal thinking."

20 Ibid.

21 Harris, Dan, *10% Happier: How I Tamed the Voice in My Head, Reduced Stress Without Losing My Edge, and Found Self-Help That Actually Works: A True Story*, It Books, 2014.

22 Weller.

23 "Alcohol Facts and Statistics," niaaa.nih.gov/alcohol-health/overview-alcohol-consumption /alcohol-facts-and-statistics.

24 Cook, Philip J. *Paying the Tab: The Costs and Benefits of Alcohol Control*, Princeton University Press, 2007.

25 Vale, Jason, *Kick the Drink . . . Easily!*, Bancyfelin: Crown House, 1999 (77).

26 "Prosthetic Limbs, Controlled by Thought," *The New York Times*, May 20, 2015.

27 Fox, Maggie, "Surgeon Promising Head Transplant Now Asks America for Help," *NBC News*, June 12, 2015.

28 Genetic Science Learning Center, "Genes and Addiction," *Learn. Genetics*, June 22, 2014, learn.genetics.utah.edu/content/addiction/genes.

29 Polk.

30 Vale.

31 Polk.

32 Genetic Science Learning Center.

33 A.A. General Service Office, "Estimates of A.A. Groups and Members as of January 1, 2015," aa.org/assets/en_US/smf-53_en.pdf

34 Alcoholics Anonymous World Services, Inc., *Alcoholics Anonymous: The Big Book—4th ed.*, New York: Alcoholics Anonymous World Services, 2001.

35 Ibid.

36 Ibid.

37 Ibid.

38 Ibid.

39 Ibid.

40 National Institute on Alcohol Abuse and Alcoholism, "Alcohol Facts and Statistics," March 1, 2015, niaaa.nih.gov/alcohol-health/overview-alcohol-consumption/alcohol-facts-and-statistics.

41 Anonymous, "Alcoholism: An Illness," in *This is A.A.: An Introduction to the A.A. Recovery Program*, New York: A.A. Publications, 1984.

42 Carr, Allen, *The Easy Way to Stop Drinking*, Sterling Publishing Co. Inc, 2003 (167).

43 Carr.

44 Polk.

45 Kraft, Sy, "WHO Study: Alcohol Is International Number One Killer, AIDS Second," *Medical News Today*, February 11, 2011, medicalnewstoday.com articles/216328.php.

46 Task Force on the National Advisory Council on Alcohol Abuse and Alcoholism, "High-Risk Drinking in College: What We Know and What We Need to Learn," September 23, 2005, files.eric.ed.gov/fulltext/ED469651.pdf.

47 Castillo, Stephanie, "How Habits Are Formed, and Why They're So Hard to Change," *Medical Daily*, August 17, 2014, medicaldaily.com/how-habits-are-formed-and-why-theyre -so-hard-change-298372

48 Ibid.

49 Vale.

50 National Foreign Assessment Center and Central Intelligence Agency, *The World Factbook*, n.d.

51 Berger, Jonah, *Contagious: Why Things Catch On*, New York: Simon & Schuster (2013), 150, 151.

52 Carr.

53 Kraft.

54 Vale.

55 Goldstein, Robin, et al., "Do More Expensive Wines Taste Better? Evidence From a Large Sample of Blind Tastings," *Journal of Wine Economics*, 3(1), Spring 2008: 1–9, wine-economics .org/aawe/wp-content/uploads/2012/10/Vol.3-No.1-2008-Evidence-from-a-Large-Sample -of-Blind-Tastings.pdf.

56 Bohannon, John, et al., "Can People Distinguish Pâté From Dog Food?," *Chance*, June 2010, wine-economics.org/workingpapers/AAWE_ WP36.pdf.

57 Kempton, Matthew, et al., "Dehydration Affects Brain Structure and Function in Healthy Adolescents," *Human Brain Mapping* 32(1), January 2011: 71–79, ncbi.nlm.nih.gov/pubmed /20336685.

58 Carr.

59 Berger.

60 Nutt, David J., et al., "Drug Harms in the UK: A Multicriteria Decision Analysis," *The Lancet* 376(9752), November 2010: 1558–1565.

61 Kraft.

62 Centers for Disease Control and Prevention, "One in 10 Deaths Among Working-Age Adults Due to Excessive Drinking," cdc.gov/media/releases/2014/p0626-excessive -drinking.html.

63 Stahre, Mandy, et al., "Contribution of Excessive Alcohol Consumption to Deaths and Years of Potential Life Lost in the United States," *Preventing Chronic Disease*, June 26, 2014.

64 Centers for Disease Control, "2013 Mortality Multiple Cause Micro-data Files," December 2014.

65 De Oliveira, E. Silva, E.R., et al., "Alcohol Consumption Raises HDL Cholesterol Levels by Increasing the Transport Rate of Apolipoproteins A-I and A- II," *Clinical Investigation and Reports* 102, 2347–2352, doi:10.1161/01.CIR.102.19.2347.

66 Holahan, Charles J., et al., "Late-Life Alcohol Consumption and 20-Year Mortality," *Alcoholism: Clinical and Experimental Research* 34(11), November 2010: 1961–1971.

67 Höfer, Thomas, et al., "New Evidence for the Theory of the Stork," *Paediatric and Perinatal Epidemiology* 18, 2004: 88–92.

68 Carr, 144.

69 "Beyond Hangovers: Understanding Alcohol's Impact on Your Health," 2010, Bethesda, MD: U.S. Dept. of Health and Human Services, National Institutes of Health, National Institute on Alcohol Abuse and Alcoholism.

70 "Neuroscience: Pathways to Alcohol Dependence." *Alcohol Alert* 77, 2009.

71 "Beyond Hangovers."

72 Polk.

73 DiSalvo, David, "What Alcohol Really Does to Your Brain," *Forbes*, October 16, 2012, forbes.com/sites/daviddisalvo/2012/10/16/what-alcohol-really-does-to-your-brain/.

74 "Beyond Hangovers."

75 Ibid.

76 Ibid.

77 Ibid.

78 Ibid.

79 Ibid.

80 Ibid.

81 "Hypertensive Heart Disease, Medline Plus, May 13, 2014, nlm.nih.gov/medlineplus/ency/article/000163.htm

82 "Health Consequences of Excess Drinking," AlcoholScreening.org, alcoholscreening.org/learn-more.aspx?topicID=8&articleID=26.

83 "Beyond Hangovers."

84 Ibid.

85 Ibid.

86 Ibid.

87 Ibid.

88 Ibid.

89 Ibid.

90 Ibid.

91 Rehm, Jürgen, et al., "Alcohol Consumption," in *World Cancer Report 2014* (Stewart & Wild, eds), Lyon, France: International Agency for Research on Cancer, 2014: 96–104.

92 Bagnardi, Vincenzo, et al., "Light Alcohol Drinking and Cancer: A Meta-Analysis," *Annals of Oncology* 24, 2013: 301–308.

93 Allen, N.E., et al., "Moderate Alcohol Intake and Cancer Incidence in Women," *Journal of the National Cancer Institute* 101(5), 2009: 296–305.

94 "How Alcohol Causes Cancer," Cancer Research UK, cancerresearchuk.org/about-cancer /causes-of-cancer/alcohol-and-cancer/how-alcohol-causes-cancer.

95 "Drinking Alcohol," BreastCancer.org, breastcancer.org/risk/factors/alcohol.

96 "How Alcohol Causes Cancer."

97 Ibid.

98 Ibid.

99 "Alcohol and Breast Cancer Risk," Susan G. Komen, ww5.komen.org/breastcancer/table3 alcoholconsumptionandbreastcancerrisk.html

100 "U.S. Breast Cancer Statistics," BreastCancer.org, breastcancer.org/symptoms/understand _bc/statistics.

101 "Alcohol drinking," *IARC Monographs on the Evaluation of Carcinogenic Risks to Humans* 44, 1988: 1–378.

102 Lachenmeier, Dirk W., et al., "Comparative Risk Assessment of Carcinogens in Alcoholic Beverages Using the Margin of Exposure Approach," *International Journal of Cancer* 131, 2012: E995–E1003.

103 "How Alcohol Causes Cancer."

104 Stokowski, Laura, "No Amount of Alcohol Is Safe," Medscape, April 30, 2014, medscape .com/viewarticle/824237.

105 "Alcohol Use Disorder," *The New York Times*, nytimes.com/health/guides/disease/alcoholism /possible-complications.html.

106 Ibid.

107 Stokowski.

108 Carr.

109 Lynsen, A., "Alcohol."

110 "Parenting to Prevent Childhood Alcohol Use," National Institute on Alcohol Abuse and Alcoholism, pubs.niaaa.nih.gov/publications/adolescentflyer/adolflyer.htm.

111 "One in 10 Deaths Among Working-Age Adults Due to Excessive Drinking."

112 Carr.

113 Turner, Sarah and Rocca, Lucy, *The Sober Revolution: Women Calling Time on Wine o'Clock*, Accent Press Ltd., 2013.

114 Carey, "Who's Minding the Mind?"

115 Koch, Christof, "Probing the Unconscious Mind," *Scientific American*, November 1, 2011, scientificamerican.com/article/probing-the-unconscious-mind/.

116 Ibid.

117 Harris.

118 "Yalom's Ultimate Concerns," Changingminds.org, changingminds.org/explanations/needs
/ultimate_concerns.htm

119 Harris.

120 Kraft.

121 Carr.

122 "Ethyl Alcohol," *Encyclopedia Britannica*, britannica.com/science/ethyl-alcohol.

123 Janet Hall, "Cancer figures prompt calls for health warnings on alcohol products,"
Northumberland Gazette, July 16, 2015, northumberlandgazette.co.uk/news/local-news
/cancer-figures-prompt-calls-for-health-warnings-on-alcohol-products-1-7361758.

124 Weiss, Marisa, "Alcohol and Cancer: You Can't Drink to Your Health," BreastCancer.org,
November 9, 2011, community.breastcancer.org/livegreen/alcohol-and-cancer-you
-cant-drink-to-your-health/.

125 Dubner, Stephen J., "What's More Dangerous: Marijuana or Alcohol? A New Freakonomics
Radio Podcast," Freakonomics, freakonomics.com/podcast/whats-more-dangerous
-marijuana-or-alcohol-a-new-freakonomics-radio-podcast/.

126 Iliades, Chris, "Why Boozing Can Be Bad for Your Sex Life," Everyday Health, everyday
health.com/erectile-dysfunction/why-boozing-can-be-bad-for-your-sex-life.aspx.

127 Arackal, Bijil Simon and Benegal, Vivek, "Prevalence of Sexual Dysfunction in Male Subjects
with Alcohol Dependence," *Indian Journal of Psychiatry* 49(2), April–June 2007: 109-112.

128 Fillmore, Mark, "Acute Alcohol-Induced Impairment of Cognitive Functions: Past and Present
Findings,:" *International Journal on Disability and Human Development* 6(2), April 2007.

129 Anderson, P., "Is It Time to Ban Alcohol Advertising?," *Clinical Medicine* 9(2), April 2009:
121–124.

130 Smith, Lesley A. and David R. Foxcroft, "The Effect of Alcohol Advertising, Marketing, and
Portrayal on Drinking Behaviour in Young People: Systematic Review of Prospective Cohort
Studies," BioMed Central, February 6, 2009, biomedcentral.com/1471-2458/9/51.

131 Bergland.

132 Ibid.

133 Goldstein.

134 Beck.

135 Ibid.

136 Hill, Kashmir, "How Target Figured Out a Teen Girl Was Pregnant Before Her Father Did,"
Forbes, February 16, 2012, forbes.com/sites/kashmirhill/2012/02/16/how-target-figured
-out-a-teen-girl-was-pregnant-before-her-father-did/.

137 Beck.

138 "Alcoholism Isn't What It Used To Be," NIAAA Spectrum, spectrum.niaaa.nih.gov/archives
/v1i1Sept2009/features/Alcoholism.html.

139 "Alcohol Deaths," Centers for Disease Control and Prevention, June 30, 2014 cdc.gov /features/alcohol-deaths/.

140 "Overdose Death Rates," National Institute on Drug Abuse, drugabuse.gov/related-topics /trends-statistics/overdose-death-rates.

141 Ibid.

142 "The Impact of Alcohol Abuse on American Society," Alcoholics Victorious, alcoholics victorious.org/faq/impact.

143 Ibid.

144 Ibid.

145 Polk.

146 Mohr, Morgan, "The Role of Alcohol Use in Sexual Assault," Kinsey Confidential, April 28, 2015, kinseyconfidential.org/role-alcohol-sexual-assault/.

147 Ibid.

148 Carey, Kate B., et al., "Incapacitated and Forcible Rape of College Women: Prevalence Across the First Year," *Journal of Adolescent Health* 56(6), June 2015: 678–680.

149 Abbey, A., "Alcohol-Related Sexual Assault: A Common Problem Among College Students," *Journal of Studies on Alcohol Supplement* 14, March 2002: 118–128.

150 Ibid.

151 Iliades.

152 Cain, Susan, *Quiet: The Power of Introverts in a World That Can't Stop Talking*, New York: Crown, 2012.

153 "The Impact of Alcohol Abuse on American Society."

154 "Impaired Driving: Get the Facts," Centers for Disease Control and Prevention, cdc.gov /motorvehiclesafety/impaired_driving/impaired-drv_factsheet.html.

155 Arackal and Benegal.

156 Duhigg.

157 Powell, Russell, et al., *Introduction to Learning and Behavior*, Wadsworth Publishing, 2012: 441.

158 Holmes, Andrew, et al., "Chronic Alcohol Remodels Prefrontal Neurons and Disrupts NMDAR-Mediated Fear Extinction Encoding," *Nature Neuroscience* 15, September 2, 2012: 1359–1361.

159 Polk.

160 Danbolt, Niels, "Glutamate as a Neurotransmitter—An Overview," *Progressive Neurobiology* 65, 2001: 1–105.

161 DiSalvo.

162 Ibid.

163 Ibid.

164 "Neuroscience: Pathways to Alcohol Dependence."

165 DiSalvo.

166 Watson, Stephanie, "How Alcoholism Works," How Stuff Works, June 8, 2005, science. howstuffworks.com/life/inside-the-mind/human-brain/alcoholism4.htm.

167 One in 10 Deaths Among Working-Age Adults Due to Excessive Drinking."

168 "Neuroscience: Pathways to Alcohol Dependence."

169 DiSalvo.

170 Vale.

171 Ibid.

172 Hitti, Miranda, "1/3 Fully Recover from Alcoholism," WebMD, January 19, 2005, webmd .com/mental-health/addiction/news/20050119/13-fully-recover-from-alcoholism.

173 Flanagin, Jake, "The Surprising Failures of 12 Steps," *The Atlantic*, March 25, 2014, theatlantic.com/health/archive/2014/03/the-surprising-failures-of-12-steps/284616/.

174 "Alcoholism Isn't What It Used To Be."

175 Polk.

176 Duhigg.

177 "Alcohol, Drugs, and Crime," National Council on Alcoholism and Drug Dependence, ncadd.org/learn-about-alcohol/alcohol-and-crime.

178 Ibid.

179 "Alcohol Use Disorder."

180 "The Impact of Alcohol Abuse on American Society."

181 Ibid.

182 "Alcohol Awareness," National Clearinghouse for Alcohol and Drug Information, 1993.

183 Vale.

184 Ibid.

185 Polk.

186 Ibid.

187 Ibid.

188 Ibid.

189 Vale.

190 Ibid.

191 Carr, 154.

192 Ibid, 60.

193 Brière, Frédéric, et al., "Comorbidity Between Major Depression and Alcohol Use Disorder from Adolescence to Adulthood," *Comprehensive Psychiatry* 55(3), April 2004: 526-533.

194 Turner and Rocca.

195 Ibid.

196 Carr, 144.

197 Polk.

198 Ibid.

199 Vale.

200 Ibid.

201 Hepola, Sarah, *Blackout: Remembering the Things I Drank to Forget*, New York: Grand Central Press (2015), 17.

202 Melina, Remy, "Why Do Medical Researchers Use Mice?," Live Science, November 16, 2010, livescience.com/32860-why-do-medical-researchers-use-mice.html.

203 Hari, Johann, "The Likely Cause of Addiction Has Been Discovered, and It Is Not What You Think," *Huffington Post*, January 20, 2015, huffingtonpost.com/johann-hari/the-real-cause-of-addicti_b_6506936.html.

204 Turner and Rocca.

205 Ibid.

206 "The Impact of Alcohol Abuse on American Society."

207 "What Happens During an Alcohol Detox and How Long Does It Last?," Hologik.biz, December 19, 2016, holologik.biz/how_long_to_detox_from_alcohol/1886-1/.

208 Polk.

209 Ibid.

210 Ibid.

211 Ibid.

212 Ibid.

213 Ibid.

214 Ibid.

215 Ibid.

216 Littlefield, Andrew, and Sher, Kenneth, "The Multiple, Distinct Ways That Personality Contributes to Alcohol Use Disorders," *Social and Personality Psychology Compass* 4(9), September 2010: 767–782.

217 Ibid.

218 Ibid.

219 Turner and Rocca.

220 Pompili, Maurizio, et al., "Suicidal Behavior and Alcohol Abuse," *International Journal of Environmental Research and Public Health* 7(4), April 2010: 1392–1431, ncbi.nlm.nih.gov/pmc/articles/PMC2872355/.

221 Pedersen, Traci, "One-Third of Suicides Involve Heavy Alcohol Consumption," Psych Central, June 21, 2014, psychcentral.com/news/2014/06/ 21/one-third-of-suicides-involve-heavy-alcohol-consumption/71515.html.

222 Carey, "Who's Minding the Mind?"

223 Horsley, Victor and Sturge, Mary, *Alcohol and the Human Body: An Introduction to the Study of the Subject*, London: Macmillan and Co, 1909.

224 Carr, 262.

225 Polk.

226 Ibid.

227 Ibid.

228 Schultz, Wolfram, et al., "A Neural Substrate of Prediction and Reward," *Science* 275(5306), March 14, 1997: 1593–1599.

229 Robinson, Terry, and Berridge, Kent C., "The Neural Basis of Drug Craving: An Incentive -Sensitization Theory of Addiction," *Brain Research Reviews* 18(3), September–December 1993: 247–291.

230 Ibid.

231 Ibid.

232 Turner and Rocca.

233 Gupta, Sanjay, and Cohen, Elizabeth, "Brain Chemical May Explain Alcoholism Gender Differences," CNN, October 19, 2010, thechart.blogs.cnn.com/2010/10/19/brain-chemical -may-explain-alcoholism-gender-differences/.

234 "One in 10 Deaths Among Working-Age Adults Due to Excessive Drinking."

235 Levitin, Daniel J., "Why the modern world is bad for your brain," *The Guardian*, January 18, 2015, theguardian.com/science/2015/jan/18/modern-world-bad-for-brain-daniel-j-levitin -organized-mind-information-overload.

236 Polk.

237 Ibid.

238 Lachenmeier, Dirk, and Rehm, Jürgen, "Comparative Risk Assessment of Alcohol, Tobacco, Cannabis and Other Illicit Drugs Using the Margin of Exposure Approach," *Scientific Reports* 5, 2015: 8126.

239 Jackson, Christine, et al., "Letting Children Sip: Understanding Why Parents Allow Alcohol Use by Elementary School–Aged Children," *Archives of Pediatrics & Adolescent Medicine* 166 (11), November 2012: 1053–1057.

240 "Overdose Death Rates."

241 Kraft.

242 Lachenmeier and Rehm.

243 Ibid.

244 Carr.

245 Carey, "Who's Minding the Mind?"

246 "The Conscious, Subconscious, and Unconscious Mind."

247 Ibid.

248 Duhigg.

249 Polk.

250 "Is There a Cure for Alcoholism?," DrugAbuse.com, drugabuse.com/is-there-a-cure-for
-alcoholism/.

251 Polk.

252 Hari, Johann, *Chasing the Scream: The First and Last Days of the War on Drugs*, New York:
Bloomsbury, 2015.

253 Stahre, et al.

254 Carr, 262.

255 Najmi, Sadia, and Wegner, Daniel M., "Hidden Complications of Thought Suppression,"
International Journal of Cognitive Therapy, 2009 (210–223).

256 Harris.

257 Ibid.

ABOUT THE AUTHOR

Annie Grace has had a unique life from the very beginning. She grew up in a one-room cabin without running water or electricity in the mountains of Colorado and then, at age twenty-six, became the youngest vice president in a multinational corporation. Success, however, led to excessive drinking and the possibility that she might lose everything. Annie recognized her problem but chose to approach it in an entirely new way. Annie's program has been featured in *Forbes*, the New York *Daily News*, and the *Chicago Tribune*. Annie is successful, happy, and alcohol-free and lives with her husband and three children in the Colorado mountains.

ACKNOWLEDGEMENTS

"Here's to . . . The ones who see things differently. They're not fond of rules. And they have no respect for the status quo. You can quote them, disagree with them, glorify or vilify them. About the only thing you can't do is ignore them. Because they change things. They push the human race forward. And while some may see them as the crazy ones, we see genius. Because the people who are crazy enough to think they can change the world, are the ones who do."
—Apple Inc.

Above all others, I take great pleasure in acknowledging Dr. John Sarno and Mr. Allen Carr (1934–2006). Dr. Sarno is the father of The Mindbody Syndrome (TMS). He opened my mind to the power of the unconscious, and this book is my adaptation of his methods to the brain disease of addiction. Without Dr. Sarno's groundbreaking work this book would not have been possible.

Allen Carr is the author of *The Easy Way to Stop Smoking, Stop Drinking Now*, and many other Easyway™ books. Mr. Carr was an incredible source of inspiration and influence on the subject of drug addiction. I, and many other influential authors, learned from Allen's revolutionary ideas, discoveries, and understanding of addiction.

Dr. Sarno and Mr. Carr will forever have my sincerest admiration and gratitude.

I would like to also thank these brilliant minds whose ideas contributed extensively to this work:

- Thad A. Polk, professor of psychology and EECS at the University of Michigan and creator of the program *The Addictive Brain*, for his neurological insight into the reward circuit and the cycle of addiction;
- Dave Gray, author of *Liminal Thinking*, for his unique and methodical approach in changing beliefs we hold that may be based on flawed reality;
- Steve Ozanich, Mindbody healing author, who furthered Dr. Sarno's work and took the time to inspire me in the earliest days of this journey;
- Dan Harris, author of *10% Happier*, for bringing practicality and humor to the journey into the mind;
- Malcolm Gladwell, bestselling author, speaker, and journalist, for encouraging us all to challenge known ways of thinking;
- Charles Duhigg, *New York Times* staff writer and author of *The Power of Habit*, for his groundbreaking work on habit and willpower;
- Johann Hari, bestselling author of *Chasing the Scream*, for his new look at addiction and deep passion for changing the way society views and treats addicts;
- Carl Jung, founder of analytical psychology, for his insight into "the shadow" and his contribution to Bill Wilson's journey to sobriety;
- Bill Wilson, founder of Alcoholics Anonymous, not a doctor or psychologist, but a man who saved himself from addiction through seemingly unconventional methods. He changed the lives of millions by looking at the same old things in a different way.